A Mountain Road

A Methodist Minister's Inspiring Autobiography

A Mountain Road

A Methodist Minister's Inspiring Autobiography

ISBN-13: 978-1479348893
ISBN: 1479348899

M MadeGlobal Publishing

For more information on
MadeGlobal Publishing, visit our website:
www.madeglobal.com

Looking back over the life of someone as important as Douglas Weddell Thompson with the eyes of someone in the 21st Century is a humbling experience. To know that Douglas was actually my Grandfather is still more humbling.

Growing up as a young child, I remember visiting his house in Uckfield, and then going quite often to visit Margret (Meg as we call her) in East Hoathly. I can vividly remember Douglas' face but I can't recall the sound of his voice. Even in old age he was an inspiring person.

Sadly my mother, Margaret Ridgway (née Thompson), passed away in August 2000. How much I wish I could ask her how much she remembered of her childhood in China, of the Japanese invading, and all the other amazing things she did together with her father. This book stands in part as a memory of her too.

I'm so proud to be able to re-publish this autobiography so that many more people can be inspired by the "little man with a great Lord". I know that my life has been changed by reading of the way he changed the world, person by person.

Thanks must also be given to Margret Thompson, Douglas' second wife, for giving me permission to re-publish this work with additional photos and resources to make it as complete a record as can be made.

Tim Ridgway
Grandson of Douglas Thompson
September 2012

Original Intro to the Book (1983)

It was a great privilege and joy to share with Douglas the last few years of his life. He enjoyed writing his autobiography and I am happy that this story of 'one of Mr Wesley's preachers' can now be shared with many friends all over the world.

My thanks are due to all those who have encouraged me to publish the book, and especially to Eric Pigott, Albert Jakeway and Kenneth Leese who have helped with negotiations and technical detail.

Margret Thompson

April 1983

Preface by Colin Morris

Douglas Thompson was as versatile a minister as Methodism has produced in the twentieth century - China Missionary, Army Padre, POW, Mission Superintendent, Divisional General Secretary and rural minister. And he excelled in each of these bewildering variety of roles.

Like most fascinating personalities, Douglas Thompson's character abounded in paradox. Small in stature and unassuming in manner, he could be utterly dominating; saltily down-to-earth in speech, his prose was often poetic in its reach. He was preoccupied with strategy but grounded it always in theology; he was an ecclesiastical iconoclast with a very high view of the Church; he was a humble man with an almost unnerving confidence in the rightness of his judgement; he was a non-University type who was immensely learned.

This autobiography encapsulates a history of British Methodism for a good part of the twentieth century, seen through the eyes of someone who helped to shape it. It is more than a chronology of events; it is a religious passion recollected in tranquility at the end of the day. Those who knew and respected Douglas Thompson will have an uncanny sense of his presence on every page; a generation which does not know him has much to learn from him about the strategy of Mission.

Colin Morris
Head of Religious Broadcasting BBC

A Foreword

A life is only seen now and again in perspective and with meaning. It is like a long march. In the Hunan Province of Central China such a march is studded with tea houses where on mountain tops the wayfarer is given cups of tea. He sits on the bench placed by Buddhist devotees on the very edge of the ledge on which they have sited the tea house and looks back down the road he has already traversed lost in wonder.

Ever the way forward is in the backward look. There is no knowledge of the way forward in his aching feet. For the heart, however, there is meaning and wisdom in that backward look which projects the traveller on.

This may be a Buddhist point of view. There is the old proverb, 'To know the way over the mountain ask the man coming down' which would support that origin.

Or there is the practice of Confucius who read tomorrow's unborn history in events of thousands of years gone by.

This is the story of a very mountainous journey seen from such peaks.

It may be that some will learn from the perspectives of the man who is coming down, tired but still walking.

Douglas Weddell Thompson

"From the mountain peak I saw a road on which the
journey was its own reward"

Contents

Peak One - SETTING OUT

Boyhood and Training

When the British Empire still existed there was a time when once a week, on a Thursday, a Peninsular and Oriental Line steamer warped out of the King George V dock carrying the King's Mail and a peculiar brand of Briton to the farthest East and ports en route.

Those black hulls and yellow funnels were arrogant in their ugliness; the P & O did not need to be graceful, it was sufficient to be the P & O. On 6th November 1925 the vessel of the week was P & O RMS *Macedonia*, full 20,000 tons, which was to sail for China and Japan. Her least sophisticated passengers were a group of twenty missionaries newly appointed to India and the East. The ship's name gave them their only comfort. 'Come over to Macedonia and help us' was, after all, the original missionary call. To the Owners, the Lascars and Goanese aboard, the name meant no more than the gamble for profits and lavish tips. To one trio of the missionaries their personal gamble — with their lives — seemed a rank outsider. The moment had come and it was awful.

Two of the three young men were seen off by their girls as well as their parents, the third was a recluse type and had difficulty in recognising a woman when he saw one. They were all leaving Britain for seven years before a furlough came round, and four of those years were probationary years in which they were forbidden to marry. Those were the days! As the ship dropped down the dock basin into the stream of the river the little party of relatives stood on the shoulder of the dock gates waving. Swiftly the winter gloom engulfed them until only a pair of scarlet knee boots, then worn by girls and called 'Russian boots', remained in sight. It was goodbye indeed. The knee-boot girl was to see China after her

four year wait, the other was never to do so. The recluse lived to
marry a female recluse, homing as on a radar beam.

The trio went below to their tiny 'inside' cabin to sort out
their luggage until they discovered, as every P & O Second Class
passenger soon did, that this job can only be done with one
person in the cabin at a time. Two went to gaze on the only world
they had ever known drifting astern and wishing that they had
chosen to serve in it. Not a hero in the bunch — there never is.

Looking back down the years from this peak experience what
lay there? How did they come to be China bound?

One of the pairs of elbows leaning on the damp rail belonged
to Arthur Preston Hadwen, a Lancashire lad who had received
an elementary education, become a Post Office engineer and
enlisted in the army in 1917. Wounded and captured in 1918 he
had spent time in a PoW Camp determined to nurse a wounded
arm which promised never to be of any further use. So well did he
do this that many never knew it had ever been damaged. He had
dreamt of going as a missionary to China for years and after the
war ended had polished his education to the point of entry into
ministerial candidature. He climbed through the Civil Service
into a Theological College. He was to experience twenty-three
stormy Chinese years, end then once more in a prison and die in
England. That was lantern jawed Hadwen, homesick for two red
boots.

Down below with priority on unpacking was James Clegg,
son of a Yorkshireman who had carved his dour way through the
life of Halifax as a Labour Councillor. James was the brilliant one
and out of that sturdy home he became one of five Halifax men to
enter the Methodist Ministry as by right. He took one of the early
Birmingham University BA degrees in Theology. His world was
books and in the end education called him out of the ministry
into the schools, but not before he had left a mark on Higher

Education in Wuchang.

The second pair of elbows on the ship's rail was mine. They were the youngest and their owner knew it. Hadwen had a whole war tucked away behind his peering eyes; Clegg had his academic confidence.

I was just me, son of a miner who with his father, had been shot out of the Cumbrian mines for joining the infant Union. They had tracked across into Northumberland and Durham seeking a pit. When I was born he was trying to pass from coal getting to the life of a 'Scot's Draper' — that is one who sold cloths on credit from house to house through the Northern villages. His wife was a girl ten years younger than he whose family thought him far below her in station, the miner being thought then the dregs of society. Her ancestry went back in history in the Scottish Lowlands in the Weddell family which had produced the sea captain who gave his name to the Antarctican Weddell Sea. Another of them — her uncle — had invented Cerebos Salt. Yet another was a Scot's Domine with the Selkirk School as his work.

Their religion had brought them together, doing evangelistic work in the slum lodging houses of Newcastle in which he preached and she sang. On Sunday nights their work was in the open air, so that among one's earliest memories is the crowd in the Big Market with my father's voice ringing out across the drunken hubbub or my mother's creating a pool of silence as she sang Sankey's solos. There was a Mission Hall — in Silver Street where the Police went in pairs on Saturdays. In the Hall a mighty washing copper full of scalding tea was always boiling with which to sober up the audience before preaching. The Mission was called the Eldon Mission and owed its title to Lord Eldon, Lord Chancellor, whose politics was a deep hatred of Roman Catholicism. Little the folk cared — there was the tea.

Such parents could not but create a home in which there was perpetual tension between the pull of gentility and the drag of poverty. This is, perhaps, the worst kind of poverty. In that home the Tyneside dialect was forbidden to us but waifs and strays picked up at the Mission or in the Big Market spoke it. To make ends meet there was a stream of 'paying guests'. There was seldom enough to go round but always enough to have at table a deserted seaman's wife perhaps, a Scandinavian girl expecting a baby, or such characters as the Black Cat, an ex-bookie's tout proud of seventy-two convictions.

The two grandparents' homes to which we children were dragged at Christmas and New Year highlighted this tension. One was thoroughly established where a herd of respectable relatives would be gathered. They would be playing cards, listening to cylindrical records on a phonograph or, the men, combining in octets to sing glees. Well clothed cousins, sixteen of them, were the topic among the women, every single cousin doing marvels at school. Here our mother was 'poor Flossie' and her man 'that Nathan'. I remember feeling fiercely proud of them both. We languished in corners dreaming of the home-made toys my father had made for us back home.

Grandfather Thompson's tiny home in the depths of Dunstan was the house of singing birds and gurgling pigeons, the canaries high in box cages on the walls and the pigeons tapping on the upstairs windows. The purr of the Cumbrian dialect spoken by my grandmother ('Come, now, them's a few fine broth.') matched the cooing of the pigeons.

He was, when first we knew him, a mighty old man working as gateman at the local gas works, who sat, great staff in hand, in a heavy leather backed chair and swore with each alternate sentence. She was his devoted attendant all the week but on Sundays, uniformed tidily, Penitent Form Lieutenant at the Salvation Army Citadel. How they loved each other; so much so that at his death — when his coffin had to be lowered from the bedroom window into the street — his parting words to her were 'Eh lass, 'tis Blood and Fire for thee and bloody fire for me'. Nevertheless the Army paid no regard, they buried him with an open air band-led service in that little street. People said that she could begin the week with a half pound of margarine and end it with three-quarters, the balance being bread crumbs.

Their only daughter, Aunt Emma, was married to Billy, a stoker on the coke ovens, and a quiet man who talked mostly with his eyes. A son younger than my father quit the ovens and swapped English slums for farming in Canada, no small transfer. I only saw him once afterwards when he returned to fight in World War I which was a free return home for so many men.

We children, all three of us, for there was my much younger sister, entered both homes timidly without making any real contact. They were both so different. In our own home playing cards were forbidden, we were not even allowed to read boys' papers; swearing was a punishable crime; singing was Gospel hymns exclusively.

Such a home had to produce tensions too, the most character forming of which for us two boys was the pull of what to do with life. On the Weddell side everyone, including our cousins, was on the 'white collar' side of life; this was anathema to Grandfather Thompson and the Dunstan family who thought the clerks and others of that world only existed to get a living by falsifying pay packets. Uncle Billy and his mates saw 'pen pushing' as degrading and unmanly. These two streams of ideas met at home. It loosed my brother out as a boy into learning to become a skilled draughtsman by sheer courage, night schools and all the strain of catching up. In the long run the Weddells won but we had the white collar basics turfed out of our lives by the Thompson tradition. We were both convinced that to leave school as soon as possible and get to work was the only way for red-blooded people.

We loved that home in spite of tensions. They were pioneer types our parents. He was tall and handsome — he could heave a hundredweight sack on his shoulder or swing it just for fun. She was small, dark, vivacious with abundant black, curly hair and eyes, as she said, 'set with dirty fingers'. He had a violent temper and would punish us, except my sister who once from under the kitchen table told him, 'You can't do me, I'm sitting on it'. My mother would intercede for us, getting in between, for she had far less evangelical puritanism in her.

He read widely using the best Bible commentaries — he once gave me on my birthday a massive copy of Matthew Henry's Commentary saying 'It will press your trousers and help my studies'. He scoured the second-hand shops, loved to paint (at which he was very good), lettered beautifully; he practised photography, his wife doing the developing which she had learned in the chemist's shop which gave the world Cerebos.

He revelled in nature study and when he took us on his rounds through the villages he would tell us the Latin names of wild plants — once and only once; we must remember. This was all the fruit of that evangelical conversion which demands self improvement as a religious duty. Yet, he never forgot the pit from whence he was digged and in which he had digged. Should he catch us cocking up a foot on a chair to tie a shoe lace he would roar, 'Bend your back boy or it's down the pit you go'.

There came one break for me in this family life. Just before World War I broke our family fortunes had sunk so low that I was sent across to Gateshead to live with the Weddell grandparents. Life changed.

They not only popped me into a bedroom of my own, which I had never had, they bought me a new suit of navy blue, my first new suit. They found sixpence a week to send me to the Higher Grade School and thrust me into the thriving Sunday School of Bensham Chapel.

The family had a pew in this great old church. On Sundays it was packed with aunts, cousins and grandmother but never grandfather. He was a preacher with the Open Brethren and on special Sundays purloined me to go off to village Brethren chapels where I was cosseted by kindly folk. I sat at table with them when they observed the Breaking of Bread and thought it beautiful.

Grandfather Weddell was a great chap. He travelled for a Gateshead sweet firm, speaking a lowland Doric which won many customers. He renewed his samples every week so the house never lacked toffees. He wrote both hymns and tunes for them. During the period of depression at home he got my father a job in the firm's warehouse — heaving boxes round.

Grannie for her part did her best to civilise me. It was under her hand that I first wore night clothes in bed instead of just tumbling in.

Then it happened. While at the Higher Primary School there came a chance to sit for a scholarship at Gateshead Secondary School (which became Gateshead Grammar School later) and my Form Master had the courage to enter me, to all my relatives' amazement. One or two of my cousins were also sitting the exam.

I passed the examination as number thirteen in the town. At twelve years of age I entered the School and the work, especially on the humanities, was no trouble to me, but I never was in the life of the school.

When I had been there a year, for some reason unknown to me I was shifted back home, which meant that every school day morning there was the walk from Newcastle to Gateshead either over the High Level bridge or, to save a penny toll, over the Swing bridge. For lunch I would have twopence for a pie or walk down to a workman's diner near the sweet factory to pool it with my father's fourpence when we both had soup. I tried to do some belated homework on the greasy table, too.

At fourteen I left the school, my course unfinished. I wanted to go to work. We thought life began at fourteen. It certainly did. My father had entered the service of the YMCA as a Hut Secretary in France by then, so it was my mother who took me to the Juvenile Employment Exchange. The character who interviewed me asked me what I would like to do and thinking of the Uncle after whom I was named, Douglas Weddell, I said Commercial Chemistry. The interviewer had made up his mind about me by then. He sent me off to The Scientific Glass Company in Newcastle. 'You'll be in science', he said.

It was a Belgian firm evacuated into England, sub-contracting the manufacture of scientific glass for firms like Brady and Martin.

I found it in the basement of a great furniture warehouse on one of the back streets of Newcastle. There were six expert glass blowers seated at one side of the long underground space at their Bunsen Burners, and another row of burners with girls making simple things. The mass of space was taken up by stored glass and a tiny little office in a cubicle at one end, a couple of lavatories at the other. I was accommodated at my own Bunsen burner next to another, senior, apprentice and began to blow. From the first day I was blowing, or at first trying to blow, thistle funnels. We got a shilling and a penny for every dozen funnels if they stood up all square. This we did all day, except when we were blowing little ornaments for the girls upstairs in the warehouse.

Just now and again we apprentices were sent off to tidy up a railway arch near by, in which we stored defunct electric light bulbs. We enjoyed this for we had sham fights with the bulbs which went pop as we missed each other. We popped far too many and were thoroughly ticked off in robust Flemish by the 'Boss', whose little side-line these bulbs were. I loved it all, and felt I owned the world, a working lad among working men, a young lad among a herd of girls.

It was my uncle Douglas Weddell who ended this adventure. I would have stayed but he said to my mother, 'Get him out of there or he'll be dead with TB before he's forty'. It was true that the two best blowers practically lived on Cherry Balm Lung Tonic, which I was sent out to buy for them.

No more Juvenile Employment Exchange; I found my next job for myself. It was as office boy in a quaint Dickensian solicitor's office where my main job consisted in being there when no-one else was, which was nearly all day. I occupied my time in copying records by hand into enormous ledger-like books of case history and generally mooning round the place learning how very murky is the world of property buying and selling. It was boring and lonely but I liked the old-world office and felt like a David Copperfield. I'd found a dead end.

Life does not deny the lowliest lad his chance, whatever Civil

Servants may do, and mine came. On the Tyneside in those days the cream of business was on the Quayside. To be a member of the Coal Exchange, the Shipping and Freight Exchange, was power. It was the power base of the Catchisides, the Keenlysides, the Lunns. From their number came the Lord Mayors of the city and the way in was to become an apprentice ship broker. How? That was the rub, for apprentices were taken at a premium of hundreds of pounds and worked without a salary.

Those were war years however. Business was heavy and difficult and one firm, Watts, Watts and Company, a London firm with twenty ships ploughing the ocean — until the Germans accounted for sixteen of them — and the Agency for dozens more of other lines out across the world, actually advertised for an apprentice. I applied and got it and with a tiny salary of five shillings a week, which the other apprentices soon taught me to augment by doing things for neutral sea captains who were not allowed on shore for security reasons.

We signed on their crews down at South Shields, we purchased their presents for their wives, fixed their Bills of Lading and saw that they had a reasonably secure place in the North Sea convoys, in which the Royal Navy had a tendency to put neutral ships in the outer tiers. Many a sea captain sailed wearing three silk shirts, or with a pair of silk stockings under his sea boots.

Back in the office there was the telephone switch-board to master, the copying of all letters, the filing of shoals of incoming ones. Gone was the atmosphere of the Dickensian lawyer; there was a large staff of typists, clerks and there were three of us apprentices. At the top level were four senior ships brokers as well as the manager. On occasions we would have to go down to the actual Exchange with them or for them and walked the hallowed floors among the Captains of Industry: budding Big Shots. It might have ended wonderfully in charge of finding bottoms for freight to Shanghai or Kingston, Jamaica — I hope it did for the other two — but for me there were other things planned outside my ken or control and it all summed up into learning skills which

were employed in very different circumstances. Life was for us
more than work. We had busy weekends and evenings at our
disposal. In the simple ways of our times our world was, pre-
eminently, our girls, and in the second place, and with them, the
streets and diversions of the streets. In wartime England our city
was a prime target, with two or three of the greatest armament
works in the world within it, as well as the strategic river itself.
'No mean city.' It was under a heavy 'black out' and just made for
penniless teenagers. We ranged through it like stallions on the
hills.

The companion girls were all out of the same 'mission' circles
into which we were born; their tiny homes, in most cases, backing
on to Armstrong Whitworth's great factories. They were of our
own age and shared our own world-sampling interests. Boys and
girls we ganged up with others like ourselves and simply went out
to get all we could, at the price we could pay.

Long strolls through the blacked out streets, quieter places,
shop doors, the edges of the town, like the Two Ball Lonnen
which was a Mecca of couples; chip shops; anywhere was good
enough for us.

Saturdays were times when all picture houses were open but
we were broke — Saturdays were a problem and that problem the
Methodist Church solved for us and thousands. With the help
of Joseph Rank, father of the great family, it produced halfway
houses to the Church in its great Central Halls. They were large
halls with cinema organs, seating at their smallest some 1,200
people on tip-up seats, brilliantly lit, vibrant. Mother of them all
still is Westminster Central Hall.

They came to our aid with Saturday night Concerts at 2
½d. and the half-penny was tax. They were Music Halls refined
to a Christian standard, light music, comedy and song; artistes
appeared who later became famous names. They were havens for a
host of people for whom public houses and 'Empires' were taboo.
We joined the throng. With the entrance money, and some chips
afterwards they were nicely within our range.

Sunday evenings were even more difficult than Saturdays. What was there to do? At the Central Hall, having got used to the place on Saturdays, we found that the evening service was about as enjoyable as the concerts. They cost only the collection, and some funny things happened to it! With the mighty cinema organ, the choir, over a thousand voices in the congregation, special music and brave lighting they were terrific.

Our particular Hall was the Westgate Hall of the Newcastle Mission, the parent of three centres of the mission. The Ministers of these Halls were a special breed. They had a skill in oratory which left politicians away down the field — as Winston Churchill later was to tell candidates for parliament. They talked about things which we understood in language we could follow and a manner which put them on our side. Alan F. Parsons was the particular minister at Westgate Hall in those days, a master of his craft. Years later I was sorry that we got across him for he died early in a struggling London Church, worn out.

It was the seating of the Hall which was our downfall. Long curving rows of tip-up seats were arranged on rising tiers above one another so that each seat could be seen from the rostrum on which the preacher stood. This meant that the girls who sat on the row just below us with their long plaits of hair falling down their backs, became fair game. Someone suggested tying those plaits together through the backs of the seats. When the next hymn was announced and the girls tried to rise to sing, it was mayhem; they could not rise and the seats went clop, clop, clop, as they attempted it.

Mr Parsons looked up from far away on the rostrum, my brother and I had rolled up our hymn sheets and stuck them behind our ears. 'Will the Stewards kindly eject those boys with cigarettes behind their ears in the back row of the gallery', the Minister said. We were enraged — cigarettes indeed. We resisted, and it took four Stewards to get us out. There we were, in the street and the black-out and our friends, and our girls, inside. It was the end of the Westgate Hall and our friendships for us.

As the Chinese say, every difficult situation has a built-in
escape route. In this one it was the Superintendent of the Police,
Mr Dale, a member of the Central Hall congregation who
pointed it out. Deeper into the slums of Newcastle, he told us, was
The People's Hall, sister to that from which were were banned.
We found it on Rye Hill, a slope leading down to Armstrong
Whitworth's. It was an old chapel transformed into a mission hall.

The programme was different, but one thing it did have, a
young Men's Club, some forty young fellows led by an older,
thriving businessman, Mr Haggle, who made hawsers and ropes
for the ships in the river at his Haggle's Rope Works. A lady of the
congregation cared for the young women and there was an old
Wesley Deaconess, Sister Sarah Page, whose biscuit bonnet and
grey uniform gave her entry into both and linked them. She was a
gem, as are so many of the Order.

We tried it, liked it, and stuck; we didn't know it but we were
growing up. The young women of the People's Hall were all of
an older age group than those we had known, perhaps in their
twenties, and they interested us more than the young girls we had
previously larked with.

The great thing at the People's Hall was the Sunday night
service. The total seating of the Hall was about 800. In an older
style building, the effect of nearness was as great or greater than
in the modern cinema type building. The galleries went sweeping
round the whole interior until the folk in the end seats seemed to
be over the preacher's head. The vast audience 'clustered'. Wesley's
Chapel in the City still has this character.

When the congregation rose to sing in this proximity there
was released a tremendous, compulsive emotion. In the preaching
there was a strange 'undercover' immediacy as though every word
was a whisper in the ear rather than a declaration. The Minister
at this Hall was the Rev. H. Taylor Cape, a born Central Mission
type with a warm, embracing personality.

The day had to come. One Sunday night with the Hall
crowded Mr Cape chose to talk on a most unusual text, probably

because of his love of Hebrew and the Old Testament. 'For the bed is shorter than that a man can stretch himself on it; and the covering than that a man can wrap himself in it', Isa. 28:20.

What had this to say to me? I had tumbled into a rumpled bed with my brother ever since I remembered, except for that period when my Grannie had put me into lovely clean sheets at Gateshead. We had quarrelled, my brother and I, about the sheets, even to stretching a divider made of knotted ties down the middle. Something — experience longed for, freedom, the cramp of life, the inadequacy of the open air appeals I had heard dozens of times in the Big Market — rapped on my heart.

This man was talking about a wider life, my hope, a faith, which reached out ahead. The old Methodist phrase dating back to John Wesley, 'recumbancy on Christ', meant a new lease of life at all points. When he made his appeal I got up from the back of the gallery and wound my way down innumerable steps to the body of the Hall and down the central aisle to the Communion Rail — to find that my brother had followed. Mr Cape folded us in like two sons.

A great dawn broke across my life. I felt as though the whole world had been re-created. 'Something lived in every hue Christless eyes have never seen.' The next morning on the way to work I felt as though the cobbled street was singing praises. Our mother was thrilled and wrote to our father out in France and soon there came from him two pocket New Testaments in which he had written 'saved to serve', 17th February 1917.

I don't know what would have happened to that sudden glimpse of 'Life' had it not been for the tender concern of H. Taylor Cape. The whole content of the Christian Faith was still unknown to me. I could not live out a life on that one moment's beauty. He knew.

Within a week he had me down at a street corner of the bustling Scotswood Road and on his 'soap box' — 'just to tell the folk in five minutes what happened to you'. I lasted three with my tongue feeling like a matchbox in my mouth. But I had confirmed my decision by my own lips.

He arranged for both of us to go to his home once a week to study the religion he had passed on to us, and that follow up was really the foundation of my personal faith. He had been trained at Handsworth College, the Theological Institution at Birmingham. He simply took down his own personal notes of all he had learned there and slogged through them. This was too much for my brother, his religion was not to grow in that way. Religion became the spirit of his life, but in his own personal way, which thrived on Christian music, kindliness, generosity and a great devotion to his mother and family. This was his 'bigger bed' to his end.

I was fascinated by the studies as, week by week, Mr Cape went through his notes on the Old Testament, New Testament and systematic theology. Most evenings at home I sat at the books which he recommended. It cost; especially on summer evenings when I would look out of the window on a bright world and wonder what had happened to me — choosing to be alone with books rather than out there.

It was inevitable for my mother's connection with the Christian Endeavour Federation that I should be asked to speak at meetings of Endeavourers in many places and I conquered the 'matchbox' condition. So it was that Mr Dale of the Westgate Hall and the Police, invented the sobriquet of 'The Boy Preacher'. I didn't thank him for that! I found myself on trial on the Methodist Plan.

The war ended. I saw its end outside Newcastle's St Nicholas cathedral with its strange Wren, Lantern Tower. The ship broker's office backed on to the Cathedral Yard and on the 11th November 1918 I was copying letters at the window which looked into the Yard when the bells rang out with a crashing peal of every bell in the tower. We all dropped everything and rushed to the crowd which was gathering in the square outside the Church. They kissed, they hugged, they danced, they sang, survivors of a holocaust. No more torpedoed ships, no more drowned seamen, no more neutrals to prey on. There's a price to pay for everything.

It was 1919 before my father came home from France, having stayed on at Marseilles to serve the Indian Army going home through there. The YMCA service had made him and he was given the new YMCA Centre at West Hartlepool to open, an occasion of much ceremony presided over by Princess Louise. My people moved there, save for my brother who stayed on with his firm.

I broke my apprenticeship to ship broking and found a job with the *Northern Daily Mail* in the heart of West Hartlepool. It was the premier newspaper in the area and later produced Eric Pigott who became the first professional Press man to edit the *Methodist Recorder*.

In the mornings I was behind the counter vetting and receiving classified advertisements, then out and about in the afternoons cub reporting local events, and in the evening getting the paper into the hands of news boys from odd premises in town. That was the rough bit. To be in an empty shop surrounded by thirty or forty yelling lads all anxious to buy and sell and wanting to be first out on the street, while getting the cash and number of papers right, was no sinecure, particularly when an irate parent threatened to 'fill your bloody mouth with broken teeth'.

There were several thriving chapels in West Hartlepool but there was no Central Hall and though I was by now 'on Full Plan' as a Local Preacher I wanted on. There was a Mission at Old Hartlepool some three miles away and to it I went and so met the Rev. Garrett Udy, a Cornish minister, stationed there. He was vintage central hall material. I helped him in open air services, but did most of my preaching round the Circuit and when free went to a Primitive Methodist Church which had scores of young folk and was situated opposite the YMCA. One chapel to which I was sent sometimes was, strangely enough, at Greetham where Cerebos had its factory.

It was a good life, with work I liked on the paper, the' Y' as home, sometimes helping my mother in its canteen and always mixing with chaps just older than I, and it became idyllic when I found that at Seaton Carew, a nearby seaside resort, there was a little chapel which had young children and no leader for them. I teamed up with a Seaton girl about my own age, Ethel Leech, to operate a Sunday School and we did all kinds of things with these children. A whole summer I lived in a tiny tent on the beach reading in my spare time and late at night by candlelight lost in 'Young's Night Thoughts'.

Garrett Udy was the man to end it all. This strange man, who himself left the Methodist Ministry, said to me one day in his manse, 'You should go into the Ministry and your way to do it is to get time for more study by going as the lay missioner to a country Circuit. I'll get you one.'

I thought this one over in my tent and applied for the post at Richmond, Yorks, and so in that September of 1921 I was into the full-time service of the Church.

It was a complete transplant. I arrived in time for the spate of Harvest Festivals, not knowing a blade of grass from barley. I had fourteen chapels in which to conduct Harvest Thanksgiving Services for congregations whose life was the land, for even the town folk lived by the land at second remove. I talked to them about the harvest of the sea and their fellow workers who ploughed the deep waters. The other half of England's food supply.

I was put to live with two delightful people, in Ryder's Wynd, an old gentleman who was a joiner, and his devoted daughter. He was a carpenter — his chief joy was making coffins — and hers in making good Yorkshire food. He was a fountain of Dale's lore and she, though never at church, turned her home into a sanctuary. I had a room way upstairs littered with books, and there I studied in the mornings.

The Circuit had one Minister, the Rev. Herbert W. Pates, a bearded old tiger nearing the end of the ministry, whose beard was intended to hide the scars of smallpox which he endured in a 'plague ship' in the Thames mouth years before. He got round the churches in a Morgan three-wheeler while I did it on a cycle. I was allowed to have a bath in the manse each week provided that I blew the organ for his daughter's practice.

In those days the programme was simple. There were no special week-night youth groups, etc., to organise but simply one preaching service at each place following extensive and thorough visiting before the service in the afternoon. This meant four week-night preaching services and three on Sundays. One Wesley Guild — that pioneer of youth movements — in the town was the only chance to hear other people speak.

There were younger people in plenty in the town church and in particular I used to drop into a flat, where three girls teaching or in business chummed together, after I had finished my night meeting and cycled back. Farmers' sons joined in these late night sessions.

One of these girls and I became specially fond of each other. She was much my senior and worked in a local garage. I sometimes went over to her home in a nearby Dale and she came on occasions to mine. There grew up between us an understanding which when I got into Inland China I lived greatly to regret. I came to see that to transplant her to that environment would be sheer cruelty and ended the connection. She lived on in the North Yorkshire scene and raised a family in it, but I still see this as one great mistake of my days. I have always been grateful for the friendship of those years.

The months sped by as I went through the many tests demanded of ministerial candidates — the written examinations, the vote by the Quarterly Meeting of the regional churches, then the interview by the District Synod, which took place at Barnard Castle. There were five of us offering in that District that year. I can still feel the terror of being the fifth in the line standing before all the Ministers of the Darlington District. When doctrinal or biblical questions got no adequate answer up the line the questions bounced down for me to stop them. There still remained my own quota of questions. My own Ministers — Alan

Parsons, Taylor Cape and Garrett Udy were far away in other
Synods.

Those quiet mornings in Ryder's Wynd saved me. The Synod
sent me, with one or two of the others, forward to the national
conference with a unanimous vote. My Superintendent was
delighted with his candidate.

The Conference July Committee is a formidable body
composed of College Tutors, other pundits, high officials of
Methodism and senior Ministers. It met for the north of England
in Manchester's Didsbury College, on this occasion presided over
by Dr. Findlay, who put most of the questions to us as we stood
in hatches before the Committee. Mercifully the system provided
one already trained senior student in charge of us all — a body of
over a hundred candidates. He, it happened, was going to China
in the autumn and I grew to know him very well.

The Committee had before it all the dossiers of the examinees,
our background story, our education, our written examination
results, the votes of our own churches and of the Synod, topped
up with the opinions of its own particular examination. It graded
the men in four grades — 'no doubt' was 'A', 'nearly all right'
'B', 'doubtful' 'C' and 'rejected' 'D'. On these results the whole
Ministerial Session of the Conference, about 300 ministers, based
their final vote. I found myself in 'A' group and was told by one
of the ministers that I would be sent for training to Handsworth
College in Birmingham.

My father had by now left the service of the YMCA and was
pastor to a congregation of 'Free Church of England' people in
Halifax. It was therefore from there, in the company of James
Clegg, that I went up to Handsworth College in September 1922.

No words can ever express the debt I owe to Handsworth. It
opened the world to me and set my feet in sound ways of study.
The Staff was incomparable: Dr T. G. Tasker was our Principal
and House Governor, Dr Frederick Platt, with Dr W. F. Lofthouse
and Dr Wilbert Howard, taught us and loved us, nor must we
omit the Assistant Tutor, A. D. Philipson, who endeavoured to

fill the gaps in our general education. Dr Henry Belt followed Dr
Tasker in our last year.

It was part of the genius of Methodism in that period before
Government Grants that she took us without charge, if necessary,
into such a place. It was also an act of grace that such men as that
Staff should give their lives to us — as Dr Howard once said 'As a
ladder up which we climbed'.

We rose early and were in classes all the mornings. With Dr
Tasker for Church History, Dr Platt for systematic and pastoral
theology, Dr Lofthouse for Hebrew, Old Testament studies
and philosophy, Dr Howard for New Testament studies and
Greek, with Mr Philipson for English language and literature
and supplementary Greek. Dr Howard also fitted in a course
on 'Primitive Life in the Early Church'. Dr Lofthouse included
modern Psychology based on the newly translated works of Freud
and Jung within his philosophy.

Afternoons were our own to go out and to take part in sports,
with the exception of visits from a part-time tutor in elocution,
Mr Robinson. The evenings were packed with exercises, note
revision and the preparation of passages for coming Greek and
Hebrew lessons. Occasionally there would be a visiting lecturer
such as Dr Deissmann of the German Church or a private hour
with one of our tutors in his home. Private hours were given to
some subject chosen for its appropriateness to our individual
future work, as when Dr Lofthouse did a study of Afrikaans with
a man going to South Africa.

We worked. That did not, however, prevent a busy student
life. We played football, cricket, tennis, squash and hockey. The
more personal life was served by the traditional breaking up of the
whole student body into Firms — a group of four or five students
who were mutually akin — for teas and outings. Mine was Frank
Mussell, the College Chairman, who since has spent a lifetime
in Rhodesia and Zambia, John Watson who went to South
Africa, James Clegg, Fred Bramwell who failed the medical test
for overseas service but who weathered a life of British northern

circuits, being a southerner. Such friendships last a lifetime
though the 'Stations' might put us seas apart.

It was this Firm which at the 1924 Election captured the key
of the College Tower and flew the Red Flag from it to celebrate
a victory over the head of a Midland brewing firm. This was
possible because we had scrambled over roofs to hang an aerial for
a crystal set in Mussell's room and so had the news in the dead of
night.

There was also the Rags Committee on which in my second
year I served. Its task was to torment the First Year students into
humanity after their passage through the heady experience of
passing the Conference's tests. It organised a spoof examination
in their first week on spurious questions with loaded answers.
For instance, 'What is the relationship between cotton, shirt
and wooley' was not a request for an essay on the West Riding
but a reference to the fact that all three were the names of senior
students. The true answers were revealed at the Christmas dinner.

It was part of the official discipline of the College that a First
Year student should conduct a service and preach once to the
whole assembly. The service was the subject of a criticism session
on the following Saturday morning under the direction of Dr
Platt and later of Dr Bett, a terrifying experience both for the
preacher and the critics.

Apart from its academic life the College was organised as a
self-governing community with 'Tables' as its parliament. The
dining hall was set out with one cross table at which the senior
year sat and the other two years running up to it. As soon as the
evening meal was finished a session of Tables began — anything
and everything could then come up for discussion and decision.
Debate and delegated responsibility became familiar to us. Such
tasks as College Secretary, Plan Monitor, Missionary Secretary,
College Doctor, bell boy, 'getter up', lights out responsibility, were
all allocated at Tables.

Sundays were different. Half of us were out taking services
at chapels at places throughout the Midlands. Reports on our

services, we knew, came back to the Principal and gave a basis
to the Plan Monitor and the Governor in sending us to suitable
chapels. Not to be sent out was a real rest; we would go to hear
Dr Spurr of the Baptist Church, the successive preachers at Carr's
Lane Congregational Church, George Robson at our College
Church in Somerset Road, a model of intimacy in style. There
were days when at the Cathedral they had specially known figures
such as Dean Inge.

Our weekend appointments provided our pocket money. The
fees which we received were pooled and divided among all the
men whether they had been out or not.

Pastoral life involved being a member of a Mission Band in
serving a needy church in the Black Country. Mine was at Greets
Green, beyond West Bromwich, where the home craft was making
ships' chains in backyard sheds. It got me into trouble for staying
out all night.

We acted as team to a Connexional Evangelist running an
evangelical mission from this church and that involved a late
night procession round the local pubs during which we picked
up many folk who followed us to a service in the church. After
the service ended a chap grabbed hold of Fred Proctor and me
and asked us to take him back to his wife. He chose Fred because
of his lovely tenor voice and the solos he had sung in the service.
'She won't believe I'm changed if I go alone', he said. We took
him home and at his request poured a bottle of beer he had in his
pocket down the drain outside the house, saying a prayer as we did
so. His wife was at the stove cooking him a meal when we went
into the tiny, bare house. He, stone sober, flung his arms round
her and said 'Everything's going to be different, the ministers
have brought me home'. In 1966, forty-two years later, when my
name was in the news I received a letter from him. He was living
up north and told me he had held every lay office in a Methodist
Church and at eighty wanted to say 'thank you'.

When Dr Tasker carpeted me for staying out he told me there
was a life of evangelism ahead but now I was a student and needed

everything the College could give me. He was right, though my
parents would not have thought so.

Those halcyon days flew on to their end. It was the practice
for students to go out as Probationer Ministers for four years,
continuing their studies as they worked in circuits, then the
Conference ordained them. There was an exception in the case
of men going overseas. They were ordained at the beginning of
probation.

As I had been gazetted to the Hunan District of China I
was joined to a small group, including Clegg and Watson, to be
ordained at Carlisle Central Hall in 1925. It is the habit for an
Ex-President of the Conference to preside over such services and
Dr Tasker came to officiate. We were the last group of dozens to
be trained by him both in Germany and Britain. He was assisted
by Bramwell Evans, known as the Romany Minister, minister
of the Central Hall. The crowd in a Central Hall had begun my
journey, a crowded Central Hall blessed my ordination.

There followed eight weeks at the Selly Oak Colleges on a
course of study doing phonetics and linguistics, to help us learn a
strange language, hygiene and some medicine.

Our last glimpse of our beloved Handsworth was to go back
there at the start of the new term to be 'Rolled off'. This was a
great tradition. We walked between two lines of all the students
down the long corridor which had been our home shaking
hands with every man while the whole College sang, to the tune
Canada,

> And let our bodies part,
> To different climes repair,
> Inseparably joined in heart
> The friends of Jesus are.

So the preachers sang in the eighteenth century when some
went to Sierra Leone and others to Antigua. Charles Wesley is
deathless.

Peak Two - TWO'S COMPANY

First China Years

In the burning heat of the summer of 1929 I left the Siang River town of Yiyang by launch bound for the provincial capital, Changsha. This was no official business trip but at the prompting of the Methodist Conference far away in Britain, for it was the year of the end of my probationary ministry. At Conference I was to be admitted as a life member of the Wesleyan Preachers. It was the high spot and goal of the seven years of probation in Britain, China and India which had flown away in my life journey. It also gave me the privilege of marriage and that brooked no delay.

Getting married in China at that time was no simple job for a foreigner. One could be married by a Consular Official at a British Consulate but that meant travelling to one and was equivalent to a Civil marriage in England, and did not satisfy the Church's rules. One could be married at a Consulate and subsequently have a religious marriage in a Church but that meant that the religious ceremony was simply what is now called 'The Service for the Blessing of a Marriage'. The one place at which the religious ceremony included the civil was at Holy Trinity Cathedral, Shanghai. There the Dean would allow the marriage of a non-Anglican provided he registered as a 'missionary' rather than a Minister — an interesting distinction — and the marriages were registered in batches, when the list was long enough, in Britain in Parliament as 'Marriages beyond the High Seas'. Couples never knew that date. The Dean of Shanghai at that time was the charming brother of the cricketer Sutcliffe and he revelled in this early precursor of Anglican/Methodist Union. The bride was returning from England to China and would disembark at Shanghai.

At Changsha I met the Rev. Stanley K. Lamming who had

generously agreed to come with me to Shanghai — which after all
was eight hundred miles away — as Best Man, and we boarded a
river boat and sailed for Hankow, the next stage on the journey.
The sheer relief of that river boat's Western style bath and cabin
and food baffles description.

Changing river boats at Hankow we arrived in Shanghai
three or four days before the wedding day, booked for 25th July,
the day on which back home Conference was receiving me — we
cared little about the time difference which actually made us
anticipate Conference! I had booked at Beaman's Guest House in
the fashionable part of the city. Lamming went to the Missionary
Guest House down in the heart of the city. Ring buying and other
shopping gobbled up one day. On the second day the P & O
Liner docked and we met Gladys off it and got her gear through
Customs wondering what on earth she made of the man she had
come back to China to marry. I decided that these nursing sisters
are hard to shock and seldom do what they don't want to do. I
had promised a fine senior missionary wife up in Hupeh, whose
life in China had been no bed of roses, that I would 'give her time
to settle down to get her land legs and a new vision of you'. 'It is
horrible to rush a girl into marriage still with the ship's winds in
her ears', so Mrs W. F. Allen had said. She had told me that being
let down the walls of Wuchang in a basket in the first revolution
was not so frightening as getting off the ship in the morning,
buzzing off to the church and being a wife in the afternoon. We
'did Shanghai', had a pre-wedding supper in the 'Yellow Jacket' —
a well reputed Chinese restaurant, taking Lamming everywhere.
The following day we wandered round and in the evening we went
to an open-air cinema. We saw little of the picture, though in the
front row of deck chairs, as we talked to catch up on news.

I had booked Gladys a room with bathroom at Beaman's and
it was from there we both left in a taxi on the morning of the
wedding (very early, about seven o'clock), picked up Lamming
and set out for the Cathedral. On the way down to it Lamming
suddenly asked, 'Where is the second witness; we need two

and I'm only one'. Consternation! He hopped out of the taxi and sought one. He went to the China Inland Mission's office, borrowed a young girl clerk and arrived at the Cathedral in time.

The Cathedral was empty and silent as we arrived and made our way to the tiny Lady Chapel. By and by one lonely Indian Christian came in to the early morning Holy Communion — a steward on a ship in port. Mr Sutcliffe appeared, robed, and there and then, with our beloved Lamming, the sporting English girl and one Indian Christian as congregation, we made our vows before God one to the other. This was truly a peak moment in life and was crowned by the early morning Breaking of Bread.

The Dean came back to Beaman's with us — the Indian guest and girl witness could not — for the wedding breakfast, which really was a breakfast. It was by now nearly nine o'clock and we were all four hungry and it was already about 90° in the shade. I have been since to many such events but that fried egg and bacon meal remains quite unparalleled.

That evening after dark we boarded the *Lungwo*, Jardine's Queen of the River Fleet with Lamming to see us off, bound for Kiukiang, the port for Kuling holiday centre in the Lushan Mountains. We lounged around the ship on deckchairs keeping the fact of our newly-wed status a secret from the few passengers on board and looked back down the days in which we had been together in Hunan and the years of separation in which Gladys had been Home Sister at Manchester Royal Infirmary. What a Probation it had been.

———————

When it began I had arrived in Shanghai with my two colleagues, Clegg and Hadwen, at the end of 1925. Then the Chinese had no right to stop any foreigner bringing in anything he cared to bring. This was a spin-off of the Unequal Treaties. Furthermore, they could only charge five per cent *ad valorum* on any article coming in. I had with me among my heavy luggage

one box I had never seen. It had been mixed in with mine by
the Mission House at home, breaking their own regulations,
and the young Chinese Customs officer insisted on opening
it, quite by random chance. The first things to come out were
women's underclothes, the second a silk dress and so on to the
bottom. This young officer, himself a youngster, looked at me,
said 'You travel alone?', winked and put it all back and had it
nailed down again. Everyone carried gifts in his baggage anyway
and he thought he understood. I decided I was going to like these
Chinese. It turned out in the long run I was carrying the trousseau
of an English lady doctor.

Gladly leaving my boxes to be handled by the coolies we were
stuck into rickshaws and taken off to the Missionary Guest House
which housed missionaries passing through. That evening Clegg
and I took a stroll down the North Szechuan Road, which we
didn't know ran down to the Japanese Concession and the barbed
wire frontier of the whole Concession which was international
Shanghai. We had gone but a mile, soaking in the place, when a
white plain-clothes policeman hove up along side. He said, 'You
new here? Don't go any further down there. Scallywags are always
fighting with the Japanese troops, it's not very healthy.' China was
complicated, we thought, such a nice Customs officer on the one
hand and brigands on the other. We had a lot to learn.

We continued our education the next day by boarding the
river steamer bound for Hankow where Clegg and Hadwen
would finish their journeyings, but I would still have some four
hundred miles to go. We were just clear of Wushih some 5 miles
up river when, the winter waters being low, the ship ran aground
on a sand bank and had to wait for a tug out of Kiukiang to
come and pull us off. The ship listed heavily as the whole ship
load of people crowded to the rail on one side to see this great
rescue operation — there must have been a thousand Chinese
passengers. On the second day the tug arrived and fed us a
wire hawser, which a Chinese crewman in the tug bent round a
mighty towing bollard aboard his tug. The mighty pull began.

The wire grew tight and then tighter, the ship hardly stirred.
Suddenly with a cracking noise the hawser parted; it leapt like a
snake, it coiled round the crewman, broke his back like a stick of
spaghetti, and our thousand Chinese passengers burst into roars
of uncontrollable laughter. We were shocked to the marrow, not
at the death of the crewman but at the minds of the watchers.
Death a joke?

As, at last, with another hawser and another tug to help, we
got off the mud we sat and talked of this grim business. Were
the Chinese so cruel? What of the man's family back on shore?
Slowly it sank in that China had four hundred millions of people,
mostly on the bread line, plagued by a hundred warlords and their
unpaid armies, suffering flood and famine, the semi-colony of all
the Powers. What can you do, in such conditions, about death but
laugh at it? It is a daily burden. Hadwen observed that between
1914 and 1918 in Flanders, men learned to laugh at death in just
the same way. He had reason to know. China was but Flanders
stretched out into a permanent condition. Who were we to turn
away in disgust? Had not British private soldiers laughed and
rejoiced when some intolerable sergeant had toppled back into
a trench dead? Was not the English 'He's got his' parallel to the
Chinese 'Kai Ssu', 'He was destined to die'?

We arrived in Hankow within a day or two of Christmas and
I found Bernard Harvey, fuming with indignation, waiting to
act as my escort into Hunan. Our delay on the river had messed
up his plans for Christmas back on his Hunanese station, and I'd
better help him to get going fast! He was in the final year of his
probation and I was the 'Chokra'. In the shortest time possible
we were across the Yangtze River, at this point a mile wide and
unbridged, into the walled city of Wuchang (which didn't halt
us for a second), on to the Canton Hankow railway station and
into the third-class coaches on hard benches, bedding them down
with the Chinese bedrolls which he carried for the purpose. It was
Christmas Eve.

Through the rest of that day and through a tremendously

long night we ploughed our way south, surrounded by the
multi-shaped Chinese passenger complement to which I
couldn't say a word. Harvey's only conversation amounted to,
'God, can't they make this thing move, it's British?'. It at length
arrived in Changsha, the capital of the province. We rickshawed
through that fascinating city at breakneck speed and got to the
headquarters of the mission. I was lodged and told that the Rev.
Gilbert Warren, the Chairman of the District and a renowned
tartar, wanted to see me as soon as possible. I went trembling into
his bedroom, where he lay sick, to be interviewed. Here there
was no rush, no Harvey could hustle him. With infinite detail
he questioned me for over an hour on the work I had done in
Handsworth, what books, what training, what lecturers, what
the personal result in me? I answered with some enthusiasm, for
I was proud of Handsworth. I told him of Dr Howard's sharing
with us the work he was doing on the life of the early church and
of Loftie's toil over us in private hours in which I had done The
Numinous in Primitive Religion. He was more than satisfied and
I got back to life outside that dreadful bedroom, the bed and
surround piled with his books. If all the Chinese preachers, as I
discovered, were afraid of Gilbert Warren, they had a companion
in me! Yet, one of them told me that on a journey he had shared
a bed head to feet with Warren; shivering with the cold he found
that Warren had swept his feet into his bosom under his pyjamas
to warm him up. He would have died for this stern old man.

With just that one night in Changsha we crashed on our
headlong journey to, it seemed to me, nowhere. Harvey had
brought a pony to the railhead for this stage of the way and
he consigned me into the care of a couple of chair bearers. We
were off. All day long I walked alongside these two chaps as they
carried the empty chair; it didn't seem right for me, who was
obviously younger than either of them, to do anything else.

The one-stone-slab wide road snaked on and on and on, over
high hills, down cultivated valleys, now and again fording streams.
It was all indescribably beautiful. Every twelve 'li' (Chinese miles)

it wound through a Tea House at which we stopped and drank China tea or rape tea, or even chrysanthemum tea — according to the Buddhist endowment of the particular house. There was always a row of bamboo chairs or a bench seat set by the donor, which looked out across the countryside or down some ravine. What could I do but improve the hour by getting the men to tell me the names of things, and this involved some use of verbs which they, tremendously amused, taught me as I scribbled them down in my Selly Oak phonetics. It was good fun and very rewarding. Just now and again we found the pony tied up and Harvey joined us, chafing at the delay. It was a tremendous introduction to the blue hills of Han.

In the evening we came to a village which had a church. It was down at a spot where there was a confluence of waters from two streams, its back jutting out into the water on piles. It stood flat-fronted among the shops to right and left. Two oil-paper windows flanked a wide and open door. Looking in, one could see the pulpit end with texts in gay colours over the back wall. This was the worship hall, filled with benches. The left-hand wall was pierced with windows which suggested that other rooms lay down that side. Entering a door on that side we went into a room which was a guest room, built for interviews with callers and furnished well in Chinese cultural fashion, straight lacquered chairs against the walls, lacquered table in the centre and a picture of Jesus on the honoured wall. Then came a tiny open space with a ladder going up into the roof. Beyond that was the family living room, then two bedrooms and, beyond them, a kitchen with a great brick-built cooking stove. Right at the back there was a lean-to which was the toilets — out over the water with a slit in the floor as the loo. Looking down, the river could be seen, and it solved all sanitary problems.

After we had been welcomed by the preacher — Mr Chang — and his friendly wife and two budding daughters we were shown up the ladder into the roof space, where we found two bamboo chairs, a couple of plank beds and a table. We put a storm lantern on the table, accepted a huge pot of tea, spread out our bedding and were all set for our Christmas dinner. Harvey opened a tin of sardines and produced some bread.

St Stephen's Day was not unlike the original one. We said goodbye to the little family and plodded on for the last thirty miles (English). The road ran on over a mountain pass, which seemed to be intent on climbing to heaven. It dropped down into gorgeous valleys and out across endless paddy fields, where to stumble would have meant to have a mud bath, the road being a tiny wall of earth dividing the fields.

In the late afternoon we entered Pingkiang town, the streets narrow and crowded. I pleased the bearers by getting into the chair to end the journey, thus giving them some 'face', and they toiled under my weight up the long steps of the compound on a hill on the northern edge of the city. The pony, as though to mock us, wagged his shaggy head in approval.

The Superintendent Minister, Mr Pillow, and his sister, together with Gladys Wentworth, the Matron of the hospital, were at the head of the steps to greet us. Their colleagues, Miss Cuthbertson and Dr Margaret Lane, the Deaconess and doctor respectively, could not make it. Two or three years later Miss Wentworth told me that in khaki breeches and leather jacket I reminded her of some farmer from her native north Yorkshire and did her heart good by being so 'northern'.

I settled down with Harvey in the middle house of three, set in a row on a hog's back which looked down on a girls' school on one side and a boys' school on the other. The house with the medical staff was the end one (being nearest to the hospital) which finished the row on the hill. The Super's house stood on the bluff which ended the ridge and commanded a stupendous view of the whole town lying below us.

This was it. I was at my station but could do nothing until I could talk with some ease. I was found a young fellow who had a good classical education and a clear voice and began to conquer the language. He was with me three hours of six days a week and

I put in another five hours each day and found it fascinating. Ministerial missionaries had to learn not only to speak but to write and read Wen Li, the classical form of the language. This was so that we could write our own letters and read those we received personally, in order to be free of the swindles which were the fate of commercial foreigners in China, on the one hand, and be able to use the Chinese classics in preaching on the other.

I was young, straight out from the battle with Greek and Hebrew and I found it all entrancing, thanks largely to Dr Lofthouse's insistence on the overseas students' attention to language. At the end of a week or so I could order from our servant the things I needed, allowing for mistakes, as when Harvey heard me order boiling water for a shave and said 'I hope you get it!'. After a month he told me I must learn the formula for consecration and distribution of the Elements in the Communion service and this I did by endless repetition, and from then on he took me on his visits to country chapels and I had this share in the service. It was a kindness which I was ever thankful for and which I imitated when in charge of others later. After six months I was made to preach to an audience of Christian Workers in the schools and hospitals. My one great mistake in this ordeal was to use a lighthouse as an illustration of the sermon's theme. There wasn't one within a thousand miles! The mistake was homiletical rather than linguistic.

There were other things to worry about. Our compound was an island of peace in the scene of war and disorder. The eastern side of the Circuit ran up to the mountains of Kianghsi, the home of bandits, unpaid soldiery and war. Consequently the hospital never lacked wounded men and women. Sometimes it was swamped with them. Men had to be put in the women's hospital on makeshift beds and no beds. They were often difficult to handle. Miss Wentworth was often at her wit's end to cope with the rush. She sent us a note which said she would be glad of the help of 'able-bodied coolies' but didn't want any quasi doctors. Would we come? We went, on her terms.

In the May of that year down at Shanghai there were great
riots and disturbances in the streets. The international forces and
police found them extremely difficult to control. On 30th May
a great crowd of students rioted in a riot of riots. They could not
be quelled by batons and police methods. The Commandant of
the international armed forces, being an Englishman, ordered his
troops to open fire and two or three rioting students were slain by
the rifle fire. He certainly preserved the Concessions in doing so
but he lit a fire of protest which swept the whole country within
weeks. The weight fell upon the British. We were the greatest
World Power of the age, and a national anti-British movement
began and captured the people everywhere. There was a boycott
of British shipping on the Yangtze and other rivers; there was a
refusal to sell anything to a Briton anywhere, even in our little
inland towns. The Mission schools were involved right across
the country — though I discovered that in shops when I said my
grandfather was a Scot people would ask 'who are the Scots?'
and I told them they were the first people to be conquered by the
English, I got my purchases.

In the midst of this turmoil I was shifted. A senior
Probationer had become engaged to a lady on his station and that
meant under the rules that they had to be separate. I was sent to
Liuyang, a circuit over the range of mountains to the south of
Pingkiang. There our compound was across the river from the
town and one went back and forth to the chapels in town by ferry.
Mr Beale was Superintendent and had his wife and child there.
There were also Dr Mary Andrews and Sister Kathleen Addy, who
worked in the hospital over the river. The second minister was
Tan chin-ching, an heroic old gentleman past seventy years of age.
I brought my teacher with me and got down to work. I never saw
this circuit's country stations because of the disturbances. On one
visit across the river I saw a poster depicting Beale as a tiger and
me beside him as a wolf, emblazoned with the slogan 'Down with
British Imperialism'. It was a beleaguered life.

One morning the Rev. Mr Tan came across the river to our

homes to tell us that there had been a town meeting of leaders
and they had determined to take Beale and me and put us on trial
before a People's Court (these were practised well before pro-
communist occupation). We would certainly be condemned and
the compound with our houses be looted afterwards. He wagged
his old beard at us and said we must leave at dusk. He would
get us native boats and have them at the river bank behind the
compound. It was a real problem for Beale. He had a wife and tiny
baby and there were the two ladies. There was also the tension of
not wanting to fly. He agreed.

That late afternoon we got together and each packed a small
parcel of hand luggage and when it grew dusk we went down to
the river bank and there were three 'hua tze' (little wooden boats
each covered by its bamboo canopy) and a team of boatmen. The
three boats reflected Mr Tan's respect for the proprieties. I had
one for myself alone. 'You will be back in a few days. It will blow
over', he said to comfort Beale. 'You can soon come back but come
only with Tang mu si' — me.

We pushed off in the gathering darkness, dropped down river
and round the bluff, with its pagoda which guarded the town of
Liuyang. We dropped still further down out of the County area.
There the boatmen said they dare go no farther and they tied up
Beale's and the ladies' boats to the bank. Mine was the last boat
in the little convoy and the boatmen were keeping well to the
opposite bank of the river. On the stern end, which was open, I
stood and watched the bank. A crowd of people were shouting at
the boat crew, 'Wait for us, wait for us'. Loyally the boatman dug
his oar deep and swept to the other two boats on the other side
and moored there.

I leaped ashore and went and told Beale we were being
pursued. The boatmen swore they would be killed if they took
us on further. Beale knew the river, it meandered dreadfully. We
could walk across one curve of the land, find the river and perhaps
find a boat owned by a man who was not a Liuyangese.

We set off in the dark across the paddy fields and scrubland,

Beale and I taking turns to carry the infant (who is now a senior
master at Lewes Priory School). It is hard to know how the ladies
in the long dresses of the times managed to stumble forward. All
three were generously built. We knew that we only had the time
which it would take the mob to cross the river, and they would be
in pursuit — they with lanterns, we in the dark. Had our boatmen
gone over to ferry them? Probably.

At last we came again to the river at a quiet little cove where
there stood one fisherman's cottage, its stilts in the river and tied
to them a little fishing boat. We knocked up the sleeping family
and offered the man an exorbitant sum to take us down the Liu
river to Changsha. He bargained but finally came to terms. This
was different boating, Mr and Mrs Beale with the baby had one
end of the canopy's interior and I shared the other end with Miss
Addt and Dr mary Andrews. I watched black beetles scurry
across the canopy over our heads and, as Dr Andrew's corset
creaked, I longed for one ro drop down and wake her. No joy! In
the morning we took stock: Miss Addy said, comfortingly, she
still had her Bible; Beale had is pipe but no tobacco; I had some
tobacco but no pipe. Nipping ashore now and again for food at
some small village we ultimately got to Changsha and into our
town compound.

One or two of our member followed us down river in a day
or two brining a few boxes and the story of Mr Tan. He had
been put up before the crowd and villified. He had said he would
do anything for China but would not give up his faith. He was
sentenced to be publically processed trough the streets but a large
group of men in the crowd knew him a the man of the hospital
and the village schools, not to mention that in town. They cut
him out of the meeting and took him through it and into the
country in hiding.

I was put with another probationer, Stanley Lamming, a
year junior to me in Handsworth, to live with Mr and Mrs Allen
out at the Union Theological College the other side of the city,
and it was a real stroke of luck for he was a sinologue of no mean

stature. He translated Hastings' massive volumes, collected a
unique dictionary of Chinese proverbs with English translations
and took a share in making the Union Edition of the Chinese
Bible. He gave us his own chinese writer as a tutor to us and
himelf supervised our work. He and his wife and daughter were
a charming family to live withm the students were round us in
college and other missionary staff on the compound made a
community. Lamming was just out. I had been down to the jetties
to see him in and had walked him back to the town compound on
a Sunday morning. On the wall of tour church, and on the streets
through which we passed, slogan shouted abuse of the British.
Inside, our church service was in progress. When we got there the
congregation was singing lustily a Chinese hymn but they were
singing it to the tune Natonal Anthem from the *Gentleman's
Magazine* of 1745 - the tune of 'God save the King'. The hymn
now is sung to a new Chinese tune 'China' and is a prayer for
the nation. I couldn't get Lamming to stop laughing before we
entered the church. I never told him that as I had walked down to
the jetty there were two beheaded corpses laying in the road and
I had hated the thought of bringing him past them on the way
back. On the way back they had gone - taken away, probably by
relatives, and the journey was fun.

The political climate was rapidly deteriorating and the
Liuyang incident was by no means unique. The disturbances were
now in Changsha too. One Sunday evening, when Lamming and
I had escorted Winnie Allen to the English language service at
Yale University College, on our way back we bumped into a great,
miles long, procession of all the trade guilds in town marching
past the Russian Consulate where a Russian visitor was being
saluted on the balcony outside the Consulate. We had to hide in
a ditch until the crowd was gone by. The whole scene, in the dark,
was stupendous — torches of flaring bamboo dipped in oil, the
guild of sanitary men with their burden of dung carrying buckets
over their shoulders, shop keepers, even the servants of foreigners.
This was our undoing, from that parade onwards we were

boycotted for all supplies and the British Consul ordered out
all Britons who could be spared from the work. Our own house
boy was gone and Mrs Allen had had enough. She had seen it
all before in 1911 in the Wuchang revolution. One morning the
British gunboat laid on launches and we took her and Miss Allen
to go down river to safety, along with dozens of other womenfolk
and children. They were transshipped into a British river boat
and sailed off, leaving Mr Allen and us to live on and do what we
could to maintain ourselves. Old Mr Allen found himself cooking
and we two ran the place. Now and again the old Chinese tutor
came in secretly with food for us under his gown and taught us for
a while and then slipped away.

The noose round the British community grew tighter and all
movement became impossible for us. From the breadth of China,
people were leaving for Shanghai where the Shanghai Defence
Force (composed of a Brigade of the British Army sent from
India) guarded the Concessions. This was in addition to the local
volunteer forces.

Our Hunan Chairman saw that we could do no more work
for a long time; schools in revolt, churches embarrassed if we
attended — it was chaos. He ordered out every one of us except
himself. Early in 1927 with Mr Allen and Lamming I found
myself on a steel lighter under the guns of the Royal Navy being
towed down river by HMS *Sandpiper*, whose crew had been
starved of fresh food for weeks. I had been in China about
eighteen months and all I had to show for it was a pass in the first
year Chinese examination and a love of the country not dissimilar
to that of my young Chinese colleagues.

Living in Shanghai was simple enough. We were stacked, all
the unmarried, in the Missionary Guest House in the heart of
the city. At first we roved Shanghai and became quite familiar
with it. I found an honorary job cataloguing the books at the
Religious Tract Society depot. Then as the time went on we
sought something a bit more alive and as party after party sailed
for home we got the Methodist Chaplain with the Defence

Force to get us posted as staff in one of the Recreation Huts serving the army. Lamming and I were sent to the Hut serving the South Staffordshire Regiment and the Punjabi Regiment, which was twinned with the Staffords. We soon learned to treat both regiments with equal service and care as the Punjabis claimed to be just as good as Staffords, except for a matter of one penny a day difference in their pay.

These troops were a revelation to me. Lamming had been in the army and had cold feet (through Trench Fever), with which to freeze me years after when we shared a bed. The soldiers got on so well with the Chinese although they knew no Chinese at all. It was almost incredible what they could do. On one occasion on the barbed wire frontier of the Concessions there was an old Chinese lady trying to get in with rifle shot whizzing all round her. A soldier shouted to her, 'Hold on grandma, I'm coming'. He leapt the wire and brought her in, carried in his arms. She patted him on the back.

As the boycott bedded down into a long-term struggle, now including a general demand for the return of all Concessions, the Home Committee of the Conference began to recall its staff. Gladys Wentworth and I, having been buddies for a long time, became engaged just before she sailed to become Home Sister back at Manchester Royal Infirmary. Lamming and I arranged the exit formalities of everyone except ourselves, always wondering when our turn would come. So sure of a return home was Lamming that he spent all he had on purchasing presents for his family.

At last the news came, by telegram. It simply said, 'Proceed to Calcutta and report to the Chairman'.

We took passage forthwith for Singapore, there being no ships to Eastern Indian ports from Shanghai. We had only a few Chinese dollars and would have to cadge our way to India. Lamming with lots more nerve than I pounced on a Baptist missionary lady who paid his excess baggage bill and, as we got to know her, said that CMS missionaries in Singapore would put us up while we waited in Singapore for transshipment. Gentle, loving people they were.

We quickly found a British India Company coaster which was going up to Rangoon in Burma. Her only other passengers were two American teachers on sabbatical leave. They complained bitterly that the first meal we had aboard was not up to the standard they had on the famous President Line ship. The skipper told them that once we were at sea they would have no complaints! We bucketed our way up the length of the Bay of Bengal without seeing them again.

In Burma we had, like two gypsies, already marked out our quarry. The Minutes of Conference indicated that Mr William Sheratt of the Bible Society was a Methodist Minister. We took rickshaws up to the Bible House and found him living alone and very glad to have a couple of young colleagues to talk to. He ran us out to the Foreign Club on the outskirts of the town, after showing us the Shwedagon Temple. In the evening he said the latest Harold Lloyd film was in town and he would be glad to have someone to go with him to see it. This we did. At the pay box he paid for his own seat and I paid for the other two out of our tiny funds. He had not known of our pennilessness I am sure, for he was a most generous chap.

On the little coaster to which we transshipped we were broke, except for the change I had received at the pay box. No 'cumshaws' for the ship's stewards, and at Calcutta I popped what was left into a phone and rang the Rev. J. M. Darlington, telling him that we had arrived, were broke, would get a taxi to his house and would he pay for it when we arrived. This he did cheerfully, for our arrival was the harbinger of his own departure.

The next day we met the Rev. A. E. Brown, CIE, a famous man who has been decorated for his work on reforestation of the Bankura area, who was the Chairman to whom we had to report. His first word to me was, 'They'll be sending us children next. Grow a moustache to give your appearance a year or two.'

He sent Lamming up to Ranigunj to act as chaplain to the

white railway staff up and down the line, a job he had vacant, and me he kept as second minister in Calcutta English work. I inherited a cantonment called Hastings, which had a chapel we had just taken over from the London Missionary Society and which Darlington had looked after until he had become very ill. A new man was awaited from England. Through the rest of 1927 and the whole of 1928 I was there and thoroughly enjoyed the work. My little Hastings Church was set among the Hooghli pilots who brought ships up the eighty miles of the Hooghli from the sea to the port and a large population of Anglo Indian families. I was in and out of all kinds of homes constantly. I saw the little defunct church get a new lease of life and was greatly helped by a little group of LMS missionaries who stood by it. Now and again I preached to the enormous congregation in the Sudder Street Church, an experience indeed. All kinds of people worshipped and crowded it, Europeans, domiciled Europeans, Anglo Indians, some Indians from different parts of India, and the contingent from the army who sat each man with his rifle beside him, for this was Army Orders.

My work included the chaplaincy to the garrison in Fort William in Calcutta and the troops at Barrackpore outside the town, to whom I preached in our little chapel there. In Sudder Street life on Sundays began early with a breakfast for the Army contingent, sometimes sixty to seventy men, with service to follow.

Into 1928 the Darlingtons sailed and I was left with it all and knew no rest; the great church, the little church, the Church Council, which was a total exercise in diplomacy with all the elements to balance in debates, the Manse next to the church to manage, and endless visiting, from homes of English gentry to simple homes of Anglo Indian folk and the chummeries of the young men who were split into an ingenious British imitation of the Indian caste system: mercantile, who had to live in a particular part of town, trade, who could not mix socially with the commercials and mercantiles, domiciled Europeans who were a world of their own, and the barracks of the Army, who ranked last and lowest.

It was extremely difficult to pass from China's revolutionary world into this system. I needed new, stylish clothes. I needed new manners, transport, which turned up in the form of an old motor cycle of indescribable date and condition and without a self start. Any soldier who turned off the Chowringhee into Sudder Street was suspect by the prowling military police, for we were the very edge of Limits and the street ended in the prohibited, prostitute area.

I began to have parties of young fellows of all types at the Manse, but could only cope with the church goers for I was living on the Army Capitation Grants only, running the Manse on a shoe-string.

Then I heard Toc H was starting up in town and joined it to find what the movement called a 'grope' rather than a 'group'. It flourished, bought a house and Mark 1, India, came into being. There, any young fellow was welcome.

Visiting entailed two hospitals, the Presidency General for civilians and The British Military Hospital for the Army, and there were always some sick to look after, church folk, missionaries from up-country, soldiers and newly-born babies.

There was then a formidable Chinese Quarter in Calcutta, with its temples and ancestral halls. I found the Hall which represented my Chinese Clan and there heard of the Christian Chinese Church and got to know the folk there. I attended their meetings and with their help I sat the second-year Chinese examination in Calcutta. I was determined not to end my days under the Raj.

As winter 1928 came round we were ordered back to China. The Movement which had thrown us out became manageable. There were now three of us China refugees in India, the extra one being Sister Maud Millican, a nurse lent to an up-country Indian hospital. She, we were to escort back to China.

Together we boarded a little steamer sailing for Singapore.

We found that Maud was a strange person to escort. She had the greatest suspicions of all men and us in particular but she was a highly competent nurse and midwife and we attributed her attitude to all the complicated confinements she must have handled. We enlarged our knowledge of the Far East on this journey by calling at Saigon. The contrast between our lady charge and the ladies in rickshaws who met us on the quayside at Saigon was quite ludicrous. They followed us along the road right up into the city offering their services. We stopped at the fine Roman Cathedral in the city centre and attempted to go in, thinking the ladies could not pursue their business there. This did not prove very easy. The vergers on the door would not let us enter until they had got down and measured the distance between Maud's frock and the ground and the distance between her hand and the hem of her sleeve. She swept in indignantly after the measurement, went straight to the water stoup containing Holy Water. 'I thought so', she exclaimed, 'it's full of mosquito wrigglers'. She turned and rent her persecutors, telling them to give more attention to changing the water rather than examining ladies' legs. Considering the length of Maud's frocks I though this was a pretty fair criticism. They had certainly wasted time on her.

We whistled through the journey up river from Shanghai into Hunan and reported to the Chairman who, with equal despatch, told us both to get down to Paoking (Shao Yang) to help the Chinese Minister to re-open our work in that circuit and to help him in his work.

Paoking is a great city which in the Empire had been a 'Fu' city, administrative centre of a quarter of Hunan. Our premises, in which we were to live, and the central chapel were set on the main East Street within earshot of all the hubbub of the city streets, the chapel flush with the street. Our residence was to be a Chinese-style house set just behind the chapel, with its rear quarters tucked into a hill. Over that hill was the edge of the town, and on the other side of it stood our hospital with two missionary houses, one for the doctor and one a ladies' house. It is difficult to imagine

two such different scenes in one tiny area. To pass from the back
of our house over the hill was to pass from mediaeval London to
a modern park. Dr George Pearson and his family had already
preceded us and were well settled in. The hospital, his creation
and built in the shape of a Chinese temple, was in full swing.
He had the hillside laid out as a small farm and he had a herd of
cows there, the gift for the most part of animals donated from
American sources by Mme Chiang Kai Shek. Probably the first
fresh milk used in children's work in a Chinese hospital was their
share in the mission.

We engaged carpenters and masons on the street and got to
work making the chapel and the-houses, Mr Nieh teh-chin's and
ours furnished and liveable. I joined with him in the evangelical
work and in searching out old members and examining new ones
while Lamming slaved away at the language. It was a wide circuit
and so deep into Hunan's backwoods that the village chapels had
not suffered too badly in the absence. Piecing together the bits
of the circuit was very trying after the highly organised work
of the Calcutta English circuit, but I was delighted to find how
much the Chinese Church in Calcutta had helped in preserving
my language. Taking a service, even in the town chapel, was an
experience, after the freedom of preaching to the host at Sudder
Street. It was far more like a diluted service in Hastings, with as
many people. Dr Pearson would be there with his fiddle to play
the hymns and the choir and organ of the Indian Church did not
seem to be too great a loss.

We worked and lived there until the 1929 District Synod
came round and the Synod pulled me out of Paoking and sent me
to join the Rev. Wu I-tang, the superintendent minister of Yiyang,
in getting that circuit on its feet again. I began to feel like some
sort of reconstruction worker.

Yiyang is a river port, on the river Tze Shui running out of
the hills of central Hunan to the Tung Ting lake which, with the
Siang, it feeds. The town stretched in one long street for some
three miles or more following the bank of the river. The street was

carved up into three wards (Pao) called one, two and three, the
third ward being the centre of the busy lumbering business. There
the lumberjacks turned the small rafts of logs, brought down on
the river, into greater rafts for the trade down river at Hankow
and built themselves little huts on the rafts for the journey. It was
here that our Mission property stood. Second Ward was the busy
shopping centre and here we had a second church. The First Ward
was the administrative centre and here stood the Yamen, nerve
centre of official life. Just beyond this the Norwegian Mission
had a compound with a flourishing hospital. Christian witness
therefore covered the town and we worked together. The town
was within the alluvial belt round the lake and one of the rice
bowls of China, getting two rice crops a year, wealthy, prestigious
and a great prize for contending armies as well as subject to
floods. In travel it had the one great advantage of launch travel to
Changsha in three seasons of the year.

I went up on the launch with Mr Wu, returning from Synod,
and found that the town had recently been the scene of a battle
between a War Lord army and a division of the National Army,
both forces in turn had billeted troops in our compound. It was
a mess. We were not out of fashion for all the shopkeepers were
busy repairing their premises.

The victorious army was in that very hour settling in to
the town in more comfort. Our premises were hanging in the
balance. Mr Wu took one look at it: behind the gatehouse, a great
quadrangle with defunct school buildings down the right hand
side, Chinese houses down the left and two foreign-style houses at
the far end. Broken furniture and rubbish littered the quadrangle
and a glance into what was my house revealed great holes in the
floors where fires of window frames and other bits had burned on
the naked floors. Mr Wu declared it was time to go and see the
general. High time! He went into his own house and changed
into formal Confucian dress clothes, faultless from the button
on his cap to the toes of his silken shoes. I tried to match him by
changing into a new set of Sun yat-sen uniform in clerical grey. He

summoned up his own private rickshaw and with me walking at his right hand we set off down that interminable street for First Ward. Shop keepers and wayfarers alike stood silently watching us along the three miles. Many of them knew Mr Wu of old. If he was going to the Yamen they expected things to happen.

We were ushered into the inner room of the Yamen by a couple of young officers and Mr Wu made a beeline for the Guest of Honour chair and sat there wagging his thin beard; the wound scar on his cheek only contributed to his Confucian dignity. No modern general moved him. He had won officer rank in the old Imperial Army of the Dowager Empress, his final test being riding a bare-backed horse round the Peking Concourse and discharging arrows into a central butt in the centre of the ring, all under the Dowager Tze Hsi's personal eye.

He began by complimenting the general on his brilliant victory over that renegade force. He said how grateful the population was for the good behaviour of his troops and authority of his officers. He wished the general a long stay and many future victories in the cause of a redeemed China.

The general digested this mixture of fact and fiction and then turned to me to ask what he could do for me as representing the aid of England in his nation's effort to modernise. I was about to reply from where I stood on Mr Wu's right hand when the old tiger nipped in smartly and answered for me. The general would not wish to see a foreigner live in great discomfort, he said, moreover we wanted to reopen our school for the children's sake in Third Ward, where it was the only school. The quadrangle was the children's sports ground. He knew that such an officer of the nation's army would help the children, an old man, and a foreign guest worker. He answered the question because the general would not wish to hear complaints from an outsider but from a Chinese.

The general did not make a personal reply but ordered up a Quarter Master and told him to go with us, clear the compound and affix a Proclamation on the gate forbidding all billeting. He personally saw us to the main gate and bowed us out.

I complimented my Super as we marched up the street with the officer behind us. He said it was nothing, and how sorry he was to thrust on me such a miserable job as to accompany him. He added that we made a good team, which thrilled me to the core. But was it just courtesy? People shouted to him as we passed and soldiers saluted.

Back on the compound I was out of that Sun yat-sen suit and into old clothes in very short order. We went and hired labour and I got busy with them on the school and foreign houses. We had the school open within a month, having made new desks and gear. I gave some attention to my house at the same time for it was to be the house to which I was in the summer to bring my bride and it needed such a lot doing to it. I got one bedroom ready and swung an old blanket over the door-less door space, put in twenty new window frames, sealed the floors, and got a carpenter on making some new furniture, and renewed the toilet facilities, which were in a horrible condition. Going about this work I detected a shocking smell pervading the whole house. What was it? I decided that the troops had left a corpse under the basement of the house. I crawled around trying to locate it. I knew some enemy had been executed, but could not find the body. Then one of the teachers told me to look over the wall. There was a pond full of stinking effluent from a brewery which lay next door. We never got rid of that smell. Then we turned to the ladies' house, which fortunately was not too bad, and repaired it, for Miss Barbara Simpson, who had been on the station in the old days was to return.

It was then a case of getting round the circuit chapels and the country lay preachers. It was a wide circuit and had many chapels. Each needed some reconstruction and that we saw to. Life was all constructing and reconstructing. Was this mission? I spent my life as a carpenter, work team boss and sniffer out of troubles to correct. It was a process which left a permanent mark on the years which were to come.

So the time sped on to that mountain top experience of wedding the lady who was to come to Yiyang and share in it, and the journey to Shanghai and holiday in Kuling.

Peak Three - A CRITICAL CLIMB

The practical rural Gospel

There are great, frowning mountains and there are lesser ones which just escape being known as hills but nevertheless can afford vistas from their summits. After all the Mount of the famous sermon Jesus spoke is no big one; and the Mount of Olives is no giant. One of the grown up hills marks the point of a change in method and work in my China experience.

One whole section of the Yiyang circuit lay in bandit country; its topography made it ideal for runaway soldiery, agitators and others who preyed on travellers. The large village of Hsieh ling kang was in the zone and I was determined that it should get no less attention because of its unfortunate location. Gladys used often to go with me on country visits, Hsieh ling kang and one or two others were journeys to make alone. I think she disliked me going intensely but put up with it.

It was a long journey, some twenty miles of winding road in between hills, through open farm lands, across two or three young rivers. Most people went in groups convoying one another through the dangers of the road. I went alone save for the loyal and good friend who was my regular bearer on all my journeys. Trudging along that road I used to look forward to one turn which revealed well ahead a hill which rose above its brothers and dominated quite a landscape. It beckoned me forward. The reason was that it was crowned on its summit with a lone tree. The winds from all directions had worked on that tree for years and had in the end shaped it into a cross which stood gaunt against the sky, great limbs etched on the blue sky or the storm clouds. That natural gnarled cross spoke to me. One day I left the road and climbed up to it and sat down under it, sending the bearer on ahead. A strange confidence and yet disquiet filled my mind. It spoke of the need to be there. The whole area needed what it stood for; that was where the disquiet loomed up. How much did we do for the millions who surrounded it? What did we bring to the villages? We brought them a new spiritual life incomparably better than they could get elsewhere, that was sure. Then we left them to work out their new experience in the unredeemed squalor of their daily life. Was that the best we could do? They tilled fields but they were not their fields at all. They became ill and many died. Whereas in England a Christian ill was the concern of modern medicine, they had local herbalists and that was it. A man might accidentally hack his foot with his hoe and have a toe half off. He bound it up and could do no more but hoe on when it healed itself, a little less efficient than before, but just the crippled chap, part of what he had been. I wondered how much interest some of the farmers were paying to the town rice shops for the seed they had sown in the land. How many children a mother must have to raise two or three — probably half a dozen.

I thought of old men sitting by the fire in little farmhouses, their eyes blinded by the smoke which could not get out of the room. There were the women, too, grinding away for hours to get the rice for one meal. 'Come from every quarter O wind and breath upon these slain.'

I underwent a spiritual conversion under that cross shaped tree. It could not be that Christ's message to these people was only in the redemption of their souls. He had been healer as well as teacher in his day. The whole Old Testament was concerned with 'every man sitting under his own fig tree' in a 'country at peace'. What was the banditry but a spin off of a poverty-line existence? From that day forward I began to collect anything and everything which taught me how to put the love of Jesus into the homes, the land and the bodies of the people. It became a raging desire which held me for years after.

I got up and finished my journey through the old ways of

mission but excruciatingly aware of its limitations. We were still in the process of reconstruction, pulling together what we had as an instrument of usefulness.

Back in town we were getting on very well, the chapels were functioning, the school was open and in 1929 had grown from the opening number of sixty scholars to one hundred and twenty-two with twice the opening number of teachers in it and Gladys' dispensary for the children and their folks. Barbara Simpson had arrived and was planning her first Women's School. Our Second Ward chapel was attracting non-Christian people. Mr Wu had chosen a Preacher to look after it who was the epitome of gentle kindness and with a cheerful smiling wife. The sort of man who had been born with Christian spirit from his birth. I loved going out preaching with him. One evening we came back late from such a 'Wai T'ang' (open air meeting) and as we got to his home at the chapel he said, 'That's funny, there's a light and I thought my wife would be fast asleep by now'. We went in and could see her head framed in a circle of light from an oil lamp. She was quietly weeping. On the table was a booklet. 'Oh', she said, 'I've heard you speak of it dozens of times but to read it for myself is so sad'. The booklet was the Gospel of St Mark open at the Crucifixion story, which owing to the Women's School she was reading for the first time.

The Third Ward preacher was of a very different character. He was Hu fu-sen, his second name meaning 'born again'. He was the second son of his mother, he was for her that son come back. He was a quick, eager man, a District Agent in the system of the church, one who had been trained to a point just short of the ministers — the doyen of lay preachers. He had been a business man who travelled much and knew his world and how to handle difficulties with ease and keep his end up anywhere. His wife, who had been a Christian long before he came in, matched him in her own way. It was she who set him on the Christian Way. He had gone away on a long trip down river and she had put away the household gods in a basket in a cupboard. When he came home he took them out, set them on their shelf and prepared an offering of rice and wine for them. She said kindly, 'They haven't been fed for weeks and weeks, they must be dead by now'. He never worshipped them again. He was changed by a joke.

He was troubled by constant headaches and would appear at a meeting with little black patches stuck in varying positions on his forehead. I once asked him about this and he told me that years before he had cut his hand very badly and had caught a frog in a ditch, cut it open and put it on the cut which had healed up beautifully. Some foreign-trained students had mocked him, but later they had read of an experiment at Nanking University where a foreign team of doctors had isolated an antiseptic in frogs and now included it in the list of foreign drugs.

The circuit stretched away down south to the old road leading down to South West China. It was an infamous road which carried the traffic in goods and in opium in and out of Central China, a scene of constant brigandage. In our part of the world the road had been dominated for years by the Kao Clan whose main residence was in a village called Ma yuan ao (the hill of the hemp gardens). A day came when the patriarch of the clan fell ill and three of the men said they would make the long pilgrimage to Nan yu shan, the southern Hunanese sacred mountain which had on it an enormous array of temples. It was a journey of over two hundred miles, and the last part of the journey had to be made making a 'kow teo' for every step of the climb to the mountain top. Thousands of people did this every year. Each pilgrim wore an apron with a large pocket to take his souvenirs of the visit to the several temples. They finished their round of worship and with the pockets full of candles, prayer pamphlets and amulets had reached the head of the steps going down the mountain when they encountered an evangelist who gave them a booklet. They stuffed it in with the rest and moved off home.

The old man looked through all the souvenirs his men had brought with them back from the mountain top. He was not feeling any better for their journey and he went back to the booklet. There was one sentence in it which stuck like a burr in his mind. 'There is but one true God', it said, 'his name is T'ien Lao Yeh' (the Venerable Father of Heaven). This sentence meant something to one who was himself an Old Man — a lao yeh. He asked the pilgrims whether they had worshipped T'ien Lao Yeh — they hadn't heard of such a god's temple. On the back of the little pamphlet there was written 'If you wish to know more of T'ien Lao Yeh find the nearest Fu Yin T'ang'. So it was that three men turned up at our Second Ward Chapel in Yiyang asking for information about a god of which they knew nothing and how Mr Jen the preacher revelled in telling them and entertaining them in his home.

That was the beginning of the work at Ma yuan ao. Most of the village was baptised into the faith and they built their own chapel with their own hands and the mud out of their own fields. One of the family, Kao Mei-ch'in, became their local preacher and they pushed out across the clan area. Within three years the one chapel became four.

One of the newest chapels was born from the life of a mad woman. It was a custom in all the villages to put mad people — mostly women — in individual bamboo cages, it being believed that the demon who possessed them was confined with them. We were often taken to them for prayers. Our preachers had elaborated their own technique for such cases. They insisted that the woman be set free and taken to the preacher's home to stay. There she was taught rhyming prayers which she had to say continually. The main features in the stories of Jesus were also told to her in simple poetry. The whole congregation took part in this treatment at intervals. It was impressive. In this village's case the woman was well and cheerful in three weeks.

This technique threw me for a long time with my Handsworth familiarity with Freud and Jung. What of the demon-possession theory? How did the whole thing work? I asked the preachers to explain it for me and their only answer was blank astonishment that I who knew so much of the Bible

found any difficulty in it. I finally gave in by resolving that God
has a much better imagination than I and has techniques up his
sleeve of which I knew nothing. The impact was greatest where a
woman was said to have a 'Ho Kwei' a fire demon. Every place in
which she lodged caught fire. One thing was certain, community
love was part of the cure. People took her into their homes,
encouraged by the preachers. On the other hand, fear was part of
the affliction. Ostracism springs from fear.

I was wonderfully happy in those Yiyang days, the work
was fascinating, it was flourishing in its new beginnings, Gladys
was coming to share in it and then she was there and as busy as
I and had Barbara's companionship when I was out and about.
My joy was to be deeply thankful for all who had opened the
door of language to make it possible to plunge into everything
and contribute to everything. My concern about the future
was wrapped up in the determination to know more of a wider
mission to which the healing service was a pointer.

Peak Four -
MAN-MADE MOUNTAIN OF THE DEAD

The Sino-Japanese War

Perhaps we might call it 'The mountain of the Dead'. A Chinese grave is always carefully sited by necrologers on a hill and is built like a man-made hill, looking down over an open vista to trees, water and hills. A horseshoe-shaped rampart is built round it with the open space of the horseshoe facing the view across the country.

It was on just such a hillside grave that I sat in the spring of 1939. It was in the province of Chekiang which is two whole provinces east of Hunan. Mrs Foster and her baby, an old German lady Miss Schaffer, Mr Stanfield and I had just rushed off a train on the railway from Hunan to the China coastal port of Ningpo, which was still in Chinese hands. We were watching the sky searching for the Jap plane of which the warning system on the train had given notice. Trains were being strafed from the air every week.

With the baby in my arms, while his mother mixed a bottle of Lactogen with water from a Thermos (my pockets had been stuffed with tiny packets of Lactogen wrapped in paper packets before we entrained), I was in thought far away from both baby and aircraft. What would be left of all we had tried to do in the years of the last decade when all of this national agony was over? I never for a moment thought that the Japanese could win; they were not only fighting against troops but against the vastness of China which would swallow them up and digest them. It was impossible to guess that years and years afterwards a Communist government would pick up the threads of much that we had achieved or attempted and expand it all into a nationwide programme. I strongly hoped at the time, however, that someone would. In spite of constant disturbance and massive troop movements things had gone well in our villages. There was so much we had done in co-operation with the Nationalist government that there was much to regret in this deadly Japanese attack. Perhaps that China was doing well was one at least of the reasons which caused Japan to attack at that point in time.

———————————

The decade began for me well enough in 1929 at Yiyang. There the countryside was enjoying a time of relative peace and order and we were going about the Church life busily. Nationwide, however, foreign relationships were in trouble as the original Shanghai incident was kept alive by other incidents in other places. Anti-imperialism was in the nation's mouth; it was used to embrace every corruption and bitterness experienced anywhere.

Such a movement could never happen without Hunan being in it up to the neck. It is the most turbulent province in the country. Mao tze tung was born in it and learned his business there. In Hunan he founded the Hsin Ming Hui, the mother of the Chinese Communist Party. It gathered together in the days of open debate about which foreign recipe suited China's national sickness best. It was originally made up of students in Changsha's higher education colleges and schools. It was in Hunan that in the Twenties Mao was given the task of organising revolutionary cells in the Farmers' Union before the sweep of the National armies on the way north from Canton. When the Nationalist government in 1928, on capturing Hankow, liquidated its Russian support and went on alone to found the Nanking government, Hunan's peace was ended and its condition produced a state of such chaos that foreigners in the province were all withdrawn.

In the middle of all these disturbances Gladys became pregnant. While we could we used to walk across the fields at the back of the town to visit Dr Fuchs of the Norwegian hospital who cared for her. He made it quite plain that with the situation as it then was Yiyang, or anywhere in Hunan, was no place to have the baby.

In the general evacuation of Hunan, therefore, I was allowed a flat in the Lutheran Building, which was in the very heart of the British Concession in Hankow. At the same time I was offered the ministry at Hankow Union Church, which was the main centre of English language worship. It was in this way that Margaret was born in the International Hospital, Hankow. A Scots doctor was in charge and a German sister led a team of German and Chinese nurses. Margaret's arrival was in the dead of a winter night in 1931. When it was obvious that the time was come I got a rickshaw and walked with it through deep snow to the hospital. After it was over and Margaret safely in a cot, the English doctor who helped told me to remember that Gladys was the gallantest thirty-six year old mother he had ever attended.

The party which was held when she came back with the baby was typical of the congregation at the Union Church. There were Chinese, European, Russian and American guests and young fellows, both officers and men, of the Royal Navy cruiser *Caradoc* and the gunboats in port at the time.

It was a great experience to prepare sermons in the English language once more and to lead worship with a cross section of the nations. There were missionaries of the town, business men, teachers and Chinese gentry in the congregation as well as the Royal Naval people. It was Calcutta over again with a wider world reference. We had a Study Class on Thursday evenings where people of these categories could join in discussion right across the spectrum of several denominations of the world Church and attitudes of various streams of national feeling expressed themselves.

The only experience to upset this world harmony in religious study occurred in this class. I planned to use Harry Emerson Fosdick's little manual *The Meaning of Prayer*. An elderly American gentleman objected strongly saying that Fosdick was a heretic. He would never open one of his books. I said we would refer the matter to the Church Council for them to decide.

This Council was a body with a constitution new to me. The Minister could not preside over it; it chose its own chairman. The representation was both national and denominational. It consequently came up rather like the UN Security Council and could be influenced in the same way by alignments of mutual interest.

On this occasion the Chairman was a Chinese business man, a banker. As the meeting discussed the use of Fosdick's book, the American who objected got hotter and hotter. Finally he got up and said he was going to leave us. He got to the door, seized the knob, it turned and turned in his grasp but the door would not open. The Chairman rose with formal Chinese dignity and said in a voice of great authority, 'Sit down, Sir! The Lord closed the door and you are not to go out.' He said that we were met in council and would remain in council until we had solved our problems. The American brother took this like a lamb and came back. I made a compromise by saying that we would use Fosdick's theme but not his book. I followed the book closely but never used it in the class and the objector sat through the whole course and said he enjoyed it.

We served with this Church and the Royal Navy happily until I had completed my first term of service in 1932 and we were due for leave. We went home across Canada, carrying the two year old through the zoological gardens in Honolulu, where she fell in love with the monkeys.

Once home we met relatives we had not known. My mother was astonished but relieved to find that Margaret was not yellow and my father had to get used to the title of 'Kung kung', the Chinese for a grandfather. After seeing the two sides of our joint family we settled down in the Selly Oak Colleges complex in Birmingham. I began to study for membership of the Royal Institute of Health and Hygiene and also became that way an Associate Member of the Royal Sanitary Institute — a logical

way of planning my new programme for the next term. The
one subject on which I could get little information was rural
co-operation. The Selly Oak staff librarian worked this one out
for me with an introduction to the work of Rural Missions Inc.
of the USA and the work in India. I consequently asked the
Missionary Society to allow me to return to China via India to
see what was doing there. There was also that which befalls every
missionary on leave in England, the constant round of weekend
deputation right across the Connexion. A man was fortunate if
he could squeeze out a month's personal holiday, though the rules
said it should be three. One of the appointments I had on that
leave was to address the annual Missionary Rally at Westminster
Central Hall. Two or three younger missionaries were to speak on
their parts of the world and — in case one of us fell down on the
job — Dr Donald Soper was to make the final speech. When it
came to my turn I talked of the need in China for a new type of
life-inclusive mission in the countryside. In doing so I mentioned
that for me the Christian adventure was a battle against the Third
International for the people's minds. I said for me the Christian
Movement was the Fourth International as the nations of the
historic Christian culture were teamed together in our efforts
within China. Dr Soper rose to make the 'salvation' speech and
made that remark about a Fourth International the main theme of
his talk. He thanked me for what he called his 'lead in' and said he
had no idea how he was going to get on terms with this audience
when we first went on to the platform.

Our leave expired and we set off back to China via India, my
people seeing us off with my mother deeply feeling the loss of
Margaret. Gladys and the child went to Kalutara in Ceylon while
I went on the Frontier Express from Bombay up to the northern
provinces.

It was just the time to do a survey of Indian rural
reconstruction for Mr Strickland had just drafted the co-operative
Law for the Indian Government and the subject was on all minds.

My first visit was to Moga high in the Punjab where an

American missionary team ran a school specially for rural youngsters who did most of their work on arithmetic and English by working with their hands on building projects and the layout of farm land. From there I went to Allahabad and the work of Dr Higginbotham, where he had turned acres of desert into fertile land by buying the sewage of Allahabad and harnessing it through long canals on to the wilderness. Then I went over into Bengal to Ushagram and saw the wonderful school compound there. Here they used the septic tank system I had studied. Before the installation, the Head Mistress told me, the sanitary arrangement was simply that the girls went one way across the open country around while the boys went the other way. When the tanks were completed the sewage was treated in them and went on to the land and solved the supply of food to the school. Then I went up to Bankura, our own Bengali station and saw how the Indian Minister had organised a series of gardens on a co-operative plan, which was producing the finest vegetables I have ever seen anywhere.

Down in southern India I saw something of the YMCA's cooperative work and went on to the Nizam's Dominions to our work at Dichpali where a Leprosy Hospital had gone in for supplying all its own food by co-operative farming. I had the pleasure of designing the first septic tank system for the hospital while I stayed there.

In this way I covered India from north to south by rail and that in itself was an education. Travelling in second-class coaches by night or day had its joys as well as its ups and downs. On one occasion I found myself stranded at Ludhiana as Cooks had made a mistake in timing a train as a morning one when in fact it was an evening timing.

I was left pacing the platform wondering what on earth to do with a whole day left in a town I had never even heard of. A little Indian gentleman came to me and introduced himself and asked where I was from and going where. I told him I was going back to China after a furlough. His eyes lit up and he told me he was on

furlough himself, from Kenya. He asked if I would go round to
his home and forthwith carried me off in a rickshaw to his little
home and charming wife. I was there for ages as the evening train
was late arriving and he would keep me until he assured himself
on the phone that the train was really signalled in at the local
station.

Day or night the trains made longer stops at certain stations
so that the passengers could get a meal. There was a first-class
dining coach to which white passengers went on such stops but
it was far and away beyond my means. I was soon down on the
platforms and among the chaps shouting 'Musselman Char' or
'Hindu Char' learning to differentiate the Moslem meals from
the Hindu meals and had Moslem fare almost the length of my
travels. After all, our faiths are two cousins if not sisters.

Once on a night sleeper I was on the top bunk of four. A
hillman — rough, bearded, lay on the opposite upper bunk
shivering with the cold. I had a fat bedroll and I reached across
and offered him a blanket, in which he gleefully wrapped himself
and soon went to sleep. A few stations further down the line
a very pompous clerkly man got in and took the bottom bunk
below the sleeping hillsman. Soon he called out 'Hey, you up
there, take your filthy blanket out of my way'. To which the
hillsman replied, 'It is the sahib's blanket you call filthy, keep your
filthy hands off it'.

When I left Dichpali, which is well away from the railway
line, I had to get to a wayside station some miles from the mission
at an early morning hour. The process our folk had invented,
however, was simple enough. The took me and a bed and a
mosquito net down on to the wayside platform, told me to go to
sleep and the guard would wake me and take me aboard when the
train arrived! Which was exactly what happened.

On one journey I was in an open coach-type car, not a
compartment, with about twenty women of all ages and two or
three men who escorted them. They were all bound for the great
temples at Madura and one of the men acted as interpreter as he

got the women to tell me all the preparations they had made and
of the gifts for the gods they were carrying. He assured the women
that I too worshipped my God and they need not be shy. Some of
the white people, he said, were like that.

I got the ferry across the Palk Straits and into Ceylon feeling
that I had met an India which the days at Calcutta had never
revealed, an India of gentle village people tilling their land and
worshipping their gods in a straight-forward struggle with nature.
Perhaps they had not the sheer vigour of the Chinese but their
courtesy made up for that. Had not the wretched caste system
held them in bondage by putting a ceiling over each man's head,
life would have been beautiful. It was very easy to assess the
difference that Christian freedom made in those who embraced it,
or in any Hindu sect which borrowed from Christians.

We arrived safety back in China and made the long, internal
trip up into Hunan without trouble. I was trying all the way by
asking and looking to get an insight into what was going on in the
country. General Chiang's Nanking Government seemed to be
doing very well. It was in command of most of the provinces, had
launched scores of new programmes to change the face of Chinese
life including health, education, banking and rural development.
He was, broadly speaking, faithfully following Dr Sun yat sen's
Three People's Principles, People's Freedom, People's Livelihood,
People's Power. This was the Bible of Nationalist China.

In Hunanese affairs all the banditry, strife and disorder had
firmly constellated round the Communist Party's Fourth Route
Army which had located itself in the mountains on the Kianghsi-
Hunan border where General Mao tze-tung was in command
at Ching Kang just inside of Kianghsi. In consequence General
Chiang had flooded the province with enormous numbers
of troops and was set to eliminate Communist power in one
encircling action. This meant peace for the counties of Hunan in
the north, the south and the west. The operational area was in the
east. The capital, Changsha, was in great fettle with Government
officials firmly in power. They had beaten off an attempt by the

Communist forces to take it, an attempt which Mao had firmly disapproved of but had to make by Party directive. This had forced his retreat into the mountain stronghold. It could only be attacked by operations based on Pingkiang and Liuyang, my old circuits.

From Pingkiang two or three divisions of troops were in a strangling operation to isolate the stronghold. They built ever-narrowing circles of forts in a ring around the mountains to try and stop raids for food into the countryside. Each fort was manned by a platoon or two of soldiers. This was sheer misery for the peasantry. There was the constant pressure of forcing men away to carry the burdens of the army. There were constant breakthroughs by the Communist army, who would concentrate on one ill-guarded fort, descend in lightning-swift night strokes upon it, burn it, complete with garrison. There followed a ravaging of the area round it, in which every pig and all the grain were captured, and then a very swift march back into the impenetrable hills. Behind this active scene lay the great reserves of Nationalist troops and the command, who were billeted on everybody and then had troops to spare. In this type of guerilla warfare Mao was the world expert and the National Army could never deal with it. At times the Communist forces would set bonfires along the tops of the mountains, visible to the town, in one flaring sign of defiance.

On reaching Changsha we were told that the Synod which had met recently had asked that Gladys and I go to Pingkiang. Our buildings there were completely occupied by troops, Brigade Headquarters being in the hospital. The Chairman gave us the privilege of saying whether we would consent to going. This in itself was a measure of the difficulty, for stationing was never questioned in our system.

We thought about it, talking it over in bed. It was my first station, we had met there, it was the only station in which Gladys had her own hospital and in which she had trained dozens of nurses. Obviously the place had to be cleaned up by somebody. It was Pingkiangese people who had asked for us. We decided that we would go. I would go in first with a Pingkiangese preacher, get the chapel back from billeting, make a snug, somehow in the Chinese house behind it, and come and fetch the family down to it. Gladys would wait at Changsha.

Mr Yu, the Chinese preacher, was waiting in Changsha to escort me back. We set off and made the journey on foot. It was a heart-searching toil. As we crossed the mountain pass which gave a view of the Pingkiang county he insisted that we kneel down on Pingkiang soil and give thanks for our return to it. In that moment I took the country to my heart, where it has ever remained.

The town had been ringed round with a great rampart which began by the river and stretched right round until it met the river again. It was dotted with 'Tiao pao', circular forts built on the ancient design in 'The Romance of the Three Kingdoms'. The whole arrangement was festooned in barbed wire. In the town there was the father and mother of all 'Tiao pao', a central refuge should the enemy break through. Troops were everywhere, but people all commented that they were National formations which behaved themselves very well and actually paid for all they took from the shops. This was a change, we had seen enough of others. We went straight up and saw the Hsien Chang (Civil Governor) and the Big Brass at the military headquarters.

We both settled into the little house by the chapel and I checked over the upper floor which seemed to me to be able to cope with the family if necessary. We then turned our attention to the Mission compound. A Brigade Headquarters was in the hospital and very comfortable there; the best Battalion of the Brigade was in our two schools and the three houses were taken over by the officers of the Brigade staff and the Battalion officers.

I tried for the house which stood first, looking over the town, in which the Brigadier, his wives and entourage were lodged. With the 'Non-Billeting Proclamation' I had from Changsha, the atmosphere then prevailing in Nanking because of General

Chiang's faith, and a fair imitation of Mr Wu's treatment of the General at Yiyang, I had the Brigadier out within the week.

To deal with stragglers, adventurers and sundry others I had a barbed wire fence thrown right round the house and garden, which fenced in our enclave in what was still a military camp. I planned to bring Gladys and the child down and as the Brigadier's aide said, 'He has several wives here, why should you not bring one'. This young fellow and Margaret became great friends and Gladys a nurse to his wife and most of the others. The Brigadier promised that if ever things reached a point when his own women had to depart he would tell me. A promise he never kept when the day came.

We set to and began to get the house shipshape. It was not such a mess as the Yiyang house had been. There had been less destruction of the fabric, but even so it took some time. There was, for instance, an enormous latrine with a thatched roof plumb in the middle of the garden and there were certain internal room doors which had simply gone.

Gladys and Margaret came down and we set up the home while still doing the minor repairs. Many of the army women came to call on Gladys and she very soon was medical consultant to most of them.

I used the army telephone to ring the Chairman in Changsha and asked him to find us a really good Headmaster and get him to pick out three other teachers to come and start our school. I wanted one mixed school, up to the Higher Primary standard. He persuaded Fu Chiangyun to come. He had been the master who helped us get Yiyang opened, and a real friend. He and I went to see the Brigadier, and after some negotiation he said he knew we would want it sooner or later and gave it back.

We entered it and began the reconstruction, which was a job indeed. There were smashed desks and burnt desks to replace, windows and doors to classrooms to put in and a general colour-wash to do right through.

While we were doing this we had a campaign through the

town and the villages to tell the world we were back in education.
This was enthusiastically received everywhere, for the school had
always had a good reputation. We had determined together on
having a Boarding School in which children from the country
could stay as well as local pupils. They came — more than half
of the children at the opening were country children who each
brought a great sack of rice with them as boarding fee.

Mr Fu was a joy to work with. We had grown together over
the Yiyang days and he had brought with him men he knew. He
had been trained in our own Normal College at Wuchang and
naturally recruited from men with the same background. We were
all at one on the treatment China needed to modernise herself.
He was a Kuo Ming T'ang member (National Party). When, up
at my house listening to my world-spanning radio, he asked what
I had done on leave and I told him about the programme I had
in mind, he was tremendously at one with it and promised help
outside the school. On the other hand, I went into the teaching
staff at the school to teach Health and Hygiene.

The next obvious target was to get the hospital going. This
was a different proposition. You cannot just close a Brigade centre
on a local demand. It had to be done higher up. It was attempted
through the Ministry of Health in Nanking and Changsha, the
Provincial Government, Yale University Hospital in Changsha
and the Chairman of the District.

After prolonged negotiation in these channels there came
(when up in Nanking the Ministry of Health became uneasily
aware that more than sixty per cent of Chinese nurses and nearly
as many of the doctors were Mission trained and that most
remarkable of all, most hospitals in China were Mission hospitals)
a realisation that this was a very' face-losing' situation. They came
up with the idea of going into partnership with the Missions
by transforming Mission hospitals into Government Health
Centres with half the responsibility each. With the pressure we
were putting on about Pingkiang what more natural than to
begin with us? This meant that Nanking got the troops out, on

the Generalissimo's signature. All of this took well over a year
to achieve, during which we lived as guests in our corner of the
military presence.

The new system had many difficulties with which as
Administrator of the Centre I was involved. We had the right
to produce the staff. The Headship of the team had to remain a
Chinese doctor who could have foreign colleagues. Pingkiang had
to pay part cost in the Government share and it was sometimes
hard to get. Gladys became senior nursing officer. We had to
establish outstations in the country and oversee them. Headaches
were numerous. It is not, for instance, every British doctor
who sees Public Health as his job; on the other hand not every
Chinese is skilled at advanced surgery. We managed somehow.

This only left the old Girls' School as an unused building. The
troops in it went when the hospital was cleared, and we turned it
into a training headquarters for village reconstruction courses. It
could sleep a large number of people and had classrooms in which
to teach them. At long last we were ready for work.

The plan which had been maturing in my mind since Yiyang
was a sixfold one. Delving deep into social studies it did not in
any way deviate from the evangelical zeal of missionary work,
it simply wanted to widen the contact of the Christian Gospel,
much as Jesus did in his own day, in Chinese village terms. The six
projects were: 1. Adult Literacy. 2. Co-operative Agriculture. 3.
Village Medical aid. 4. Agricultural advance. 5. Rural Recreation.
6. Indigenous Worship with a Chinese content. The plan
envisaged having all these operating in the same villages at the
same time. The whole thing in the beginning hinged on John
Wesley's insight in putting Local Preachers into service in his
early British Connexion. If laymen could be trained to do this by
the Ministers, why could not the other skills be done in the same
way? The Chinese Church owed much to its Local Preachers, it
could owe as much to a local school teacher or local healer.

To assess the need for such a programme it is necessary to
have a picture of the village homes. Every public service taken

for granted in the Western world or Eastern cities simply did not exist. No drainage, no power and light, no transport — all were missing. The people had among them perhaps six to a village who were literate, which meant all kinds of exploitation. The economy wavered around the subsistence level, now above, now below.

The home itself was a mud brick agglomeration of rooms with some kind of open forecourt in which much of the work of farm and home took place. Pigs and hens shared all the space, both in the home and the yard. The main room, with its front open to the courtyard, had as its centre a slate slab on which a brushwood or charcoal fire never went out, so that the room was always full of smoke. There were bamboo chairs scattered round. It really was extraordinary how much was made of bamboo. The beds might be in any room, though the parents' bed would be in some recessed corner which it filled entirely with its curtained four-poster.

The toilets were in some shed or lean-to in the yard near to the house and were cleared out now and again to the compost pits or directly on to the fields. Smoky lamps were the only light at night or, when oil was short, flaring torches of stripped bamboo. Mostly the family went off to bed as soon as a meal after work was over. Tiny children were stuck in cot-prams when they awoke and stayed in them the day long. Bigger children just wandered round the premises making toys out of anything they happened to pick up.

The farm itself was an aggregate of two acres but in pieces scattered round the village by the principle of inheritance in vogue. On the product of two acres a family lived. Rice, which was usually sold, and sweet potatoes, the food crop, were the main crops. There would be a pig or two which never left the courtyard and house. There was sometimes a goat which fed on waste land, with other family goats, round the village.

The women spent most of the day in preparing the two meals, or three in the height of summer, and looking after the children. They had no subsidiary industry. Young girls and lads either helped the father on the land or the mother at the stove, which could be outside the house or at the back of it.

The land very rarely belonged to the farmers; they had landlords who lived in nearby towns or away in the great cities. The tenant was responsible for buying his own rice seed, his own potato seed and for getting his own tools and keeping the buildings in repair. For the land, the landlord extracted fifty per cent of a notional full crop, which meant that in bad years the farmer and his family lived on some twenty per cent of what he grew. Most of them had to go to rice chandlers in the town to get seed and paid an average of twelve per cent a month for the interest on the loan. This meant that they, to a man, were in perpetual debt.

Medicine and midwifery were of scratch-help from passing herbalists and the village old women. Sickness was always seen as a visitation by evil spirits at the instigation of offended ancestors. Child deaths in particular were regarded as punishment. In the village or a nearby neighbouring village was an ancestral hall where every soul was registered and the tablets of the ancestors stood rank to rank in rising tiers of age groups, often nine steps high. Here people came when sickness struck the family to beseech mercy from the dead. Marriages were celebrated here and it was the centre for the annual festivities.

The social structure was a gerontocracy. The older man or woman, the greater the power. No man — or woman — came to power in the best years of life. A man had to be old to signify in decision making. This meant that the policies of a village council were always backward looking never forward. What had been was the guide to what should be.

On the Third day of the Third month, the Fifth of the Fifth, the Eighth of the Eighth and at Chinese New Year in February, all outdoor work stopped and the people kept holiday, visited each others homes and worshipped in the ancestral hall. Where there was any money they gambled for hours.

Where the village came into the orbit of one of our preachers it was into this atmosphere that he came. He often prayed not for young converts but for old ones. In any case he had to get things right with the elders before he could even open his mouth to preach. He was usually welcome, however, as a person with a good reputation and possessed of reading and writing, a potential ally. His coming represented a breakthrough. When a foreign missionary turned up he was, at first, a phenomenon; if he fitted himself into the pattern he soon became a trusted friend and reason for celebration.

He could not but wonder how many 'village Hampdens' were lost in this life of illiterate drudgery, what the lads could do for China if things had been different, what the girls could do if they only had knowledge with which to cope.

That literacy was the first requisite had not escaped one great Chinese, Dr Jimmy Yen, China's first representative at the League of Nations, who was himself a very erudite Christian. He had set himself the task of making a People's Literature. Out of the eighty-three thousand characters of the Chinese language he had isolated one thousand essential words, as in English we had fashioned a Basic English. He had gone on to select a Farmer's thousand, a Women's thousand, a Soldier's thousand and so on, and had produced a library of five hundred books or booklets, on the pattern of the Gospel Portions sold by the Bible Societies. His series covered life — from a booklet on 'Smut in Wheat' to a 'Book of Jokes!'.

We determined that in every village where we had influence, whether with a chapel or without, we would form an Adult School, use Dr Yen's system and teach the genuine, character-clothed, literacy to the folk. We would have nothing to do with any Romanisation or special script. We wanted the people to have their own literature in its pristine form. To do this we could not use money which we did not have, so it meant training our preachers to teach and train village people, mostly young people or children from our central school, to be the teachers. The whole system had to be self-productive of its own success. When we got going it certainly was. It spread like wild-fire as hamlets and villages in which we had no stake at all came and claimed a share in it and students became teachers at a furious speed.

The next thing which lay heavy on my heart was the life of debt. A man who had spent four terms in one of these Schools, at three months to a course of one thousand words, was popping and fizzing with ideas. Get a man who has learned to read at the age of forty-five and you've really got something. He can handle an account, for instance. He is not a blind man in the presence of a money lender.

The Rural Credit Co-operative Society was the weapon I had chosen in my visit to India. The Co-operative Law Strickland gave to India had caught a greater ear than mine. He had sold the idea to General Chiang in the same period. Chiang had ordered that there be a Farmers' Bank attached to the Bank of China. There was money for country people organised enough to get it.

A Rural Credit Co-operative is a simple structure, the simplest form of co-operation. It is so because it runs not as a financial operation but as a moral one. It was invented by a Lutheran German pastor in southern Germany long before Germany was unified by Bismark. It needs about twenty men in one place who mutually guarantee each other with all they have — an unlimited liability — who are satisfied with each other to the extent of knowing every man is honest, reliable and, in China, a non-opium smoker. They each borrow from the system a loan for a particular piece of work, a crop or a pig in farrow, anything which will give its yield in one year. They each sign in, in each other's presence, that they will repay within a year and with the capital give six per cent a year interest on the loan. The interest is split two ways when it comes in, half is left in the Society as joint stock capital and the other half goes back to the promoters for use in propaganda. In our case we determined that each man's loan would be of twenty dollars. The preachers and I never enrolled a man; we thought it best that the men in the Society vet their own colleagues.

By order from Nanking the country appointed a Co-operative

Officer for the county, in each county. We made friends with our
particular one, a Mr Chu. He was tremendously grateful to us
for our help and initiative. Helping him took me into circles of
the county I would not elsewise have known. He told me that
our men were so intelligent and asked where did we get them.
I told him we made them, by the grace of God, with the aid of
Adult Schools. The Provincial Cooperative Officer came down to
Pingkiang regularly to pay me the money to go out to the Co-ops
and to collect it from me. It was all government money. I was by
then a Member of the Provincial China International Relief Fund
Board of Trustees, and so had the privileges of a Government
official.

We kept any money I could get through the church and
mission funds for a little scheme I had for women, which was
not within Mr Chu's remit. The next-door province of Hupeh
grew cotton which it exported in bales. It occurred to me that by
buying bales and bringing them in I could get the women in their
homes to spin it into yarn which we could sell in bulk. This gave
women an income which they controlled.

To attempt the next item in our programme it was necessary
to get the elders of the villages to allow us to take from each
village a young man who could come down to our Headquarters
for training near the hospital. The idea was to put a local healer
into each village.

He had to master a medicine chest and its contents which
contained, in the first box, twenty drugs, and in the second
box, thirty. He had to know each drug, differentiate them, learn
application. He had also to know the meaning of symptoms in
the patients so as to use the right drug for the right purpose.
The little textbook ran from front to back with drugs and from
back to front with the symptomatology. He could then treat
minor ailments covered by the contents of the box and was given
an introduction slip to send more difficult things down to our
hospital for the doctors to deal with.

Part of the contents of the boxes was a store of things which the average mother in the West has in her bathroom cupboard — cough medicines, aspirin, liniments, boracic acid, digestion tablets, together with bandages, lint and sticking plaster. Others concerned Chinese disease remedies, dysentery mixture, quinine bi-sulphate, silver nitrate, iodine, and in the larger and latter box, vaccine and implements for inoculation or vaccination.

The course to know these things was not enough. It had to be matched with a course on human biology, of which the peasant was entirely ignorant, as the Chinese concept of man's interior was that it was the place of two vapours, one hot and one cold, his health depending on the balance of pressure between them. Germ or virus invasion was totally unknown as were contagion and infection.

When the student had successfully passed examinations in these three things he was invested with his box and went back to his village as its Local Healer. He was to carry on his own work and treat his patients in his spare time with no salary, charging only the price of drugs which we bought wholesale from the Chinese Firm, Kofa, which put a Chinese language label on every bottle of medicine.

If a student failed his examinations we could not allow him to return, he knew too much and too little. He stayed for another three months and did it all over again.

They could not think themselves doctors. They represented risks, but these we accepted. The present-day Chinese Government has universalised the system in its 'Bare foot doctor' programme.

Gladys, whose service to the programme was absolutely essential, could never forget the confinements she had been called to where local aid had gone wrong and the mother lay at death's door. To arrive and find an open umbrella and a hatchet lying in the room, for reasons I have never understood, and to find the women had been treading on the mother's abdomen, was unforgettable. She wanted to know why we did not do a course for midwifery on the same lines. In the end we did, and linked it to our Home-Making course which trained mothers in child care and the making of clothes and toys for children. Gladys and her girl nurses handled this one.

The Chinese are sometimes known as the 'Farmers of Forty Centuries' and accurately, for they are. The trouble with their farming as it seemed to me, eating their meals with them, was the diet's complete lack of balance. This cross-linked with a dreadful poverty and the consequent poverty of the land itself. The weary soil which had grown rice or potatoes (sweet) for centuries could not vitaminise the crops it grew. It was possible to have a whole village suffering from Vitamin B deficiency. The compost pits, essential to the land, were badly made from a health point of view, the irrigation canals were alive with mosquito wrigglers, and the fly population outnumbered the Chinese nation.

There was quite an acreage of land on the Mission compound and there were plots of land at some of the outlying chapels. There were new and improved seeds in Nanking University Agricultural College and there were new varieties back home and in the United States of America. Farm improvement is a long and patient business, which is perhaps why new nations ignore it. It took three years to get some of the crops which improved the diet from the first sowing in our land to the chapel plots and then for the first time into the hands of the farmers themselves — two years of indignisation, a year on the chapel land and then out. We gave away the seed to the co-operators. The Nanking products took less time, perhaps a year on our land. Reconstructing the composting system to the Allahabad Indore process we could begin in the first year and the oiling with rags on sticks of the water passing through the irrigation system was equally immediate. We got out tomatoes, broad and wax beans, cabbage and Irish potatoes, lettuce and peanuts, from overseas seed in the three-year programme. We got two new strains of rice out more quickly from Nanking, a dry rice which grew on hillsides free of paddy and an earlier form of paddy.

The Recreational programme required the help of the

Pingkiang Town team to begin. It was based on a club-cum-service brigade pattern, which I adapted from the Methodist Association of Youth Clubs scheme in England. The young folk got quite used to debates, a games room, and above all a drama group. When the town team was proficient at the various activities we launched them on the villages. It meant all kinds of side issues, such as the invention of an oil lamp which would burn heavy oils which the farmers grew on the land, Linseed oil for example, so that folk could see to play at night in the winter time. It was the drama, however, which really caught on in the villages. From time immemorial strolling players of the old Chinese opera had travelled the villages in the festival times. There had sprung up in the great cities the cult of 'civilised Plays' (Wen Ming Hsi). We copied the latter, a little drama of life as it was being lived and of how it could be improved.

A man would play a mother with a child, a rag puppet, which had reached the stage of being weaned. He would play the mother trying it at both breasts without success (this would have the audience in stitches) and then he would mimic the mother boiling rice porridge, putting the porridge into her own mouth and then feeding the baby with it. Then a girl nurse would appear on the scene and lecture him about what he was doing to the baby and the disease he was passing on. In the finale she showed him a bottle and bean milk which one of our doctors in the district had made from the soya bean, make him taste it and feed the baby from the bottle. All the plays were of this kind and I grew to think that every young Chinese was a born actor.

This work was best done on the stage in a Confucian Temple, where there was one, the Ancestral Hall, or in some of our chapels. Here there was always a high platform facing the dais. The preachers had encouraged the young players to believe that their activity was 'Chi to hua min tsung fu wu', Christian service to the people.

The worship programme was in action from the beginning. I had long felt that the reformed church style of worship which we had brought with us was too intellectual and difficult for the people to use when they first encountered the Faith. It did not include colour, action and formulae the people could share. The hymns were all translations of Western ones. The music was in a notation system the Chinese could not sing. They use a five note scale, for example, we an eight. To the outsider the act of worship did not look like worship. The chap who had a leg wound healed by the healer, or a new seed planted in some of his land could not come and offer thanks for just this worldly little thing. The woman whose babe the local midwifery girl had brought into the world had no way to say thank you, though this was easier because there was the action of the Baptismal Service. Indeed our only really helpful things were the two Sacraments. They did employ action for the still untrained Christian. In a word, our worship coped with the seasoned Christian who knew in his mind the meanings of things, but I wanted the whole village at worship, drawing together in that worship all that was happening among them.

We blazoned the walls within our chapels with the posters of Jesus, great stories done in Chinese costume and settings. We lifted the Cross high on the wall behind the Holy Table and put a great Bible on that table, itself against a background of a scroll saying here is the word of God, here the symbol of sacrifice. We converted to the new Hymn book which had then just come off the Press and which contained some sixty Chinese tunes and Chinese lyrics. One of these was actually written by a member of our Tze Chiang chapel. We used the gong to call people to worship and put in many responses in the worship which people could learn easily. We had scrolls either side of the main door, a Confucian Text matching a Christian one. Chinese fiddles made the music.

One of the most religious occasions in Chinese life, I always felt was a funeral procession wending its way to the grave hills. Why did we not take the Faith to the people outside the chapel walls? We began to bless the fields at springtime and at harvest;

we celebrated the opening of new rooms at a farm, visited new couples joining a family homestead; welcomed new born babies in their homes.

Life was full to overflowing operating the different sections of this sixfold plan; the days sped by from 7 a.m. in compound prayers on into the night. My diaries note dates on which ten or fifteen callers on various subjects visited my house, at meal times, at night, any old time. There were hours digging in the gardens and on the compound, hours teaching in the school knowing that what I taught would turn up somewhere in the circuit. Other hours went in the training courses and testing candidates for the medical boxes. There were women's schools to help in and always the work of administration, doing several sorts of accounts, interviewing officials, calling on offices in town, in between two- or three-week-long tramps round from village to village. There was the construction of new chapels in new places, with the supervision they needed. Now and again for the first two years there were courtesy visits from army people who brought their wives to see our way of life. There was one such army wife who was a French girl married to a young officer who would come to borrow English magazines and refresh herself with foreign conversation. There was the ebb and flow of the military campaign which sometimes brought the fighting right down near to the town, and then we had to deal with panic. Then to hear the flip flop of hundreds of straw sandalled feet in the middle of the night was to know salvation near, the army had reinforcements.

This sterile warfare of Nationalist versus Communist was the cause of some strange events. Sometimes I would go right up into the hills, from which the army had just pushed the Communist bands, to groups of our people who had survived the mess, and have a Communion Service in the wreck of some home or village inn. They were a shocking sight, the people and the land. Especially, I thought, the land. The terraces on the hillsides were crumbling, the irrigation channels fractured or weed filled. What had been paddy land had been taken over by the wild bamboo which stood in thick-stemmed forests where there should have been rice in peace. Between the bamboos could be seen the pugmarks of wild boar. All the landmarks were gone, so obliterating land ownership. On one occasion I took up a team of really old men and we spent a day or two using their memories as a record of where corner stones and landmarks had been. The area had always been so poor that no town landlord had wanted to own it and consequently our people were owner farmers there in good numbers. On one visit where I had a service on the one table left in a tea house, using tea and local biscuit for the elements, a dozen heart-tugging people shared the Meal with trembling hands; it was for them the beginning of a new day.

The took me to visit a man they said they could do nothing with, who never came out of the little shack in which he had lodged. I sat down with him and when he was sure I was not a Government official he told me how he could not sleep because he had been a troop executioner with one of the Communist groups and had beheaded with the great sword more than twenty people. He was haunted by them he said. I listened to all he had to say, talked with him and some of the people promised to visit him regularly and comfort him. We reinstated several such mountain villages. One thing I was always glad about, when we rooted out the bamboo it was carted away in man-loads to a derelict paper mill which some of the men got working again and the bamboo ended up as an asset.

The good years were speeding by; the whole country was seething with rage that the Japanese had taken the Three Eastern Provinces, what we call Manchuria, as early as 1936. Prayers in the mornings with the school boys was a matter of tears, as they prayed for China's salvation from invasion. Yet the old rivalry between Nationalist and Communist rumbled on.

Then a year later the Japanese attack began in earnest and they invaded through Shanghai, where the Chinese Army made a terrific defence. Gradually the Japanese snaked up all the new made roads which were the circulation system of eastern China, roads which peasants had made with their own hands, until they were in all the great cities to the east of us.

I could see what was coming and, using the pamphlets published by the British Government, I had built a system of trench refuges from air attack. Before ever a bomb dropped in Pingkiang we had an air raid system for the school and hospital on the sides of the hill which ran through the compound. We trained squads of the senior boys and girls to act as a warning team and as a rescue team. From the Union Jack which flew in my garden, where two boys stood looking out over the town, we had relay messengers right down into the school and across to the hospital. We drilled the children in getting into the trenches. We decided that the First Warning, which the army sounded on the great ton-weight gong of the Confucian Temple, should be our signal for putting out the Warden boys and girls, classes could go on until the 'Ching chi' warning, the urgent one — then it was everyone into the trenches.

In 1938 we had our first raid by a small squadron of Japanese Naval bombers who circled the town at low height, dipped to machine gun its centre and made off. I was praying that they had seen our flag which was painted on a great board and laid on the grass outside the hospital. They often went over us making for Changsha or the railway which went down to and touched Hong Kong. That was a legitimate target for war, had the war itself been legitimate. Chinese civilian labour, however, kept the rail going in spite of it all to the end of 1938, then took up the rails to build the Burma rail. The rails they humped by man power for hundreds of miles. A great motor way had come to Pingkiang by then linking us to Shanghai and Changsha. Except for the section to Changsha, the Chinese people took it up by simply hoeing out the earth which they had just a few months before painfully laid. Once, on the road, I was walking back from a chapel visit when a white ambulance passed by. As it did so a very smart, curly headed Chinese girl waved to us from it. 'That's no local girl', I said to my companion. The vehicle stopped and we talked with the crew. She

was a Chinese girl, a nurse, from Manila in the Philippines who
had come to fight for her ancient homeland. The Japanese were
fighting peoples not armies. They knew it in the end.

Down in the southern section of Kianghsi the Nationalist's
blockade succeeded and the Long March, so famous in history,
began in 1934. From the first they attempted to leave a remnant
army in the Southern Provinces of China and our Ching k'ang
section was among those who in Communist Circles stayed on.
There was much confusion of counsel in those days within the
Communist Movement and our group in 1936 adhered to the
plan advocated from Moscow and the Comintern, to make peace
with the Nationalist Armies in order to back up the resistance to
the Japanese and, they said, encourage the National Armies to
stiffen their resistance. They came out of the hills and were seen
in Pingkiang. I was visited by some of their officers who had come
across our Co-ops and they came to ask about our method of
organising them. Our volunteer method of inviting men to join
did not please them at all. They thought Christianity too slow. In
that year Gladys and I went to live for a month in Kyushu, Japan,
to study their village co-operative movement and I found that
they too dragooned villagers into societies.

This change of political climate reduced our troubles to only
one source of trouble and disturbance, the Japanese attack.

At this time I was joined by Cyril S. Clarke, a probationary
minister who had come to the district in the previous year and
had been doing his language study first year course in Changsha.
He was more than welcome. He was a Welshman of the Valleys
and had come up through life in the same down-to-earth fashion
as I had. Our approach to the problems of mission and to the
muck of war was identical. He was also a Handsworth man.

One of the first jobs I gave him to do was to paint an
enormous board with a Union Jack to put on the open space
within the hospital grounds. At first he bucked at this, it irritated
his Welsh national feelings, but he agreed to do it. In the first
Japanese air reconnaissance after the board was put out he sat on

the middle of the board and raised his hat to a Japanese plane as it swept low over the hospital.

In the survey of that devastated area in which the Communist forces had occupied the eastern side of our circuit we discovered that the area was rife with malaria in a very high concentration. I reported this back through the Health Ministry and it is to the everlasting praise of the League of Nations Epidemic Prevention Bureau (the forerunner of the World Health Organisation) that in the midst of the war with Japan they took action on this condition. Teams of doctors came up from Hong Kong University and did a survey, which revealed more than fifty per cent of the population infected with the disease, and set about a gigantic 'Quinine' campaign. The preachers and I went with them on their survey in order to use the local language to persuade the people to have a blood test — they were so frightened of the strange Hong Kong-ese doctors. Then there was the problem of administering the long-term dosing of the people with the quinine, so many tablets a day had to get into the actual stomachs of people over a considerable period. (Even in the British Army during the war I discovered this difficulty with our men. Officers had to see that the dose was really swallowed.) The doctors' teams were delighted that we could see to this problem by shifting Local Healers out of the west country to the area to act as 'quinine-swallowing invigilators'. On their tours the teams discovered what we had not noticed, a very high incidence of syphilis. For the first time in the history of the Bureau they planned a mass syphilis campaign with Salvarsan.

By the end of September our programme, the Government overarching programme, and the League of Nations projects were all living on borrowed time. The eastern push of the Japanese army was getting nearer and nearer. We had to shift our emphasis to the daily routine and the immediate problems of coping with survival, evacuation and what we could do in the chaos which war always brings in its train.

Refugees from the eastern provinces began to pour through.

Millions of people were moving through the country on their way into Western China, behind the barrier of the Yangtze Gorges, to which the Government had already retreated. This was the Chiang Kai-shek policy of trading space for time. Of the masses moving west, some thousands had to pass through Pingkiang and we were asked to open a transit station for them. I sited it over the river from the town in open country beside some water. There we built a village of bamboo huts, a First Aid centre, great kitchens and a modern de-lousing and baths unit. People who came to fit enough spent a night with us, then moved on to the next transit unit west of us, some thirty miles further on their journey. Many could not do this. City-bred women, having walked hundreds of miles, hobbling on tattered feet, needed longer periods of rest. Children travelling with their parents were often weary beyond description. Some came so depressed they needed more time to get back the will to walk.

It was a strangely moving experience to serve a nation protesting with its feet against an aggressor. Most of them had taken part in destroying their home towns by fire before they left, leaving for the Japanese the ashes of their homes. It had grandeur: the people's suffering rivalling the army's resistance action defeating the enemy.

We bathed them, deloused their clothing, fed them and bedded them down with blankets and straw mattresses. We patched up their broken feet, treated ailments and gave them medicines to use as they journeyed on; we, with decent Chinese rites, buried those who would never travel again.

As the weeks sped by this caravan of eastern people tailed off; the war came nearer. The human stream changed to a dribble of wounded soldiers seeking medical aid. From the end of September the light air raids trebled and the outside edges of our town were strafed from the air again. The refugee camp became untenable. We thought that these were simply 'scare raids' to soften up the civilian population, not thinking ourselves important enough to merit the full treatment.

On 17th October we were disillusioned. At that time I could not get BBC radio news on my set because the news was taken over by the pressures of the European crisis and threat of war. The Japanese news bulletins had had us a captured town for days and we knew we were not. The wounded, drifting back through us, all said the front was holding.

On the 14th of October Clarke had made a quick sortie out to Changsha to hurry up some supplies for the hospital and he came back on the following day carrying a letter from our Chairman saying it was time I got Gladys and the child out as communications through the province and out were rapidly deteriorating. The enemy had landed at Bias Bay, cutting in between Canton and Hong Kong. That was a Saturday. I had planned to go to one of the country chapels but stayed on in Pingkiang. We had a morning alarm and another in the afternoon. The first one was in our 9.30 a.m. morning service time, the second from 3.00 p.m. until 5.00 p.m. Gladys said there was too much to do to leave it all standing, and refused to quit.

On the 17th, the Monday, after morning prayers at 7.30 a.m. I saw eighteen bombers flying high, headed for Changsha. By 10.00 a.m. ten planes returned and flew over us. At 10.30 a.m. seven returned. We had everyone in the trenches except the look out team. They machine gunned the motor station outside the city across the river. At 12.40 p.m. they flew over the city East to West, following the great street through the town and put 20 bombs in a row down the length of the two streets. They circled us and put another twenty down the North to South streets. We could see from my look-out the city in one blazing chaos. Margaret had run out from the trenches and stood beside the look-out boy and me. She startled us both by letting rip a string of the most awful Chinese curses, enough to blister the ears of a coolie-carrier, as she damned the Japanese for 'destroying my lovely Pingkiang'. Between us we got her back into the trenches in tears.

There the Rescue Team boys of the topmost class were itching to get into the action and I went out with them into the town.

It was dreadful. The first home we entered had lying on the floor side by side an old woman and a pig, they had identical wounds. Both were dead and both ripped open from stomach to chest as though sliced open by a butcher's cleaver, the old lady's arm was thrown round the pig as though she had died with a frightened friend.

On the Tuesday we turned the hospital chapel into an extra ward to cope with the mauled and burnt victims as they piled up on us. The boys were out again in the town with the stretchers and tools for dealing with collapsed buildings, working side by side with soldiers and other rescue teams. The population was heading out of the town into the country and took with them some of the wounded who might have lived if they had been brought to hospital. An old British doctor passing through Changsha came down for a day or two to help us through the first flush of casualties.

Gladys had decided that Margaret had seen enough and agreed to leave and we got down to the ruined bus station to find that the buses were still running an emergency service to Changsha. We planned that the two of them should move to a circuit which was still intact down in the southern half of the District. Getting through the town was an ordeal, broken and burned people still lay among the ruins of the streets through which we passed and the very stones of the street under our feet were hot enough still to scorch Margaret's feet through her sandals. I had to pick her up and carry her. She cried like any Chinese child for her lovely town and her child friends left in it. It was all too much for a seven year old.

The next day in Changsha was infuriating. By 7.30 a.m. I was at the Government Petrol Permit department for a permit to use our mission car to move Gladys on. The alarms were sounding as I came back with the permit. When the air raid ceased I was out again to see about the car and by the evening we still had not got our petrol. They got off the next day in the early morning bound for Yungchow down on the Canton border.

I tried to get a bus back to Pingkiang later in the morning but none was going there. I borrowed a bicycle and set off down the old road. Half way down the road I came out on to the motor way and an army lorry gave me a lift the rest of the way. By the evening I was immersed in all the visits and problems of the town; it was just as well for I was very, very lonely.

The next day was a Sunday and although we had morning service at 7.30 a.m. we heard the gong ringing the emergency alarm during the service. The most urgent item on the agenda was what to do with the school, close, stay or move? Mr Fu chiang yun told us in a staff meeting that he was prepared -to take the school into the mountains in 'make shift' quarters rather than give in by closing or staying. He and I set off that very afternoon to seek a mountain refuge for the school. We tried out two mountain villages, well off the area into which Japanese troops cared to go since they could not cope with fighting in narrow valleys among the hills. Armour in the open and on roads was their safeguard. We tried T'ing Hsi Shan and a place further over in the country devastated by the war with the Communist armies, Chang Shih. On the following Wednesday the staff had all plumped for Chang Shih. The next two days went in getting the move organised and in making route maps for getting into and out of it. The staff, aided by Christians in from the area, planned to shift just about everything, including the kitchen stoves, whether for the comfort of the pupils or to deny the enemy any of the school's possessions only the good God knows.

Next of the problems was to strip the Refugee Centre of all that we could move. It so happened that the bombing had damaged our town church so that it could not be used for worship. We elected to turn it into a clinic for retreating wounded. Miss Hsu of the hospital staff took charge of this move, aided by the gallant daughter of our Yu Keo preacher whom Gladys had trained in nursing. Miss Hsu was a girl who had come out of America to take her part in saving her father's native land. She certainly did.

At the clinic we discovered that troops, wounded, coming down the roads from the east and north were suffering from severe infestations of scabies which made life miserable and caused them to scratch their wounded limbs, so making their wounds worse. We added a new bathing facility and a clothes fumigation plant at the chapel to cope with this. Clarke and I would spend hours rubbing soldiers down with sulphur ointment and fumigating their clothes, while the girls dealt with the surgical wounds.

Life could not stop at field work of this sort. Night after night I worked till the morning had come on circuit, hospital, provincial and co-operative accounts to keep things straight, and secure smooth supplies. It was the co-operative finances which astonished me. They came in regularly from the most difficult places, largely prompted by patriotism in the peasants. One man turned up on my doorstep with his society's money stuck all over his body, fastened by tape from one of our medical chests and with two pike-bearing comrades to guard him on the road. They demanded to see my own credentials before they would part with the money. They would not take any out for a new loan but said, 'We will come again when we are rid of the little dwarfs'.

The Japanese, not being content with having levelled the little town, kept on raiding and raiding from the air. The worst was on the 8th December when a squadron of planes came in singly and each plane swept over the town for twenty minutes dropping bombs where they thought the people might be. This ingenious technique made the whole raid last all the daylight hours. One bomb scored a direct hit on the deep shelter just behind the Confucian Temple but fortunately did not penetrate it.

Meanwhile our vacant buildings filled up with women and child refugees who came on to our land for protection, the stories about women who fell into Japanese hands were not nice. It was necessary to register everyone and refuse all men. Some turned up, even two young officers came in over the wall and had to be ejected.

It was now December and I was scheduled for leave in the Spring. I remember marking the day when Albert Leigh, who was to succeed me, sailed from England. I was very loath at that time to think of leaving. We were so engaged in everything; I was sorry to think of what Leigh was to come to and realised how much he would have to rely on Clarke for all kinds of information. I compiled rolls of members right throughout the circuit, in English and on a 'stroke' alphabetical system of Chinese.

We learned about this time that the Japanese had split into three columns to come down through Hunan and link with their force then coming in on the south coast. They were under orders to penetrate to and converge upon Henyang — the city central to the province. This would bring one column right through Pingkiang, their left flank. It would also mean that Gladys' refuge down in Yungchow would become a theatre of war. Would we ever get out? Would we spend long periods in two different concentration camps? Then as Christmas came I was relieved of any anxiety about her and the child, for a stranger came through from the south and brought me a letter written in Yungchow just as Gladys and Margaret left there on a Red Cross lorry bound for Haiphong in Vietnam.

How near the enemy had now come was demonstrated by a band of civilian-led guerillas bringing in a Japanese prisoner who had been so hungry that he had laid down his rifle on the grass and was lying on his tummy trying to tickle a fish out of a stream when the boys pounced on him. He was condemned by the Governing Officer of the town to be put in a cage and exhibited to the population. I went and pleaded that this contravened the Geneva Convention on Prisoners of War. I was told that the act was necessary as the populace would learn what a Japanese uniform was like and that their physique was so similar to Chinese. I won half a victory by having his exposure cut down to two days, after which he was sent back to camps.

The hospital itself had problems. Ever since we became a Wei Shen Yuan the Chinese doctors had been short-term appointments coming and going. Dr Outerbridge, the only long-term missionary doctor — a Bermudan — was taken away to supervise the drug-line down into French Indo China and was in charge of all supplies for all the hospitals. Our doctor staff was one temporary doctor who was very soon called away by the provincial authorities. He had once before in north China been in the hands of the Japanese and was in any case anxious to go. We had no doctor.

The Chinese nurses, however, were of a higher calibre. They elected to keep the hospital open at all costs, with one proviso, that I would sign the Register of Surgery should they have to do any, as to sign it contravened the nursing code of the profession. I was therefore present for all surgical operations and signed up for them. I discovered how strange are the ways of a round of ammunition which hits a man in the shoulder but is recovered anywhere in his body a day or two later. The nurses were sure that if they had to go they would pack emergency boxes of midwifery and medical equipment and join the school behind the barrier of the mountains. The two leaders were the girl who had left behind an American citizenship to fight for China, her father's native land, and Miss Chang the daughter of our Yu K'eo preacher, a Pingkiang girl whom my wife had trained. She was a tower of strength in the hospital or the street clinic.

Those weeks between our October destruction-raid and the end of the year were a strange mixture of work, emergencies, friendship, planning, worship, counsels. We carried on trying to get our last draft of the local healers trained and out. We kept our classes and worship services going.

We got involved in the life of the town in new ways. I got roped in with the Roman Catholic Priest, Father Wang, a Spaniard, into doing certain civic duties when the Hsien Government retired on Changsha. We were in charge, together, of the Hsien granary which contained the town store of grain and saw to it going out in rations to people, and ultimately to its being carried away out of harms way. I had the town fire tender — an old machine which was on fixed wheels and needed twenty men to pump its great arm when in use — stored in my garden. On one occasion when part of the Roman Catholic premises was hit by a bomb we rushed this thing through the town and saved the Church itself from destruction. Once one had a complement of twenty pumpers it put up a most efficient stream of water, so long as the twenty kept it filled up.

Other routine things went on remorselessly. Clarke's Chinese examination, for instance, was due and between us we got it in. Between these things we tidied up our premises, renewed our flags on the hospital and bedded down our women refugees. In doing this on one day we found the corpse of a soldier lying in the mortuary, which quite belied the use we were making of the buildings at the time. He had to go. We cremated him on a giant bonfire.

Towards the end of the year the Hsien Governor and his staff returned — he had been in trouble for leaving and was brought back by a Government Censor, Mr Hsu Ching-yu, who had been a guest student with me at Handsworth in the days gone by. We had great fun talking over the contrasts of when, with some others, I had taken him round Bourneville and shown him round Birmingham.

This melting pot of war relationships seemed to count for such a lot. About the time of Mr Hsu's visit a woman was brought in who had lost her husband and her child in bombing and been mutilated herself. I went to see her. I found that she belonged to my own clan — she was a T'ang — and her depression was monumental. She didn't want to live. When we stripped her off to see her wounds we found one leg was gone from the top. 'What good am I like this', she moaned. As the girls saw to her stump I got a large sheet of paper and we laid her on it and I sketched right round her body preparing to order her an artificial leg. We promised her she would have one leg, all the way from Europe, and she would even get a new husband proud to have her. 'Shall I dance again at the New Year Festival?', she said. Not this one but the next, we told her.

Christmas day came along and our team determined that nothing would keep us from celebration. It rained and that was the symbol of our good Christmas. The church was decorated, and sixty people were at the morning service. We had a house party of 51 at the nurses' house. In the evening someone gave Clarke a duck and we had it for supper. In the afternoon a wandering -postman turned up with two letters — however old — from Gladys and Margaret. It was Christmas indeed.

The year 1939 began among us with the traditional Methodist Watchnight Service which has a close affinity to Chinese ways of celebrating the beginning of a year. We blended into it the dual note of Tennyson's Hymn

> 'Ring out wild bells to the wild sky,
> The flying cloud,
> the frosty night;
> The year is dying in the night;
> Ring out, wild bells and let him die.
>
> 'Ring out the grief that saps the mind,
> For those that here we see no more;
> Ring out the feud of rich and poor,
> Ring in redress to all mankind.'

and Wesley's New Year hymn

> 'Come let us anew
> Our journey pursue
> Roll round with the year
> And never stand still till the Master appear.
>
> 'His adorable will
> Let us gladly fulfil
> And our talents improve
> By the patience of hope and the labour of love.'

We sang, we prayed for China and for a new sense of responsibility in Japan and as the first minute of the new year dawned we had silver bells ring to mark the passage into the year, which was a change from the rough beat of the air raid gong.

I made the first duty of the new year a journey round all the parts of the circuit to which one could go. I walked on ice-bound roads up to Chang Chia Pei and looked over our property and met the members, then on to Tze Kiang, the beri-beri village, where I had a look round the work being done by the co-operators and had a service and baptised two or three new members. From there I went to K'u Ling a new centre which was entered over a pass in the mountains, from which we could hear the argument of the guns. I slept there in the chapel on a couple of pews. After breakfast the next morning I went on to Yu K'eo, the mother centre of this area, for a chat with Mr Chang, the preacher there, and together we went on to another new place, Pi Yuan T'ung. There I made friends with the Hsiang Chang (Area Officer). This place looked as though given a chance we could have a large development. I left there at seven the next morning and made my way by the pulverised motor road, passing wounded troops and struggling supply lorries, back into Pingkiang. It was difficult to think on that war torn road that behind the mountains there were such peaceful villages as those I had just visited.

After this refreshing journey, doing the work for which I was there, it was back to the ruins of Pingkiang and all it was demanding. One new experience was the affection which the General Officer commanding the area began to show in visiting our house. It was probably triggered off by a group of Korean Volunteer guerrillas who came to the house to hear the foreign news on the radio, copy out the headlines on wall posters and then run them in behind the Japanese line to post them there on the walls.

General Yang-sen would bring his wife up to the house with him and they would chat about the world and the way it wagged. They had both been trained in Paris and loved news of the outside world. His overseas travel undoubtedly made him very appreciative of the way the Korean lads prosecuted their little bit of psychological warfare. He slowed down all the desk jobs I had to do, and they were legion.

On 14th January, Albert Godfrey Leigh turned up quite unheralded. He had got a lift on a military rice-train up from the coast and come down from Changsha on foot. He simply arrived unwelcomed but very welcome.

The next day or two went in escorting him to the Hsien Chang, the military commander, who gave us a wonderful lunch, and showing him the various activities of the Mission in Town. Fortunately Clarke had just got back from his first unaccompanied run round the circuit and was able to share the visits with us. We were for the moment three Handsworth men together loose in the heart of China.

On 4th February I left Pingkiang as I had first entered it, under my own steam on the old road, the only difference being I had a bicycle with which to ride the smoother bits. A whole mass of friends saw me out of the town gate, and peddling and walking as hard as I could I made Changsha in the evening about nine o'clock. There our headquarters had been bombed out and the work had been moved to the Hunan Union Theological College site near to Yale University. I found a bed in a Canadian home.

The next ten days went in Synod in which I was responsible for the English translation of the Minutes with Mr Li chang-hsu who was responsible for the Chinese basic copy. He was a most charming fellow. Nearly blind, he became a Minister in spite of everything and later was the Christian Liaison Officer with the Communist Government. There was an enormous Synod party to say goodbye to Mr Stanfield as well as me.

On the morning of 17th February at 8.00 a.m. we boarded a train which ran on a remnant of the Canton Hankow Railway to Chuchow, in Kiangshi. There we were to change to a train on that strange railway which ran to within 180 miles of the China coast at Ningpo. It was a remnant of rail still in Chinese hands which skirted, on Chinese Free soil, through country occupied by the Japanese, always subject to bombing but ever repaired and kept usable. It was the perfect example of the futility of fighting against China's vast spaces. At Changsha the staff had cheerfully sold me tickets right through to Chin Hua, the point within reach of the coast, 800 miles through occupied China.

Our party was J. H. Stanfield, the retiring Chairman, a Miss Schaffer, a German lady who had given her life to China, Mrs Connie Forster, a missionary wife and her baby son John, and me. My pockets were stuffed with little doses of Lactogen to make sure that young John got his rations and we carried all the articles to service him. If anyone got through it would be young John.

The whole journey took four days. On the first day we rumbled right across Kiangshi, our neighbouring province. On the second day on the train all went well, except one air-raid warning which did no more harm than interrupt John's meal which he had half on the train and half on a grave-hill. We arrived at Chin Hua, the end of rail, at three in the morning of the third day but were allowed to stay aboard until 6.00 a.m. when I scuttled off and went to look for the China Travel Service, that most indomitable of Chinese services. I found it and went and brought the ladies and baby to rest there while Stanfield and I searched round for baggage, and tickets. Stanfield went off to contact the China Inland Mission station. It took more than two hours to wheedle our tickets out of the Authorities and get the China Travel agents happy with our luggage. We all went to the CIM to swap war news.

On the fourth day we boarded a bus and tore at furious speed over the most incredible road until a tyre burst and we slithered to a heap as the bus halted. The driver changed to his spare tyre and we resumed our headlong drive until just four or five miles from the spot at which the launch awaited us, a second tyre went. That was it. We had no second spare and had to get out into a little village and wait for another bus to come and rescue us. Nobody worried, passengers said we had done well to get so far. In fact it gave everyone a chance to eat at the village inn. The relief bus arrived and we got down to the river and the launch and arrived in Ningpo, the only Treaty Port still in Chinese hands, at nine o'clock to be welcomed by our mission staff whose house was not far from the bund where we landed. Stanfield and I shared a bed, I clad in borrowed pyjamas belonging to our six-foot host. I could have slept on a clothes-line.

The next day we rested, went round the work of the Ningpo staff and sorted out our baggage into individual loads, for at this point our ways parted. We even attended a musical evening in the town at which there were thirty foreigners, the biggest clutch I had seen for years.

The only way to get to Hong Kong was to go away from it up the coast to Shanghai and transship into anything there which happened to be calling at Hong Kong. I boarded the coaster, *Hsin Peking*, and at Shanghai transshipped into the Dutch vessel of the Japan, China-Java line *Tzisidane* doing her round. *Hsin Peking* got into Shanghai at 7.00 a.m. and there was only time to regularise my passport and get myself vaccinated as we sailed for Hong Kong via Amoy on the 3.00 p.m. tide.

She proved to be a real haven for three restful days. I had been sorting out baggage and living the war so long I had not had time to examine the contents of my own heart and mind. This lounging round *Tzesidane* gave me the chance to do so. I discovered that there was too much of China's sorrows in my heart as well as in my head. I had not given enough of both to remembering that I was going out into the great world with its own problems and had forgotten what family life was. I took a hint from the commercial life of Amoy, which with the Japanese occupation of the town had simply switched its life to the island on which the foreign people lived and did its world business from there. I began to turn my mind into an Amoy island.

Peak5 - ITALY AND THE APPENINES

With the Army, free and bound

The peak of the next phase of my life came in the middle of World War II in Italy, on Campo Concentramento, 70, at Monturano a village at the foot of the Appenines near the coast of the Adriatic.

The Prison Camp was the home of eight thousand young fellows captured by the Germans on the Western Deserts of Africa. We were billeted in a disused silk factory which had failed as a business proposition and had been turned over to military use. The great warehouses had been filled with three-decker bunks closely bunched together as our dormitories. The old machine hall had been cleared as an assembly place and sundry other buildings served as sick bay, offices and store rooms. Outside our compound, but within its own wire, were the quarters of our trigger-happy guard, a whole battalion of Italian troops.

The whole camp had been ringed round with a double barbed-wire fence, beyond a trip-wire, and in it were built watch towers which each housed a Breda machine gun. These the guards always had in on the camp. On the great gate which admitted to the camp was emblazoned the Fascist motto, 'Struggle, Obedience, Fight'.

Just inside the wire of the perimeter the prisoners' feet soon wore a track which we called 'the circuit'. It went right round the compound. People trailed round it at all times of day. It was the circuit of despair. On it men took exercise. Many of the men had come to the camp from the infamous camp at Benghazi. Most who came from that camp had contracted dysentery; some came to us moribund before we ever had a chance to help them. I buried thirty in one month, laying their bodies in the civilian cemetery at Fermo. Those who walked the circuit were fighting off

death, staggering back toward life, trundling round that circuit in
a fierce but unbelieving effort to live until the end of the war.

Early one morning in May 1943 I was walking the circuit
when the sun caught the hill some ten miles away. It was a
beautiful sight. The village which, as ever, crowned the hill was
itself dominated by the village Church which stood out like a sign
against the sunlit sky. It was so sane, so ordinary, one could almost
hear the villagers going through their daily life, the shout of its
children. Away to one flank of the hill village the sun caught the
great loom of the Appenines looking down at the little hill. The
whole scene brought back to me the Psalm, 'I to the hills will lift
mine eye, from whence cometh mine aid'.

My eyes came back to the stumbling feet trudging that circuit,
feet in straw sandals, feet in broken boots, all very weary feet.
Feet of men who just thirsted to stay alive and forced their weary
bodies to take exercise round that infernal circuit. The beauty of
the hill was not speaking to them.

I fell to reflecting on the work I had done with Dr Lofthouse
at Handsworth years before on the Hebrew of that Psalm. I
recollected how we had discovered that in the stout Hebrew of
that age the text should be read as beginning with two questions
which somehow the English translators had missed. Shall I lift
my eyes to the hills? From whence comes my strength? In that far
off age the hills were the sites of the little, pagan, fertility godlets.
Look to them for strength! Whence cometh my strength? Our
strength comes from the Lord of heaven and earth. Psalm 121
is full of confidence in God's protective care. 'He will not suffer
thy foot to be moved.' 'He will not slumber nor sleep.' 'He shall
preserve thy going out and thy coming in; from this time forward
and for ever.'

There was a message for those trudging feet after all. It was a
moment of deep spiritual insight which went with me through
four such camps and three years of prisondom.

———————

We came home to England from China when the war clouds were darkening over Europe. Those of us who had lived a while outside the English world, subject to the news of foreign nations daily, had the knowledge that the coming European war could not be avoided. We knew that the USSR had a pact of mutual assistance with Germany and that Japan too had a quarrel of her own to settle over European presence in her world of the East. We could not believe that Britain would survive the coming conflict. She was too tired after the first phase of World War I. This thought, that we were saying farewell to the homeland on this visit home, dominated my thought throughout the furlough year.

The news which we heard over the ship's radio on 15th March about Albert Leigh deepened this sense of finality. On that morning the Japanese had put in one more raid. The people on the compound had taken refuge in the trenches as the planes stooped to bomb our compound — all except a band of some twenty refugee children who instead tucked themselves into the cellars of the second house. Albert, parading the compound, saw this and dived into the cellars to have them out. A bomb hit the house, it collapsed and a great beam fell across his chest and killed him on the instant, the watch on his wrist still ticking away.

We learned later that the town Government saw to his burial on the Christian Grave hill which they decorated with a banner wrought in silk which said, 'The Spirit of the Christ'. That was well done.

We got home stunned by this loss. Why had I survived so many raids over long months, got Gladys and the child out, and Albert go down after a brief three months of superintendency in Pingkiang? We saw Mrs Leigh and I took her up with me to unveil a plaque in Albert's memory in the new chapel of Handsworth College. His widow was granted pension rights by the Church as though he had served forty long years: but my concern was that he had not.

I began to think of the two million or more young Britons who would soon be caught up in a losing war. How many young dead would that produce just as senselessly as Albert? Should I not line up with them and give what there was of life to these British lads as I had tried to give in Pingkiang to Chinese lads? Would that carry on Leigh's story of service?

A year of Furlough from missionary service is no sinecure. We lived in four corners of the country in borrowed houses or quarters. I had my ration of week-long deputations up and down the country. In all I went to eleven Districts of the Methodist Church on long-stay tours of meetings in various churches of the District. They could be anything from great congregations of five or six hundred people to Women's Meetings in afternoons with fifty to fifteen women. They could be Children's Clubs, Boys' Brigade Services or classes in homes, and all the time staying in different homes, which I found the real trial. I did the following Districts in this way: York, Manchester, Sheffield, London North East, Plymouth, Newcastle, Exeter, Cornwall, Isle of Man and Lancashire.

This was in addition to the meetings which arose by individual approaches, from people one knew or were in the neighbourhood in which one was living. It was as tiring for the missionary wife who lived much alone and wondering when her husband would be home, and for how long.

I had contracted with the Edinburgh House Press to prepare a book on rural mission techniques and was very keen to get it done and done well so that, when at home, in addition to preparing material for deputation there was always this assignment to see to and visits now and again up to London to see the Press.

This could have been just the normal furlough drill which so often has sent men back to overseas work from sheer exhaustion. In this case it was complicated by the uncertainty about what was to happen, to Britain, to China, to us. Going round conferences such as Swanwick, there was very little to be deduced from the counsel of people there.

The day after the war finally broke out I wrote to the Mission Headquarters and told the Secretaries there of my feeling about

the war, the challenge of masses of young British men in the
services and the apparent co-ordination between my last days
in Pingkiang and the needs of such experience among our own
Forces.

I got a qualified approval from the Officers of the Society on
4th October. I was somewhat disappointed by the remark of the
China Secretary who asked me whether I was attracted by the
wearing of a uniform! A cable came in from Cyril Baker, who was
acting as Chairman in Hunan, saying that they blessed my going
and counted me as the Chinese Church's contribution to our war
effort. This cheered me up no end and banished the cynicism
about glamorous uniforms. I made the application to the Royal
Navy, Army and Royal Air Force board of our Church and was
interviewed by them. They said I was just on the limit of the age
group required in the bevy of new chaplains they were seeking
(Methodism had to give 12 per cent of the expanding chaplaincy
corps). The thing dragged on into early 1940 before I was finally
commissioned into the Royal Army Chaplain's Department. In
my own heart I knew the right thing had happened.

I was immediately gazetted to the Essex Regiment of infantry,
a Territorial Battalion which was then stationed in Witham,
Essex. In theory I was the 'Other Denominations' chaplain for
the whole 121 Brigade while living in one battalion. In fact when
living in a particular unit the chaplain soon becomes far more
intimate than that. People accept him as a part of their own
communal life. I was never unduly troubled with denominational
rivalries throughout my years in the Army.

On posting I went straight down to Witham and found the
Headquarters of my unit established in Barclays Bank in the High
Street. Here I slept on the floor for quite a period until Gladys
came down and we found a lodging in the town.

I was introduced to the Commanding Officer who did not
seem too happy to receive me. He greeted me by saying, 'I suppose
you are more acquainted with Women's Meetings than a lot of
young fellows, Padre'. This with a whole pack of young officers

standing round listening in. I was riled and replied, 'No Sir, I'm just back from the Sino-Japanese war and masses of Chinese lads'.

I felt a tap on my shoulder and turned to find that it was Major Charles Newman who was in command at the time of the HQ. Company, who said, 'Can I have a word with you Padre?'. We turned away and he said to me, 'Never hint you know anything about war or Active Service to the Colonel, he's never seen it, if you take my meaning'.

It was a good hint and I followed it. All too soon Major Newman was seconded away from the battalion to lead the attack on Narvick in Norway where he won the VC. The Colonel of whom he had cautioned me proved to be an enlightened and just CO. He was a stickler for good order, neatness and protocol but none complained of him.

He demanded, for instance, that I speak to Battalion Parades in Witham Parish Church and when there was a protest from the incumbent (who had begun his career as a non-conformist minister and become a stiff clergyman) the Colonel declared that King's Regulations was his Bible and it said he could command me to preach to the troops from the chancel steps, as he could any officer, if necessary.

Though I spent very little time in the Mess and much with the men and around in the community, I found the cadre of officers a most likeable bunch. They were nearly all Territorial Officers — as were the men — and in consequence we had a spectrum of British manhood, from a parson's son to sailors from Burnham-on-Crouch. We were known to the rest of the Army as 'Swede Bashers', though many were boys from the Essex parts of London. It was very easy to get to love them all. When Gladys came down to join me she made her impress on the younger officers by finding their wives digs in our several locations which were just outside the area where the Colonel would not have wives living.

This was particularly so when, very soon, we moved out of East Anglia up into the different world of Northumberland for training with carriers and the duties of guarding that glorious coast with its miles of sandy beaches. The High Command had decided that an invasion would be just as convenient for Hitler up there as nearer London.

We moved first to Throckley in the Tyne valley, then to Wooler, where we fought again some of the battles against the Scots of long ago, and finally to Haltwhistle. From each place we had small units out in villages near the coast. In each place I got local churches and chapels to open halls as canteens and rest places. In Belford, one little town, I had troubles in this respect. The leading local lady refused to do anything for the Army; she said the Authorities had refused to let her join the Home Guard. She took me into the garden, set up a target at the bottom of it and put three bull's eyes on it with three rounds of 303. 'What do you think?', she asked. 'Best shot in Northumberland', I replied in Northumbrian. 'You belong here', she said, 'I thought you too were a southerner.'

The whole move was a gift to me. I had come home and acted as the interpreter as well as the parson on the unit. The men's difficulties with the language were only matched by the ease with which they found their way into the people's hearts. We had followed a none-too-good regiment and had a lot to do to rescue the Army's reputation. There were stacks of romances which lasted.

I though that compulsory parades would be a bind and was prepared to fight them, but I didn't. Old soldiers who had come back for this war said, 'We couldn't come if they weren't compulsory. We wouldn't have the nerve.' 'We like singing with the band, a short talk, all but the inspection before parade. We'd miss them. If we came as volunteers we'd be called holy.' They had a point and I took it and concentrated on getting inspections (including the nails in men's boots) removed to a different time.

It was a tremendous thrill for me to enter into this Church Parade system which went back to the times of Cromwell's first chaplains. After all, Milton had gone before, there was a standard to maintain.

It was an even greater joy to do smaller parades out with companies and platoons away on sites off from the Headquarters.

There were a sergeant and a corporal who played the cornet and a fiddler who would go with me to see to the singing and it mattered not at all that the father of one of them ran a public house in Witham. The Battalion had allotted a driver to me who would never make a soldier, but he had been a chorister and saw to the supply of Army hymn books and often chose the hymns. We were a real team and what sermon tasters they became! We operated on the sands of the Embleton beaches, in the courtyards of stately homes, often with the staff joining in; any old place would do. Just now and again we acquired a parish church and really went to town with the organ. The vicar of Belford who was an addict of butterfly collection, said, 'take the Church, my dear boy, use it'. We did, adding our instruments to his organist. Our Brigade area was from just south of Berwick to just short of Newcastle. They were busy Sundays.

I had acquired an empty shop in Haltwhistle and put a begged library of books in it for the chaps to use when these days of English soldiering drew to their close.

We were all given 'jabs' of a secret nature — though as the bottles of serum were all marked YF and the clerks who had access to King's Regulations could look up YF, some of us knew that Sierra Leone was involved. We were dished out topees and khaki drill too and that set us all saying goodbye to sweethearts and wives.

Of course it was to Glasgow we went and boarded a trooper! She sailed after the dockies had done all they could to ruin the officers' steel uniform cases by stamping on them, and joined a convoy of 70 ships in the Kyles of Bute. The Royal Navy took us on from there. The whole convoy headed north until there was no more daylight. We then turned westward and crossed the most northerly part of the ocean until in the middle of our journey we were heading down the coast of the Americas. Off Brazil we shot across the South Atlantic making a beeline for Africa.

It was nearly Christmas by this time and I was up at the crack of dawn to prepare a Communion Service in the saloon. I was wondering who would turn up to share it, there had been such a party the night before. Suddenly there was an unmistakeable bang, a whistle and a shell exploded on the sea surface just beyond us. I nipped out on deck just in time to see, away across the sea, the flash of the second shell which actually went over us and hit the next ship in the convoy. This was no submarine stuff but a surface raider attack. I looked for our own guard ship, a little bucket of a sloop; she seemed to turn in her length and let fly an answering shell with her tiny gun. Off she went in the direction of the flashes from afar; it was a Royal Naval 'David' challenging a German 'Goliath'.

I never got to the Communion but I chanced to see one of the most gallant actions of my war. I spent the next half hour waking sleeping officers, one of whom said as I rolled him out, 'If this is a joke, I'll murder you, Padre or not'. The convoy scattered ship from ship and we made port under the surveillance of that most incredible of aircraft, the Walrus: the only aircraft which is actually propelled by its inboard screw.

We came to after our adventure in the harbour of Freetown, one of the world's great harbours. Ashore the city spread out before us in its tropical luxuriance. Half of the tin chapel-bells seemed to me welcoming us. My Roman Catholic colleague had been a missionary here and, leaning on the rail, he told us all not to expect too much. Hot, noisy and messy, was his summary.

I thought it looked very attractive. The town's gleaming white houses climbed a beautiful hill known as Signal Hill. Behind the town a great mountain shaped like a couched lion towered up, which gave its name to the whole colony and protectorate: Sierra Leone. The harbour was alive with shipping, much of it Naval. 'Nelson' lay under our noses. The whole scene produced a cheerful hum of busyness. I decided I liked it.

We, the first expeditionary force from Britain for a century, however, were there on business. Just north of us was the Vichy

French port of Dakar and off from it lay the islands of Cape
Verde, a Portuguese possession. Dakar was a well developed base
for Axis Power, marine, sub-marine and aerial power. It tormented
all our convoys going round to the Middle East, as we had reason
to know. Could we stop espionage over the Vichy border? Could
we occupy the Cape Verde Islands and so neutralise Dakar? As
we were there reinforcing land power so the Royal Nigerian
Artillery had come up as gun power and the RAF was stepping up
its strength by bringing in 'Sunderland' and other more modern
aircraft to replace the dear old 'Walrus'. The Royal Navy was
there in strength having failed, it is said because of espionage in
Freetown, to take Dakar unaided.

The battalion disembarked and we were led to a railway
station on a narrow-gauge railway. We packed ourselves into
its quaint open carriages and began a twenty mile run into the
Protectorate, the chaps' eyes wide open with astonishment as we
rumbled along. We came to a wayside station called Benguella and
detrained, where we stood in companies on the baking platform
while we were issued iron rations, having had no food since
disembarking. As we stood there a signaller came up the platform
and said to me, 'Padre, there's a Black Parson in civvies down
there'. I went with him and saluted an iron-grey parson dressed
immaculately in clerics. 'Good day Sir, it's nice of you to see us in.'
'Good day Sir', he answered, 'My name is John Mark, and I'm the
Superintendent Minister of the Songo Mission of the Methodist
Church into which you have come. Welcome!' I laughed with
sheer joy and said, 'Well met. I'm the Methodist chaplain of this
mob you're welcoming.' He fell on my neck and embraced me.
I introduced the signaller, telling him that the lad was a local
preacher. He kissed him too.

We went back to the Signal Section and I introduced him
to the whole bunch. 'You've got a five mile walk yet', he said, 'I'll
walk it with you'. One of the lads offered him some cheese on a
biscuit. When the command to fall in rang out he lined up with
the platoon and, carrying some of our heavy gear, he marched

off with us. It was a very hot five miles but that platoon never
noticed. They had a guest. Black can be beautiful!

The walk ended at a perimeter camp cut in a forest which was
still being constructed for us. Mr Mark introduced me to several
of the workmen, including their 'boss' who was also one of his
people. This man always attended any church services I had in the
camp as did a number of others in his team of workmen. Once
a lad came to me and said, 'That boss fellow is supposed to be
religious but I heard him swearing like anything'. I took the lad to
see the man. 'No lad', he said, 'You heard me saying "Jesus" shifting
those planks? That wasn't no swear, that was a prayer. He helps
me to lift the big ones. He wouldn't be no good if He didn't come
when I needs help, would He?'

We worked hard on that camp, sweating off the ship board
fat and getting acclimatised to the country. Every day was a route
march and firing practice and all the skills which make a good
team of soldiers: signals, transport, field cookery and — worst of
all — long marches wearing gas-masks, in full service kit. Night
marches were best but for the wretched plague of mosquitoes
and the stinking anti-malarial ointment on our legs and faces.
It proved a near impossible task to get the men to wear their
'short-long' trousers with the bottoms tucked in over their knees
and smear themselves with the ointment which, as it grew stale,
attracted the insects rather than repelled them. We had to start
each day with quinine, which the men believed ruined their
sexual potency. 'You've seen my daughter', I used to say to them,
'I've spent my life taking this stuff. The number of those sick from
malaria and footrot grew to high proportions. It was a choice, in
a way, between the two. Exposure meant malaria, closed up foot
and leg wear meant footrot, which spread from the feet up the
legs.

After we had completed the basic acclimatisation we moved
from the perimeter camp down to a new camp right on the
beach at a village called Lumley, which was much nearer to the
town. This was much superior. We lived in huts actually on the

beach and the men were in the sea bathing every day in the late
afternoon. We had the most glorious sunsets, with the bugles
blowing the 'retreat' out across the sea. Our work, too, changed.
We took to small cutters and were out on beach-storming
exercises with other units, one defending and one attacking
the beaches. Our long marches also took us not into the bush
but through the villages of the Colony itself, with their warm
southern English names. The men from Burnham-on-Crouch
now came into their own; they became famous boat handlers.
Now and again we had the horrible job of going out to pick up
Merchant Navy crews, who had been on torpedoed vessels, from
boats in which they had starved, and some died before we could
fish them ashore. They were in wretched states and we took them
off to a Reception Centre in Freetown to be re-clothed, fed and
repatriated.

I enlarged my parish by taking in gun sites of the Nigerian
forces scattered round Freetown for anti-aircraft duties, many of
whom were Christians and enjoyed a short service. They were
under orders never to shoot down the regular French plane which
came snooping in once a week, they had simply to keep her up
too high for reconnaissance. One young British officer with them
got browned off with this and told his team he would give £1 to
the gun crew if it did get shot down in some fashion quite outside
Orders. The very next week it did.

We were within the orbit of the Freetown Circuit Plan of one
of the town circuits and I preached on the plan at Murraytown,
Freetown Wesley, and other spots. By now I had four or five chaps
who were local preachers and they too appeared on the Plan
and took services. They in their turn found a nearby Countess
of Huntingdon Chapel (a species of Methodist movement gone
Congregational) which they teamed up with and nursed back to
life.

Wednesday afternoons were still free and I looked round for
things to do. Mr Mark said he would take some forty men out
into the wilds of Sierra Leone if I wished. I organised a couple

of trucks which took us to the end of metalled road in the
Protectorate and there we began to walk through banana groves
and tall hard wood trees. At the foot of one Mr Mark showed the
boys an offering of wine and rice. He told them it was the village
holy place for villages round about and asked them never to
disturb such a spot. He at last brought us to a headman's village.

The headman came out to greet us with the two riflemen the
Government allowed him. He led us all into the central square
of the village on which he sat to hear cases. He asked if we would
like to see the village dancing team. I hesitated a moment. Would
the chaps behave? Then I thought I knew them well enough to be
ashamed of myself.

The girls came out naked to the waist and with very tiny loin
cloths. They were golden yellow, being Fanti people not Negro,
and as they danced they made a charming picture which we all
clapped tremendously. The men had brought tins of bully beef
and biscuits for a meal and we all ate together.

The headman then asked if we would like to see the crocodile,
and who would say no? He took us off to a long shed at the end of
the village. In its gloom we could see the trunk of a tree which had
been split down its length and, with his legs clamped in between
the two halves sat a man whom the headman said had not paid his
head-tax of one pound. One chap fed him bully beef and before
we left his fine had been paid by a whip-round.

The chaps kept up this standard of behaviour wherever we
went. Once in a village called Waterloo we wandered round
seeing the place and an old, old woman called us to settle on
her verandah. We sat round her and she said we were the first
troops from England she had seen since she was a girl. She asked
a corporal, 'How is the good Queen Victoria'. He never batted an
eyelid and told her the good Queen was safe in the arms of Jesus
and her grandson now ruled in her stead. 'It is good', she replied,
'He will rule like his Grannie'.

One of the difficulties about our afternoon bathe was that
European women had for years strolled along the Lumley beach

in the sunset. Their presence to most of the men meant wearing trunks or diving neck-deep into the sea whenever one appeared. Many of the women had Naval officer companions with them which made our disappearance the more urgent.

I discovered through local friends that across the mouth of the Lokko River there were miles of uninhabited beach from which we could bathe. I tapped the Adjutant for the hire of a launch and took parties across there.

On our first visit we all stripped off and laid our uniforms in rows along the crest of the dunes and raced off into the sea. Someone looked back and shouted. We all looked, and there were numerous little black heads sitting among our clothes. 'Clothes chaps!' someone shouted. Everyone lumbered back up the beach to the rescue. We arrived, puffing, to have one little fellow say, 'You swim, we keep watch!' They were all scholars from a nearby Mission School.

My daily chore was censorship. There was a high percentage of married men in the battalion and only four married offices. Every letter home had to be censored and after two young officers had been heard by the bar steward laughing over a quote from a letter there was a near-strike. The order went out that only married officers censored married letters. In practice, the CO being one, three of us censored most of the married men. Naturally the Padre came in for the brunt of it. I became familiar with hundreds of women in Essex villages through letters.

I had a requisitioned tent which held my library, games and an office and there I spent hours censoring. One lad came in carrying a boot box which was full of his wife's letters. 'They're all right', he said, 'I've read all hers and written replies to all she said in between the lines of hers'. I fingered through them, dozens of them. This was the end. I told him that the Government made me read his but I had no authority to read hers. Did he want me to read them? That woke him up, he didn't mind, he said, but she might!

We had a great hall which could hold the whole battalion and

did when I gave talks on the progress of the war and the range
of international politics — no easy task. I got an offer from The
Methodist Boys' High School to give a Sunday night concert
in it. They came down, numbering fifty, under the care of their
Mathematics Master. He told the battalion that they would sing
the songs of their fathers. Spiritual after spiritual rang out for two
hours in the lovely voices of the boys. The master told the story of
the rescue by the Royal Navy of the fathers and grandfathers from
slavery of these very boys. 'That is what Freetown means', he said.
Our men joined in singing some. One they were still singing on
the Western Desert when we got there.

> 'Rather than be a slave,
> I'll be buried in my grave
> And go home to my God,
> And be free.'

The nurses' choir from the town hospital also came down
to do a concert, dressed in their best gowns, pretty as a picture.
They became the only ladies to be entertained in our officers'
mess. There was only one snag in their visit. English overseas often
changes its vowel values. We do not care for our language when
it gets overseas as do the French. The compère at this concert was
a male nurse who introduced each solo item by saying, 'Our next
item will be sung by a norse'. This sent the Essex men from villages
into fits, they knew much more about horses than they did about
African ladies. As each nurse came on to the stage they gave an
impression of horses' hooves which the nurses, fortunately, took
to be encouragement.

After a year of this West African life the battalion began to
show signs of wear and tear. Our casualties by foot fungus and
malaria mounted to nearly three hundred men and reduced the
fighting strength to some seven or eight hundred men; the War
Office decided we had had enough and we were ordered to leave.

We embarked in a Norwegian merchantman turned trooper
and sailed for the Middle East. It was a voyage of which I

remember little for I went down with malignant malaria the day we embarked and spent most of the voyage feeling as limp as a wet rag and in the care of our battalion doctor who says I reached a temperature of 106 on several days.

I was back in working condition by the time we reached Durban, where we unloaded a large number of our sick. Here the CO ruled that no man who could not wear his boots and puttees could be allowed to go ashore and enjoy the massive hospitality of the local people, who took car and coach loads of the chaps out to see the sights of the area.

I was able, however, to take many in slippers to the canteen in the heart of Durban which was run by the Methodist Church in the centre of the town. 'We will not expose them to the population', promised the ladies of the Church. They also laid on a breakfast for the men who went to Church on Sunday morning, which increased to large numbers the men who said they were nonconformist!

From Durban we embarked in *Isle de France* which, with all the other great names in the shipping world, was doing duty as a trooper. Not beginning our voyage from a Home Port we were short of cigarettes and other supplies which, fortunately, were made up to us by a generous gift from *Mauritania* which was carrying a contingent of Australians. Five of these great liners arrived safely at Port Suez and we began an new life.

We found ourselves camped in a tented camp on a very dirty piece of desert just alongside the oil refinery at Suez where the stink of oil infiltrated everything. From there we provided the small units which were scattered along the canal to guard it and operate the winches which stretched an anti-bomb rope net across the canal at night. Others had the duty of guarding the maze of docks each night, which the Italians bombed with great regularity. Here we suffered our first Middle Eastern casualty — a young officer was struck by a fragment of shrapnel which pierced his tin hat.

My own work became very complicated. Fortunately the

Transport Section had scrounged me a motor cycle on which I used to ride just about the length of the canal to visit the scattered groups, and the Methodist parson who operated a Methodist Soldiers Home not far away could help with the care of the men back at the battalion base. That motor cycling was the limit; every road had a coat of oil which dealt treacherously with the back wheels; the sand, when one left the road, dragged at both wheels and tended to lift the tyres and tubes off the machine. The ever-resourceful Transport corporal dealt with this by screwing washers with bolts through the tyres and the wheel frames to anchor them on. This mysterious bike had at some time been in the hands of the enemy and been recovered from them wearing an ingenious Italian air filter which kept the sand from its innards; a cross bred Enfield-Fiat!

After a tour of this duty we were moved again and found ourselves entrained for Palestine, where we came to rest in the Sidney Smith barracks at Haifa. It was here that we were finally torn from our Essex Brigade and selected out to become the base battalion of a new Indian Brigade of what was to be The Tenth Army. We lost our CO, who was sent off as Port Commander of Port Sudan, and we came under the command of a Regular Army officer whose active service record was as long as his arm and we were brigaded with one battalion of Ghurkas and one of Sikhs newly out in Iraq from India.

So, off to Iraq we went, in our own trucks. Once through Nazareth we entered the tip of Jordan and down to Mafraq, whence we followed the now disused pipeline out across the desert. Once away from the tourist sites I felt myself really in Bible country and so did many of the men.

In a covered truck with a herd of them I was constantly showered with biblical questions and through a mouth covered with a scarf against the cloud of dust the column raised, I preached some very Old Testament material to an unexpected audience. When we got to the end of a day's run we got down to pitch our tents near people who could have been Abraham on his

journey the other way. Covered in the dusty sand we must have
looked pretty much like him ourselves. Indeed, standing round a
camp stove with the other officers one young fellow said, 'Here we
are Padre, Abraham and Lot but our sheep are men.' One section
of the track stuck in my mind with the gift of a new insight. Just
into Jordan the desert ceased to be sand and was covered in great,
monstrous rocks, round smooth and brown, which lay round in
various sizes from tennis balls to higher than a man, like a mass of
bread rolls — an obvious clue to the trigger which suggested the
temptation of Jesus, 'Turn these stones to bread'.

Once into Iraq we shot off north-easterly toward Mosul, the
hills around which it now appeared were our destination. On
those hills, just before Christmas, we found masses of tents lying
on the ground un-erected, spotted with snow. With a group of
lads I got one square Indian Army pattern tent erected and a fire
going inside it. It filled up with men as they finished erecting
the tents assigned to them and I got the gramophone going with
Christmas songs and we sat round singing until, in one mass, we
fell asleep.

We were five miles out of town, it appeared, because our terms
with the Iraqi government dictated we could not live in centres
of population. Our presence had two motives. One, the Turkish
frontier was nearby and a German attack through Turkey was
anticipated; two, we had to train into integration with the two
Indian Army battalions. The two duties matched one another.
We trained as we dug out defences on the frontier, doing which
I discovered that the Indian Army Signals attached to them were
largely Madrassi men many of whom were Christian.

I had not been long there when I was visited by two Iraqi
gentlemen, one named Jaleel Daoud (David of Galilee), who
begged me to act as pastor to their Christian Church down in
town. Their minister, an American missionary, had left in the
Rashid Ali rebellion and the Church was bereft.

I found this place. It was behind a mighty protective wall
with an iron bound gate in it down in a part of Mosul banned

to troops. I said I could only help them if my men could get to
worship in it. This they wangled out of the Military Command.

On Sunday afternoons a whole party of us sallied off down
to central Mosul to that iron-bound Church. Veiled women in
complete purdah knocked on the gate and entering the courtyard
they zipped open the purdah and stepped out in bright everyday
clothes. Many of them were graduates of the American University
in Lebanon. The little Church was very beautiful and soon filled
up with people; our Army presence really made it uncomfortably
full.

We had a bi-lingual type of service. An old retired Iraqi
minister using Aramaic for language led the service and translated
for me when I preached, and the British soldiers sang in English
matching the Arabic of the local hymn book. I had never dreamt
that one day I would hear worship in Jesus' language and be
translated into it. After service the whole congregation had tea on
the flat roof of the church buildings.

Mosul was a fascinating place. Just outside it are the ruins
of Nineveh with their statues of the winged bull, with its great
ramparts, and inside of those ramparts the Indian Army was
operating the Field Hospital for the troops stationed round. A
hill nearby was crowned with a magnificent mosque dedicated
to the Prophet Jonah — Nebi Junis. The streets in town were
old, narrow markets bustling with life. Just a truck ride away was
Erbil, one of the oldest constantly inhabited towns in the world
crowning a great mound full of the rubble of long centuries.

Our work near Mosul being finished we moved down country
to Ba'quba fifty miles north of Baghdad where the Euphrates and
Tigris come near to one another, where we began to hack out the
second line of defence. It was historically wonderful. When first
we began to dig we claimed back from the sands shell cases and
impedimenta of the World War I troops who had dug there before
us. Modern digging goes deep and below where our fathers had
dug we began to discover ancient ornaments and utensils which
had been used by Babylonians centuries before us. We struck

into an ancient Babylonian cemetery and came upon many tear
bottles, beautiful, iridescent things meant to contain tears of the
mourners. One ladle with a twelve inch handle surmounted by
a bull's head all in pure silver marked some Assyrian occupation
of this southern territory. We became quite popular with the
National Museum of Iraq in Baghdad.

While on this site we reached the Jewish Passover and I was
successful in getting our new CO to give the Jewish boys from
East London (of whom we had quite a number) permission for a
few days leave. Then I went into Baghdad and interviewed a rabbi
who secured homes for them in which they were welcomed to the
great family feast of the Jewish nation.

As a *quid pro quo* for Christian boys who were keen on Bible
knowledge I got permission to take some truck loads of men on a
sightseeing trip to the ruins of ancient Babylon where we camped
in houses of foreigners who had been driven out by the war.

It was a wonderful experience to walk by Abram's canal which
flowed round the ruins, to see the great idols and mighty walls
and study that portion of the scriptures on site. Baghdad — the
modern successor to Babylon — was different, a sea of narrow
streets, slums and offices. The only place to which troops could
go was the YMCA, an American one, run by a devoted couple to
whose quarters the young Crown Prince would come as a little
lad, in his own Rolls-Royce marked 'Iraq 1' on its number plate.
He would climb up on the lady's lap to be loved. In the history of
Iraq he was murdered shortly after reaching manhood.

Livelier than the great mosque and the official buildings were
business girls of the town whom one saw leaving their homes,
wretched shacks surrounded with bustee, with no water supply,
out of which they stepped as modern young things as neat as great
ladies and went off to work like girls getting off a London train. It
was sheer conquest.

Two things happened which affected my own life in this
period. The first was a new posting; which did not come off.
Another battalion of the Essex Regiment passed through the

Middle East bound for Burma. A posting came through for me
to transfer to them because of my grasp of Chinese. The posting
came too late, the battalion was already on the sea.

The other was an offer to remain as an Area Chaplain in Iraq
which meant serving each unit as it turned up there and just while
it remained in the area. I thought this one over and over but in
the upshot I decided that it was my duty to stay with the lads with
whom I had begun my service and see them through to the war's
end. Our relationship was too intimate to break up.

Meanwhile on the Western Desert front the German forces
had entered the fray supporting and ultimately displacing the
Italian. This determined our fate. We moved back through the
desert track, this time via Deir Ez Zor and Damascus to the
Holy Land. From there with scarcely a rest we pushed on in our
trucks down into Egypt, through Cairo without a stop and found
ourselves back on the deserts of the west. It was a choking, tiring
run and the jeers of the Cairo population did nothing to cheer
us. Crossing the Sinai in particular was bad. There the sand is
particularly fine and silvered us from head to foot. The tarred
track across it was so insecure that any driver who used his brakes
was 'on a charge' for he tore off the road surface.

We camped a day west of Alexandria and then enbussed again
and threaded our way, through masses of troops coming down,
to Merza Matruh where we dug in or took over the diggings of
others before us according to the luck of the draw. I inherited an
elaborate hole in the ground which dated back to pre-war Arab
wanderers and thought myself lucky till I tried to sleep in it. Then
fleas; I could sit in it and see hordes of fleas hopping toward me
from all over the floor. I decided that it was better to be bomb-
blasted than to be eaten and took my ground sheet out into the
open air.

The men were busy on patrols over miles of desert in open
trucks. It was the time of Rommel's great advance and when they
did see his tanks or troops it was a case of evasive action. They
were so armoured and we so naked of all superior weapons. The

chaps stalked Germans like deer in Scotland. One young officer
with a truck load of men stalked a German tank until all the
people in it had got down to relieve themselves then he swooped
in and captured the German crew and fired their tank. This sort
of warfare was all that could be done without tanks (or with only
the little Valentine) against the German heavy tank strength.
People will never know how the Western Desert Force fought
in those pre-Eighth Army days. Did the War Office not know
the Germans were coming in strength when they took away our
heavier Churchills and sent them to be lost in Crete?

We blundered on round Matruh and down to Daba via
Fuka and then went back to a place joining on the well-prepared
concrete defences of the South African Division, out on the naked
desert southwards where we filled in the gap which lay between
the well-defended South Africans and the great impassable
Depression called the Qattara Depression through which the
Rommel force could not come. We were there to hold a line in
front of El Alamein while the Command got ready its counter
attack — which we never saw.

We soon found out why the place had not been prepared for
defence before we arrived. Under a thin layer of sand the ground
was one great slab of slate inches thick. We dug and dug, until our
hands bled, with any tool which would split that slate slab. Fire
pits, slit trenches, holes for vehicles and, my own responsibility,
the Regimental Aid Post which the doctor and I had to see to. We
could not 'dig-in' our own truck for it would be used to carry back
wounded to the rear while we stayed put just behind 'A' Echelon,
the force in contact with the enemy. Wire went up dividing us
into blocks, mines were laid though there were not enough to
surround our defence and what we had were Egyptian which went
off when they felt like it. I dug out my own slit trench to sleep in
behind a hump near the RAP. We were heavily bombed the first
night and I presume that the bomb crews reported back that their
bombs did not set off any mines on our rear. Later it was from
that rear line that we were overwhelmed.

The battalion was dreadfully short of water. The nearest water point was out of action and our drivers had to go miles to get any. One water truck out of our four was already gone. A pint a day was the ration. In the RAP we scrounged an extra ration, Harry Nesmyth, the Water Corporal, realising that we needed it. In the night three twenty-five pounder guns came up, of the Leeds Territorials, and were sited near us with a mountain of ammunition beside them. 'There's a fine bloody target' commented the doctor.

The morning of 1st July 1942 dawned to a brilliant start and I sat up in my slit trench wearing a tin hat which I hadn't worn when I fell asleep. 'You put it on in the night when we was bombed' said my Driver George. The air was full of rifle fire and mortar cracks. We were engaging a German Engineer unit who had arrived on the wire in troop carrying lorries. Our mortar men, under a vicar's son, drove them off.

I pushed off down to the Second in Command to get the news. He was quite sanguine, we had driven off this attack and there was not likely to be another, he thought. I had hardly got back to the RAP when we were amazed to see trucks of our own Regiment scurrying down the desert and past our line making for the rear. 'It's all yours' they shouted at us gleefully. It was; as they faded away German guns opened up from positions near enough for us to see the sand swirl up and their flash as they fired. Our twenty-five pounders replied with an extraordinary rate of fire; the enemy fire seemed undisturbed. Rather it ranged in and took on a new, sharper sound. Boston aircraft flew over us and attempted to silence them. Between their sorties and the German reply there sprang up a rhythm of noise and silence. A group of bursts from out there silenced our gunners. By this time I was in the RAP hole with a group of drivers, who could not get through to the front to pick up casualties, and such wounded as they had brought in.

I had made an arrangement with Corporal Nesmyth that I would go round the fire pits with him on his afternoon trip delivering water. In the late morning he rolled up to station his truck near the RAP. As he wheeled the truck round to station it he saw me standing outside the hole and grinned and made a sign that he would like a cup of tea. I dashed into the hole to turn up a Primus stove to make it. There was a crashing explosion, I looked out and saw that the gunfire had hit Nesmyth's truck. He was still at the wheel upright, his mate was lying against the shattered windscreen pumping out blood from a leg wound. I rushed over and found Nesmyth dead, cut loose his comrade, for they had roped themselves to the truck. I yelled for the doctor who bound up the leg. Then I lifted Harry Nesmyth down and laid him on his truck's own camouflage net and took from his pockets all the little things a man carries: his wife's portrait, his child's too and the little Methodist Prayer Wallet which I gave to chaps who came to church. He had never done that. He must have asked George for one. He had a grin on his face still and I could imagine him saying 'Watered the whole ruddy lot and no time for a cup of tea!'.

By this time the whole scene was dominated by a fury of noise. The crack of artillery seemed to be coming from all directions, the deep rumble of tank-tracks playing an obligate to it. Trucks went swishing by, and the rapid fire of small arms was everywhere. In our rear the noise of battle was as insistent as in the front. German infantry was coming at us in armoured trucks and the boys in the fire-pits were cursing the amount of ammunition which was bouncing off them instead of finding a true target. It was the classical picture of an infantry unit facing an armoured assault; flesh and sand against steel and armour-piercing fire. I saw one tank, its turret gun blazing, sit on the lip of one fire-pit and mow down its three men with one burst of fire, including two boys who were keen churchmen. So it rumbled on from pit to pit.

I dashed back to the RAP which had in it the group of drivers of evacuation trucks and the few men they had brought in. The drivers had their rifles by them. One or two chaps picked them up. A tank rolled along the edge of our hole sending the wall crumbling down on us. I kicked the rifles into a corner and said to the lads 'It's all over, watch what you say'. A Panzer NCO entered the RAP. My first thought was how grey and tired he looked, but his automatic rifle stuck out in front of him menacing the whole group of us, which it could have taken with one burst. I walked toward him and said 'No, we are Red Cross Personnel'. He said 'Yes' and waved for us to move out. I got the lads up and we filed out.

Outside was his detachment. I looked around and could see a rifle trained on us in a nearby fire-pit. I knew it was George's pit. I shouted 'Come out George, we're in the bag'. I rashly waved my arm beckoning him out. The next moment I was lying on the ground, felled. I put my hand to my stomach and it came away covered in blood. One of the German's rounds had shot me. I had seen too many stomach wounds in China. I was less afraid of dying than the physical tedium of doing it. 'O! Lord let it be quick', I prayed.

Then George was stooping over me and tearing away my bush-shirt. The NCO who had winkled us out was standing beside him and George was talking to him. The NCO pointed to a stretcher, told four of the British lads to put me on it, and the last I saw of him he was pointing out to them the way to go.

It was a desolate trip, resistance was over, there was a great drift of Essex men off in the same direction as us. Our own long-range shelling from the El Alamein line crumped down round us — too late. We arrived at the German Command Post, a tank and an armoured vehicle. The boys dumped my stretcher down beside it. It was Rommel's own vehicle. There was a stream of men coming up to my stretcher wishing me well or saying goodbye.

A German doctor came up and wished me good day as he examined my wound. 'A wounded doctor!' he said, crouching one leg either side of the stretcher. 'I am not a doctor', I said. 'What then?', he queried. 'I am a Chaplain', I replied. He reared up above me, ceasing for the moment to be a doctor and shouted 'It serves you well. Why does your Archbishop say the German troops fight a dirty war? Have we been dirty in our war? He lies.'

I replied, 'I don't know anything about Archbishops, I am not of his Communion'. 'Ha! You are Evangelische?', he said. 'What you doing here?' 'Just my job, like you!' He knelt down beside me, looked again at my stomach and said, 'I cannot save you. You will die, but not for three days if you do not eat or drink.' I asked him his name and he changed once more standing over me. 'Why ask my name?', he said. 'I like to know doctors' names', I told him, 'we are of twin professions'. 'Just that', he said, 'It is Schlegel'.

He turned, called up an ambulance and ordered men to put me in it. George, with his usual eye for a chance, got three of our boys to pick up a gunner with a bullet wound through both knees and had him laid on the other stretcher in the van. I was very glad of that gunner and I hope he was glad too. The German driver winked at George and stuck up one thumb, recognising the Transport Circle on George's battledress.

He was the nicest of chaps, that German driver. He drove us like Jehu across the open desert, knobs on the stretchers cutting into our backs. He came to a Field Dressing Station and was turned away, he drove on to a Hospital Unit of the Italians from which the Chaplain emerged, wiped my face and kissed me. He gave the gunner a lime juice and said there was no room for us there either. We drove off again and finally came to an Italian Hospital where the driver persuaded the staff to have us put in two beds from which they had just taken out two dead. The driver stood at the end of our beds and said in tortured English, 'It is near Sidi Barani'. He saluted with a 'Heil Hitler', took a receipt for us and went.

We were packed out in that ward, all the beds full and men lying on mattresses between the beds. The RAF had caught a Division coming in from Jersey, fresh young lads, but now scarred with horrible burns as well as bullet wounds.

One of them was put next to me. He had third-degree burns all over his body. When they peeled off his uniform, none too kindly, skin came off with it. He was obviously dying. He raved endlessly, thinking himself at some Jersey café demanding

Chianti. Then he went back home and called for his mother, 'Mutter, wasser bitte'. He was only a lad and childhood was not far away. His arrogant demanding from some Jersey waitress was the military veneer, the real lad asked mummy for water which he could not have. I reached across and stroked his hand. It was enough, he responded and fell quiet the faintest of smiles on his ravaged face. He was dead next morning.

Relationships between the Germans and Italians were desperate. German doctors were round hectoring the Italians and insisting that they treat their own men, pushing the inefficient Italian orderlies round.

It therefore fell to a German doctor to deal with me. He probed down and down into the wound looking for the bullet and not finding it he stood at the bed's end playing with my army equipment. Then he found what his forward colleague had missed. The brass buckle on my webbing belt had a neat furrow cut in it.' This saved your life', he said. The round had hit the buckle and glanced off before rupturing my stomach wall. He packed the hole with gauze and said I would be OK.

On the second morning I was surprised to see a very neat British soldier standing at the end of my bed. He saluted and said I'm New'. I told him I had only been around a couple of days myself. New was his name he said. He looked at the bowl of thin soup I was eating and said he could better that. He disappeared and came back with a thick macaroni from the staff cookhouse. I decided he was a batman, I was right. His officer was a Brigadier whose foot had been shot off.

In the Italian system a Brigadier was classed as a General and this prisoner was no small beer to them. In another private tent he lay with his captain aide-de-camp. New was with the Italian NCOs. It appeared that the Brigadier was to be evacuated to Sollum Field Hospital that day. Did I want to go asked New. The Brigadier invited me.

I went. The Field Hospital was housed in the old Italian Army barracks and we came to rest in a real room with only one corner shot away by a shell. An Italian Colonel-doctor attended to us most graciously until the Captain became a bit peremptory — as staff officers will — when the colonel's tone changed, 'You are not the Brigadier, you will remember that', he said sharply. New appeared with a very satisfactory meal.

This blissful situation was not long for me. Next morning I was classified as walking-wounded and tottered into a truck laden with Sikhs, Italians and Germans and driven to Tobruk. It proved better, the ward I was put into was still being run by its South African staff under a burly staff-sergeant. It might have been St Thomas's! I no sooner got into the place when a cheerful voice called my name and said to another chap swathed in bandages round his head that they'd got the padre too.

He was sightless this chap in bandages and the burly staff-sergeant had to keep off the flies while he ate some soup. 'With all the guts you got you'd think you'd be bigger', I heard the staff sergeant say. It was wiry little Wiseman of 'C' company.

'I always wanted to get you by yourself', he said, 'what happened to Bill the Swede basher in the end?'. My heart gave a jump. On the hills of Iraq, on a stage lit by car headlights, I had told the chaps a serial story about Bill, fitting the incidents to our lot. 'Well', he said, 'you left the poor sod reading a letter in which his girl broke it off when last I heard.' I remembered and cooked a reply, 'She followed with a letter in which she pulled up her socks', I lied. 'I didn't think she was a girl to drop a chap in it', he replied. We talked long, Bill, who had a bullet in the base of his lung and would die, and Wiseman, who remembered the serial story I had told the folk on the Iraqi desert, here in his blind prison life. I wondered when it was that I had really preached to these men. Was it in Services or in other circumstances all together? I couldn't tell; probably Jesus had suffered the same difficulty.

I was not left long to enjoy the company of these two. Within a day or two I was hustled out to a lorry with a Sikh or two and some Italian wounded and we were driven back along the coast to the little town of Derna.

We were now in the hinterland of the war and came under the full blaze of the second-line of war treatment. It was an Italian tented General Hospital to which we came, run by nuns who were more tainted by war-fever than the German troops who had taken us. The Superior who was acting as Matron, in particular, didn't want British people in her care. When she went round the ward in the evening, as she did every day, she averted her head when she passed the four beds which contained us. She threw four toffees on to each Italian bed but missed us out. She never knew that two or three of the wounded Italians corrected her discourtesy as soon as she left the ward. A young 'professori' a university lad, would come and sit on the edge of our beds and talk to us in English. We had great fun in discussing the fact that most of the Italian sick called frequently on St Agatha for comfort. I told the young fellow that St Agatha was an English saint of a different temperament to the Matron. He told the others and the prayers went up.

A particularly nasty piece of work was the Italian doctor who did dressings every morning on a table in the centre of the ward. The chap in the next bed to mine was a young British Lieutenant whose calf had been completely penetrated by a high-velocity bullet. This wound was always packed with gauze. The doctor would stand over him and lecture the troops. 'See, you malingerers', he said to the Italians 'how this officer endures pain'. With one ferocious tug he took out the old gauze but never won a single moan out of the lieutenant. He then put the new gauze in with one mighty push of his forceps. I was always the next patient and he repeated his performance on my tummy.

It was this lieutenant who caused our privations to be turned one screw farther. The Superior did talk to us on one occasion. She informed us that a Bishop from Benghazi was to visit the ward and she wanted our top sheets changed. We were to be washed and had better behave ourselves.

He came, robed and very, very fat. His face was a flushed port-wine red and his head was crowned with a flat, ecclesiastical hat which had a silken vine decorating it; from this hung down beside his ear a bunch of silken grapes. I looked and wondered what connection this had with the vine of which Jesus spoke. From the next bed there came in a loud voice the Lieutenant's opinion, 'My God. It's Bacchus.' The Superior heard and understood this reference. When the Bishop was departed she came over and cancelled our total food ration for two days.

I was now getting up and walking the perimeter of the hospital each day watching the traffic on the main road nearby. I spent my time wondering what news of me my wife at home had. I didn't know that the news had been forwarded to her that I was 'missing presumed dead'. That premature news I didn't know until I arrived in Bari in Italy where I met the people who had filed this information.

Being still alive I was hoisted out of hospital and sent up to a quaint building on the hill outside Derna where I was thrust among a group of about twenty New Zealand Officers, with one Northumbrian stuck in among them, together with two or three South African Officers for good measure.

As I was being 'processed' into this camp by a South African Warrant Officer who ran the place for the Italians, a black South African soldier told me he was one of a large group of black prisoners who were incarcerated next door. He asked if I would go out to them and hold a service with them. I told him I very gladly would do so and we fixed it for that evening. I was given a thin soup as a ration as I passed through. The black soldier stopped me in the passage way and tipped into my bowl some soup of a very different calibre which he had purloined from the Italian mess. An hour later when I was in the room with all the others the Warrant Officer came storming through and said to me, 'You don't go to that service, all fraternisation is forbidden'. I replied, 'What are you doing?'. I had put my blanket down beside a South African Officer and the other two lay just beyond him. The lad next to me said, 'The day when you get home won't be so cheerful for you, I'll say', and with this one in his ear the Warrant Officer left us.

These three South Africans had escaped and trudged down the desert for days until one night they slept in the ruins of an old tank. By bad luck the Italian Recovery Squad had investigated that particular tank at that very time and the three were scooped up again into captivity. They were in shocking condition, their feet being lacerated and blistered beyond recognition. Their advice to the others who sought to escape was detailed and accurate.

Walk south, they said, until you're beyond the battle area then strike east until you are behind British lines and come up behind them. This, however, needed a compass. I had the only one, no bigger than a tiny wrist watch which had been given to me by my father and lay in my trouser pocket. The Northumbrian captain was the leader of those who planned to go from the next truck in which we were to be shifted. I got alongside him in the scrum and passed it to him, 'Take this and stow it somewhere', I said to him, 'there's work enough for me right here'. He gave it a quick glance and said, 'Duties do differ, don't they?'.

That truck trip arrived very quickly. We were all shunted off toward Benghazi to a place called El Marj Barce. On the way the escape plot was to wait until a lonely part of road and there a couple of chaps were to attend to the driver and his mate at some twist in the road which separated the party from our truck load of guards. Just as they were ready to execute it a German Staff Car with its escort whizzed passed us and the escape was abandoned.

At Barce we were thrown into a huddle of captive officers of Indian and British Forces all wrangling for a place to sleep. We were to be listed here as PoWs ready for export out of Africa.

The contrasts among the Indian Army prisoners was the most interesting point about being in this camp. Some of the Indian Army men were among our best friends. They would queue up for a beef stew which was the ration and tip it into the dixies of British officers — themselves not eating beef, feeding up their colleagues. Others, nearly all Sikhs, were approached by the

Italians and offered commissions in the Army being raised by
the Japanese in Burma to fight for the 'freedom' of India and a
number accepted the offer and were taken from us to a spot of
their own.

Once registered we were taken off again back to the place
we had inhabited at Derna and locked in it until we could be
flown to Italy. By this time I had clubbed up with the three South
Africans and was helping the youngest one, with his terrible feet,
to get around.

The day came to fly over the Mediterranean. A posse of guards
came in one morning, by no means pleased with the duty assigned
to them. Some of the New Zealand officers said we ought to have
prayers before we flew out and we gathered round in a big clump
while I led a short service. I opened my eyes at its end to see all of
the Italian guards on their knees, their fixed bayonets poking up
among the prisoners. They feared the RAF as much as we did.

Down at the airfield Italian bombers were coming in in twos
and threes. There was one man among us who said he could
manage a plane and the escape thing came up again. As the
German troops got off the plane, we were lined up to enter it and
an Italian officer came along checking names and in doing so he
winkled out this particular officer, and another escape plan fell to
the ground. One machine gunner was stationed in the plane with
his gun trained on us sitting up forward, and two others stood
by the ports on either side. The thing that shook me was that
the pilot had his little son, aged about eight, with him up in the
cockpit. It seemed the pilot was sure he would get easily across to
Italy. Which he did.

We landed at Lecce on the toe of Italy and were put into the
local headquarters of the Italian Red Cross. Here we cheered
up — there was running, pure water in the courtyard in which
men revelled. There were Italian girls and boys who came in to sell
us fruit and buns. To them we were not prisoners but customers.
Many, finding we had no Lira, gave us fruit gladly.

We entrained and found ourselves parked at the camp at Bari.

It contained hundreds of officers some of whom were of my own battalion. We were first put into very lousy quarantine quarters wired off from the general run of prisoners but we were actually given Red Cross parcels as our rations. I pooled mine with the three South Africans and we messed and slept side by side. The quarters had a little wired off open space and the men already out in the big camp crowded the wire round it picking up news.

I was at the wire one morning when a young Lieutenant of the Essex Regiment came up, took one look at me and said, 'Good Lord you're dead'. I assured him that I was alive and he rushed off to bring a posse of old comrades to have a look at me. We were each given a card which said we were prisoners of the Italians and were being treated well, which we could send home if we simply signed it and added nothing. I signed it and sent it off, though some would not admit to being Italian captives. I knew what it would mean to my wife and daughter.

Out in the big swim I was parked to begin with in a corner occupied by 21 chaplains, all the fruits of the capture of Tobruk. They were employing themselves with mutual discussions and chaplains' get-togethers. There were only two of my own church there and one was very sick indeed. The other and I looked after him until he got back on his feet again. I discovered that there were many of our own men outside our wire in a 'Men's Camp'. On just one occasion I got through the wire and had a service with them and a reunion.

The South Africans baled me out of this Holy Club and I went to sleep in a hut occupied by the Second South African Police Battalion. They were all Afrikaners and read their Bibles, and prayed on their beds each morning. My companions were as different from them as I was but they tolerated us.

I gave one talk to a session which was designed to occupy people's time which had been organised by Major Brooks of my own unit; I talked to them about General Chiang Kai Shek's Nationalist China. But I was really longing to get out into a less refined atmosphere with more work and when the Command sent out a notice asking for chaplains to volunteer for work in men's camps I found myself joined to two others, one an Anglican and one Roman Catholic as a team to go to such a camp.

Padre Coates, the Roman Catholic and I had to support the Anglican padre, who was terribly crippled, all the way to a tiny little village called Monturano which was up the rail as far as Porto San Georgio and then on an electric rail to the camp. The nearest city was Fermo. The camp was an old silk factory and contained within it the mulberry trees of that trade. There were great storage barns which had been converted with three-tier bunk beds, the central machine shop which housed more people and a row of office buildings which now housed the Warrant Officers and sergeants who were running the day to day life of the camp. One of the bigger buildings was operating as a hospital ward and two South African doctors were housed in it.

When we arrived there were about two thousand prisoners in it. They included the wreckage of my own battalion, who gave me a great welcome. The two South African doctors were soon repatriated and replace by two British doctors, one a lapsed Methodist, the other a Jewish doctor of the Hepworth clothes firm. This was PG70. It was in its infant days when we arrived and soon grew to be eight thousand men. It was guarded by a whole battalion of second-rate Italian troops who were very fed up with the war. We were put in one little corner of the hospital block and were technically regarded as an offshoot of the Italian Officers' Mess, that is, one major looked in on us every day, our food came from their mess and the Italian padre under whom we were supposed to work came in from the Theological School at Fermo when he felt like it. Under his cassock he wore a British DSO for service with our troops in the First World War. Often he had delicacies from homes he knew secreted under his surtout which he fed to Roman Catholic boys.

Fortunately there was plenty of open space in the camp. The mulberry trees caused it and we could walk round the perimeter as exercise. There was one corner on which we could light fires

and 'brewing up' there became part of the pattern of life. It was
extraordinary what we would burn to get a cup of tea. There were
those who even burned the pockets out of their own clothes.
'Embers' became a universal cry as one group finished brewing
and offered the remnant fire to others.

On getting into the camp I was 'taken over' by an Essex lad
called David Mordecai, obviously a Jew. His welcome was, 'Jesus,
it's good to see you'. He caught hold of my arm saying 'they said
you were dead, let me take you to the sergeant-major, he's got a
brew ready'. The sergeant-major was Camp Commander and had
an office and a cabinet of other sergeants, some very decent chaps
among them. They gave us the 'grif on the camp while we drank
tea.

Others arrived daily. There were at that time no Red Cross
parcels and no cigarette ration. The place was very lousy, there
were not enough beds and men were sleeping on the cement
floor. The Italians were still adapting the warehouse, into sleeping
blocks. There was a very long list of sick people and other men
were very 'bolshie' and wouldn't obey any British order. The
Italian staff that they contacted every day was mixed. One was
an American-Italian from the Bronx. He was the worst. Another
was decent, he shouted, 'watch your knives' as he went round
searching for knives.

Would we please each select a Batman as the lad who did
it got an extra bread ration as an employed person. He said to
me; I couldn't find a Methodist, sir, but there is a Welsh lad
who belonged to the ' Presbyterian Methodist Church of Wales'.
I settled for him and a very nice chap he was. New, who had
arrived before us, now parted from his Brigadier, was thoroughly
miserable in this sea of men. He was attached to Ogilvie, the
Anglican.

We wandered round followed by these new batmen and
went to the block which held the hospital. I smelt it. I was back
in China immediately. It had that stale brown smell of surgical
penury. The doctors had rigged up enclosures in which to live

made of Italian groundsheets. One greeted us, the other just
grunted with that strange peculiarly Boer grunt. The first was
a likeable man with limpid brown eyes and a quiet intelligent
manner. They were both clinically frustrated and hated it. They
were surrounded by well-toothed disease and could only do so
little to help. They saw in every sick man a demon of disease
which their best effort could not banish. Cawood, the younger
doctor was halted by the war on his way to a fellowship in
obstetrics, to dwell with no tools among lusty men.

One officer was our interpreter — and spy — an aristocrat,
a Bourbon by descent. He could bring us things we wanted and
charge our account. He had a mistress in Rome and he told us
proudly that he was marrying her. Four and a half months later
he told us jubilantly that he was father of a son. I nearly lost his
friendship, for a demon possessed me to remark 'Your Mussolini
is omnipotent. Your nation needs men and here you produce a
son in just half the normal time.'

Our 'Boss' was our other contact Dom Mario, a Roman
Professor of Theology. Orders to us from the Camp Commandant
came through him. He talked to us in a mixture of Latin, English
words with Italian suffixes, and gestures. He was an irrepressible
person whom all the boys loved tremendously. He could make
them laugh.

Bursting through this ring I found the men eager for services.
I began sessions of evening prayers. We met in a half constructed
barn by the light of one weary electric bulb, the worshippers
standing in a great huddle of blanket-clad bodies. They wanted
to sing lots, but we had no hymn books. We used the old Scots
way of a man who knew a verse singing it and the men following
behind repeating it, until I got the Bourbon to buy me exercise
books, pens and ink from Fermo which I dished out to volunteers
who wrote hymns. This proved an amazing process. We could all
remember first and last verses. We 'cooked' whole verses until one
lad turned up with what was left of a single copy of the Church of
Scotland Hymnary — the rest had been used for other purposes.

I got a tremendous appreciation of the character of the ancient biblical copyists.

Life soon patterned out; the wolfing of a scanty meal, a tour of the billets, a conference of the writing group, preparation of a talk for prayers, a word with each sick man, prayers and then a chat with Coates, sitting on our beds delousing ourselves. He became a dear friend; our dialects coincided, his Durham and mine Northumbrian.

Ogilvie tried terribly hard, had his Sunday service but couldn't cope with anything else and he was packed off to the civilian hospital from which he was repatriated. This meant that Wilfrid Coates had his 550 Catholic boys and I had the rest to serve; thousands of men, Anglicans, non-Anglicans, Jews of whom there were twenty or thirty who had courage enough to keep their name tags which proclaimed their faith in spite of Italian phobias about Jewish things.

I was lucky the Italian command had in its care two YMCA mobile canteen workers they had captured in the Desert. They classified them as soldiers, and I inherited them both — Ray Davey from Ireland, a Presbyterian who entered the Ministry — Jim Barker who was his vicar's right-hand man in a Herne Hill parish. We became a team and soon there gathered round us an Anglican candidate for the ministry, David Greaves, and then another, Gillespie, and two or three Methodist Local Preachers and we could tackle anything.

Our Sunday Service was, at first in a half-built billet, then in the open air in competition with a Housy-Housy school. It grew larger and larger. Jim made a choir, Dom Mario, our 'Boss', got me hymn books from the Geneva Committee which became the World Council later. He got me a Bible through the Vatican from our London Publishing House. We called the whole venture 'The Church in Camp'. If you were a prisoner you were a member.

We used Anglican, Methodist, Presbyterian and Baptist orders of service and, after a training course for preachers which I ran, we took turns in taking the services.

We grew into a real school on weekdays. One day I was sitting under a mulberry tree thinking of home when three chaps joined me. They wriggled and chattered then they got round to it. Could I have a class for people who wanted to know the truth about religion. They were really just bored. We sealed the bargain by sharing my last Italian cigarette. The classes grew until there were twenty such groups in camp. Later a sergeant who was not in sympathy with the managing NCO's sought me out. He said, 'I'm a communist, you're a Christian, will you tell me the secret of getting classes together. I want to teach Marx.' 'By all means', I said, 'anything which gives these chaps an inner life of thought goes with me.' Years later when I had returned to English church life I had a letter from him one Christmas which told me he was a Baptist Minister.

I had taught Chinese students for so long, but they came to me to compare one faith with another. These British lads had never had any philosophy of life — it just happened to them. One lad summed it up, 'I wake up in the morning thinking about something'. It took the whole team of us to cope. I prepared a little card of Reception into Church Membership which could be acceptable to all denominations in England. For years after the war I had acknowledgements of them coming from all sorts of corners.

The most painful part of the work was the number of men who just curled up and died. We created a Covenant system whereby people who came to Church made a solemn covenant to hand me the names of any men in the billet (where it was so easy to be quite forgotten on some high corner bunk) who did not get up and shave in a morning. And later, when they at last came, put Red Cross parcels under the pillow to worship instead of eating their contents.

It was amazing how many men got no letters at all from home. On the other hand I got letters given to me by the Commandant in which people said that they were getting no letters from the men. Then there were what I called' crooked' letters. One such came from a mother who wrote that if her son had lost a leg he should be repatriated; why wasn't he? I went to look for this chap and he hopped down from a three tiered bedframe's top bed. 'How's your stump?', I asked him. He said 'Stump, Sir?'. 'The stump of the leg you lost, according to your mother's letter.' 'Oh that', he laughed. 'I wanted to make sure she sent me a parcel with fags in it.'

In the end I got chaps who did get letters to lend them to us, and cutting out the personal stuff we made a Common Letter. It was really surprising how much the Censors of two nations had missed when we sewed so many letters together. 'The man with the cigar has met the eagle on a warship', was one quote. Churchill had met Roosevelt. A special team led by a newspaper man edited this lot.

The time came when Red Cross supplies began to arrive. The problems changed immediately. We left the problems of starvation and physical weariness behind and had to cope with the problems of fed, lusty men cooped up in their strength. Jim Barker was selected as Confidence Man — trusted by Italians and British alike — to have charge of the parcel store-room. He had conquered the Italian belief that YMCA was a branch of Free Masonry, which Mussolini had banned. We got our parcels by the peculiar system of one parcel to each seven men, to be eaten straight away. The Italians thought this stopped hoarding items for escape plans. I found myself presiding as referee at food divisions in some groups of seven. Some things were easy but to measure a tin of condensed milk into seven equal portions was a problem. Chocolate was of high points value. You could trade it with the guards for anything. If one man chose a whole tablet he got little else from the parcel.

In those well fed days I began my old habit of telling a public serial story out on the open space. I cooked up all sorts of titbits both from active service and homelike into an endless story which attracted tremendous crowds of men with nothing to do but listen.

The dead were the cause of a tussle with the authorities. I
buried thirty-one in a year. They were buried in a corner of the
civilian cemetery of Fermo. At first I went up with only the coffin
and two guards. We hated this. So did Dom Mario our Senior
Italian Chaplain. They gave us a Guard of Honour of Italian
troops. Finally I got a Guard of Honour of British soldiers. It had
to be smart. We made it so. The Warrant Officers got together.
On each occasion twenty men dressed spotlessly in borrowed
clothes, a cap from one man, a battle-dress blouse from another,
trousers from a third. They marched through Fermo's main
streets like guardsmen with an Italian lieutenant and I walking
just behind the hearse. People would kneel as we went by. Some
of them would follow right to the graveside. On the way back it
was different, our men winked at all the girls they saw. Men were
getting scarce in Italy and every wolf whistle got a response.

The latest influx of prisoners we had nearly put us back to the
first days. The great camp at Benghazi was being cleared as our
troops conquered in the Desert War. Even the Commandant and
his staff complained about these men. The whole batch was a mass
of disease. They all had dysentery, they were all emaciated, most
had chest troubles. They were rolled off the train which brought
them in like parcels. Among them I found my own George. He
couldn't stand and his chest condition was terrible. I joined him
to a friendly seven and got him into the hospital unit. A friendly
Italian batman stole me a litre of country wine from the Italian
mess and as I poured it into him he said, 'Good Old Teetotal
Thompson', and fell asleep. My Welshman resigned at once and
George got his extra bread. David Mordecai I knew had been
cobbling the Italian shoes and was a millionaire in fags. I met him
at my Jewish Services each week. He didn't even smoke. He gave
George a supply of cigarettes from his store.

The coming of these wrecks into our midst confirmed every
rumour we had heard and the hints in the Italian Press which
Padre Coates read daily. The camp went wild with excitement.
We had to deal with new problems. There were men who were

afraid to go home now that it was near. They had quarrelled with
their wives or fallen out with a girl or had not written for months.
Our guards changed too, became more chatty and fraternised
more. Two even sang at a concert and only collected from the
Commandant a reprimand for doing so.

It was at this time that I struck a personal problem. Major
Calderai, the Bourbon, told me that my name was down for the
next repatriation as I was the oldest of our team of doctors and
padres. This went through me like an arrow. I thought about
Gladys whose letters were coming in telling me she and Margaret
were counting the days. Gladys was nursing in Hunmanby Hall
public school for girls. Had she not done so she could not have
paid her way on the meagre allowance the War Office provided.
Margaret was at Trinity Hall school and rapidly growing out
of childhood into young womanhood. Her Mother said, 'she
certainly needs a father at this stage'. The victories in the Italian
Front gave her reason to hope that our reunion was near. (That
was one side of the situation.)

On the other side of the picture I had never discovered among
the men that my age was a hindrance to them. Sometimes age and
experience had been an actual help. It so happened that that very
day a man was sent to me who had just heard that his wife had
gone off with another man. He told me all about his love for her
and how they had lived happily before the war took him. I tried to
make him see that no action of hers could really destroy what they
had had. His own actions, thoughts and prayers were the keys to
getting her back. 'If you could teach me to carry her in my prayers
right through this with love, I'll manage', he said. I promised him.

The next day a chap who was so lousy, filthy and still looking
as we had all looked at the beginning, came and said in a cultured
voice 'I'm lousy, do you mind if I sit on your bed?'. 'You're lousy
in more ways than one', I told him as he sat down. 'What's your
trouble?', I asked him. His story rolled out. He could not stand
prisondom like other 'regulars' and working lads. He was a
musician. He was a mess. He showed me his scabious hands with

their long fingers. He couldn't stand filthy language, the never-ending topics of conversation, sex and filth. Could I get him a 'repat' he asked.

I probed out his background: Public School; gentle home; privilege; there they were. He really felt that men should lean on him and in fact he leaned on them, carried by newspaper boys and rough working lads. He was really sick of himself. If he got his repatriation he would be damaged for life. I promised to get him into one of our Christian 'sevens' where he would not hear filth and might even help with our music.

These two men did for me what they never knew. The thread running back to the German lad and the emaciated young South African held firm. I contacted the Bourbon and told him to get my name off that list. His eye gleamed as he said, 'Si! si' You love the men too much.' The decision released such abounding energy I knew somehow it was right. I did not then know the price to be paid.

Our next flood of good news came through a visit to the camp of Major Comba, a chaplain of the Italian Church of the Waldesi. He was serving with the Alpini Regiment. At first the Commandant would not let him in saying we had no Waldensians among our men. I was called to the Commandant and had to swear that I regarded him as my Superior. He got in and we sent a message round the camp calling folk to meet him. A mass of men turned up. I wondered what he would do, he was a product of Edinburgh University, Ray Davey knew his son. I trusted him to have a true word. He told the story of the Prodigal Son and asked the men to forget they were prisoners, forget the war and centre their minds on their own prodigal-selves. He spoke of their loyalty to their homes, their wives, their children. 'How do you shape up?', he asked us, 'are you not prodigals all as am I?'. 'Let us repent together', he concluded 'in the prayer that Jesus taught us to share.' He led the great surge of prayer and gave an Apostolic Blessing. The men gave three great cheers. I had never expected to hear such a crowd cheer an Italian.

In spite of his invigilators he managed to tell us that the war was moving quickly to an end in Italy. The Allied troops were coming up through southern Italy. His news was confirmed a few days later when the Commandant informed me that a party of doctors and chaplain were coming to us from southern camps judged now to be in the war zone.

The next day Padre Willis, a New Zealand Church of England chaplain and the doctors arrived. They cramped our quarters but were welcome. Padre Willis soon fitted into our Service pattern and was a help to us all.

One morning — which happened to be the anniversary of my wedding — we actually saw the Italian Officers playing football with the portrait of Mussolini which had hung in their mess. This was it; Fascism was gone. The word swept round the camp and the next six weeks were filled with optimistic rumours. As the Allied advance slowed down in the south the structure of camp life wobbled dangerously. Some very pointed slogans appeared as graffiti concerning the Eighth Army.

The day dawned on the 8th of September 1943. First there came a rumour, then swiftly our guards became hilariously happy, then Italian Officers were among us slapping backs and offering their cigarette cases round. War with Italy was over. BBC news blared through the camp's loud speakers.

On Thursday the 9th a great congregation gathered in the open air round the boxing ring and we celebrated worship. There was a strange uneasiness in my mind and I could not talk to the congregation in tune with their wishes. Instead I told them that we were deeply inside of Italy; that there still were Germans in the country; that our freedom was not yet. I besought them to stay in Camp and not to attract German attention or annoy the surrounding villagers who might ask the German Command to deal with us.

The camp could not be held. Most of the chaps simply wandered out for walks through the wire they had destroyed, now that the Bredas pointed outwards. A tiny minority went out

for 'vino' and women and by the evening returned home drunk.
By the next day the Commandant visited us and asked for better
order, he was having visits from local gentry who said their villages
were disturbed.

Our camp administration was the Warrant Officers, the
senior doctor and myself. The Commandant told us that two
Italian Divisions were round us, that police were down on the sea-
road to watch for any German moves. His information chimed
with news items from the BBC and our own scout parties who
were watching the main roads. Above all, the incoming officers
from other camps brought with them a copy of a notice of the
British High Command which said that prisoners should be kept
in camp until British soldiers arrived.

Our duty therefore seemed plain enough. We believed that
the men's only risk was in bumping into retreating Germans or
stimulating any cells of Fascism in the villages to seek German
protection from harassment. We put Coldstream guardsmen
in the gates as guards, using abandoned Italian weapons. We
organised lorries full of toughs to whip in any stragglers.
Still there were incidents: the worst when two of our men
patronised the same brothel as was used by German troops. The
Commandant was furious. He called together us Chaplains and
told us we must persuade the men to better behaviour.

Major Parkes, the senior doctor, and I went on the intercom
to address the men in camp. Major Parkes retailed to them all we
had just heard from the Commandant and I followed up with
an appeal to the men to keep together and stay in camp. I hated
doing this in the end. The speeches were warmly received by the
mass of the men who had their own protest about the minority
expressed for them. That night I joined the patrol on the back
wire of the camp but all was quiet.

The next morning the last of the loyal Italian soldiers were
gone, which some of the shrewder prisoners took as a distinct
sign that they should go also. We sent out two of the most reliable
warrant officers to visit another camp which was some thirty

miles away. They sent back a message that they were lying up outside the camp they had gone to inspect and saw that camp emptied by the Germans. They had seen the ruins of another large body of campers most of whom had been killed while out of their camp.

The Commandant sent for us again and read to us an order from Rome which said, 'This zone is controlled by the German authorities. PoWs must return to their camps on pain of death.' I spoke once more to the whole camp and told the men all we knew. That included the fact that German troops were pillaging the farms all round us taking cattle, pigs and crops. The countryside was eaten out. In the evening the BBC ridiculed this Rome announcement. I said that the staff would authorise and ration small well organised teams of men who wished to go out on genuine escape sallies. Some Commandos and bitter people took this up and we had nearly a thousand go out in this way. That left seven thousand, about a thousand of whom could not have walked a couple of miles. Others had lost all interest in getting out.

On 17th September while the men were having a check by the warrant officers I was called to the camp gate where I saw German motor cyclists of the 25th Regiment of the 5th Panzer Division drive up and throw a cordon round the camp. We were prisoners all over again. My heart was sick as I thought of all the hopes represented by the men then paraded within the camp. A 'feldwebel' told me that his unit was simply passing through and that he would guard the camp for three days.

A murmur like a great communal sigh went up from our men as they saw German troops mount the towers round the camp. Others went round collecting up the abandoned Italian arms but they acted too late, a Sergeant Major Byers preceded them extracting the bolts and throwing them into the cess pools. There's a lot to be said for Sergeant Majors.

The night was hideous with light-trigger firing. Prisoners got through to the Command section of the camp and dropped out of the windows and so to freedom. Verey lights sprayed the place with weird light as the Germans tried to stop this. Other prisoners began to pile up anything which could be moved and started a bonfire. The men ferreted out two German soldiers of Polish origin and bribed them to fire over the heads of prisoners going out through the gate they guarded.

The next morning the Panzers were gone and new, fresh German troops were around. They turned out to be newly from Europe and we knew then that the Allied assault south of us was halted and that the Germans had declared the Italians enemies and formed a German line south of us.

I was overwhelmed with depression for I had taken a lead in keeping the men together and felt I had let them down. I was so sore that the world around me seemed a dreamlike fantasy of which I was only a spectator.

The mood of depression in the camp changed to one of ironic, sullen humour. Notices were stuck up round the place for the on coming British forces. 'Tired of waiting, we're off to Germany, see you later.' 'We were the Eighth Army: what are you? Tortoises?'

The first draft of two thousand men were entrained and left. My George among them and several others of my closest friends. Slowly the camp was emptied until only a remnant was left which included all the British Officers of which, with new additions from other camps, numbered seventeen. The new ones told similar stories to our own. We were to entrain at 11 a.m. and mustered to walk out just before that time when we discovered that Padre Willis' luggage was lying there but no Padre Willis. We closed up and formed files of four and went to the camp gate. We got as far as the train on the camp railway siding then we were marched back again.

Then we saw the German teeth. The 'Hauptman' pulled out his revolver and simply said, laying the nose of the revolver on his watch. 'In half an hour I shall kill one in every four of you.' We sat down on our kitbags to wait the half hour. It was ironical, we had no idea Padre Willis was going to do this, there were Warrant

officers standing by, anyone of whom would have filled that
seventeenth gap, nor could we do anything about finding him.
One of the doctors began to moan, to our intense embarrassment,
Italian officers came and went among us, the Commandant came
to say he could do nothing for us. After twenty five minutes I was
talking to a fellow Northumbrian warrant officer when Willis
turned up covered in wisps of straw. He told the Hauptman
that he had been asleep. 'You are to have sleep later' rejoined the
Hauptman. Willis told us later that a Maltese officer had offered
him the chance to hide.

At Porto St Georgio we were put into a small steel railway
truck with one grill high up in one wall and supplied with an iron
cauldron as lavatory and locked in. The guard informed us that if
one man escaped he would shoot the oldest man among us. That
honour lay between Major Parkes and myself.

Once the train moved off it was as though the whole world
changed. The dreadful sense of responsibility rolled away. It
felt like a holiday. There would be nothing to do but sleep, eat
German bread and sleep again. Italy was 'kaput' and we with it.
Had I but known.

We were five nights and five days on that train. My last vision
of Italy was on the platform at Verona where our train was stuck
because of traffic jams. Another train laden with Italian youths
was at the opposite platform. They were going to forced labour.
We shouted to them, threw bits of Red Cross rations to them
and cigarettes. We missed their truck doorways as often as not. A
young Italian woman came down the platform giving fruit to both
trains and she began to ferry out gifts to the other train. After
three trips she was seized and beaten by a German guard. She
cocked her hands on her hips and screamed her rage into his face
until he slunk away. I was glad that my last sight of Italy was of
their magnificent women who seemed to do all the work and have
all the courage in their nation.

We lost our front-line guard at the Udine Pass and collected a
bunch of nervous, fussy little women of lighter calibre. They were

afraid to let us out even for a five minute trip to a lavatory. At
last we were ordered out on a siding. We got down, all festooned
in straw, untidy and miserable. The scene about us was of empty
derelict huts and barbed wire. We climbed into trucks and were
whisked off to another camp which looked from the outside
brisk, polished and orderly. Over the main gate it was designated
as being 'Stammlager IVb'. Having been thoroughly searched we
were packed into one hut in a side street of what seemed to be a
town.

We saw before us two-decker beds arranged in groups. In the
centre of the hut was a table and a cooking range, at the far end
an ablutions unit. To us it looked palatial. We deployed across the
beds looking for vacancies of which there were few. It was a meal
time and we helped ourselves from buckets of boiled potatoes,
which we had not had in Italy or for two years before that. The
whole complement was from Italian camps and we soon found
that our experience had been the common one. The air was thick
with escape stories, only one of which jogged me. It was the story
of 'Jenks', my crippled companion back at Derna. On Punishment
Camp 5 he had had himself bricked into the wall and only
escaped death because a German officer tapped the wall and heard
it was hollow.

We were free to roam this great camp. It contained forty
thousand prisoners. Most were Frenchmen. It had beer halls,
a canteen, a library and massive cooking houses all of them
dominated by French people. The main street ran straight for a
mile with off streets branching out. Wired off alone were huts
for Russians. It was the Russians who stood out. The French were
settled in, they even had French soil in a casket in the canteen.
The Russians were slaves. They were in groups of ten or twenty
hauling muck-carts, doing all the dirty work. Many just stood
around, listless, erect corpses. When they moved they hobbled
on cloth-bound feet or aided with sticks. They stank of decay. We
found that they were largely simple village levees run over in the
great German advance into the Ukraine and disowned by Russia.

A Russian doctor told me there were thousands buried in the forest nearby.

Here was the thing we fought, laid out in front of our eyes. Master Germans, English a little lower, Frenchmen a little lower than us, some Dutchmen below that and thousands of Russian helots dying at the bottom of the pile. I heard our British lads from Dunkirk and the Desert boo when twenty Russian prisoners pulling like dray horses and ten pushing behind, dragged the sewage cart through the camp, commanded by a Frenchman.

The Germans made a mistake and ruined that camp by taking in so many men from the Desert. They were different. They denied salutes, they wouldn't be cropped, morning calls by German corporals were greeted with catcalls instead of polite salutes. One German officer was refused a salute by an English officer as he walked through camp. He slapped the Englishman's face who felled him on the spot. A handful of Dutch officers grabbed the Englishman and 'lost' him.

Massive misery of this calibre always presses hardest on some lonely figure. He carries the weight. In IVb the person was a German Cavalry Sergeant of the First World War. He had been a prisoner himself in Russia and it took him seven years to get out of Russia, with a Russian wife. They found their way from Siberia out into the Pacific.

He was more than a trifle 'fey'. He venerated the stars. One was his own particular discovery; his star told him cosmic secrets. The star gave him stern messages. Europe was to be a place of suffering for a hundred years. There remained nothing worth while but deeds of kindness and dressing the wounds of the world. He agonised over the plight of the Russian prisoners, pitied the English. He picked out Dominion officers and when one had never heard of Schiller his eyes lit up like an evangelist in a pub.

We caused him more suffering for he was in charge of us ex-Italians and was our interpreter. He would stand at attention while some Hauptman annoyed with us harangued him in all the curse words he could muster often for twenty minutes in a go. The

Wachmeister (Cavalry Sergeant) simply gazed into the heavens. Said one New Zealander, 'If he does speak it will be to correct his grammar'. Once he did speak to say, 'If you have understood some of the words the Hauptman has used you will please forgive; he is angry'.

When we were allocated a hut on the derelict camp for services and our class and our worship programme was going again, I was under an order to submit every sermon in notes to the authorities. This was a bind. The Wachmeister came to my aid offering to take a notebook with several weeks' talks in it, 'If you stray from them in the moment I will not listen'.

The camp could not settle down. They began to select work-parties to go out to mines, farms and dumps. The Germans dictated but the prisoners wangled the results. No man of the rank of corporal could be sent out under camp law. We promoted chaps not well to corporal. On the other hand David Greaves who operated one of my classes discovered his whole class was going on one party. He stripped off his two stripes and went with the class. Other groups had our lay preachers in them. Ultimately, Ray Davey was gazetted to have a wandering ministry across the outside teams.

Then the axe fell on me. Three Chaplains and one Jewish doctor were told we incited the men to unrest and with one thousand of the liveliest ex-Italian men we were taken away to Jacobstahl, the derelict camp we had seen on first disembarking.

I discovered that my sin was having preached a series of sermons on Amos, my favourite prophet, and other minor prophets. They were a bit hot and the Wachmeister had not thought the Jewish prophets taboo. It was therefore appropriate that I should be consigned to where the Jewish internees had been before us. Round us lay Russians who were ill, mostly with tuberculosis. The compound was old and decaying. One hut which Padre Day — my C of E colleague — used for worship had a whole wall fall out. In the huts the beds were simply long shelves. Sixty men filled up the shelves in each. There was no lighting until we demanded pressure lamps. There were no paths, we simply ploughed through snow and slush.

The men were proud of their banishment and indulged in a holiday of German-baiting. RSM Hodgson of the HAC, our leader, had a gentle deceptive way of crucifying Germans. 'Who took that ton of coal Sergeant Major?' would ask the officer whom the men nicknamed Harry Wragg. 'I don't known Lieutenant', breathed Mr Hodgson, 'do you think it was the men?'.

The men were fascinated by the Russians and would crowd the wire to lob Red Cross tins over to them. An armed guard would shift them, they came back. The Russians shared our cesspit and knew that by crawling under the seats on our side they could enter our camp. They came in groups of half a dozen and had night entertainment with our men, leaving before dawn.

Later the detachment of Russian Women Doctor Majors incarcerated alone within the Russian compound sent a note saying that they thanked us but they didn't like the way we lobbed parcels over. Could we conceal the food in bath towels when we went for baths, which we shared with their compound. This became a habit with us all. The 'Queen' of doctors answered by doing tooth repairs on our chaps instead of doing what was her duty — just yanking bad ones out.

Our own quarters were with the sergeants who woke us every morning singing 'I love coffee I love tea, the Java and me, a cup, a cup, a cup of coffee'. To tell the truth more went in bribing Germans than was brewed. I remember waking one morning to see a rat pulling my sock through a hole in the floor. On another occasion some chaps got schnapps through the Russians and drugged the guard in one dark corner with it while they took ten tons of coal from the guard quarters in a long string of ant-like movement.

We Chaplains were ridiculously happy. Cooped up in our tiny room we sat round a little fire at night when the day's work was done and chatted about what we each had done in services and visits round the huts; sometimes at concerts we had organised in huts. The Roman Chaplain was a quiet, shrewd and twinkling man who would listen to Padre Day argue that Christianity had reached its ultimate in his church. I would sit until they reached a climax and then intervene to give a Freudian analysis of Popes and offer a social science explanation of ecclesiastical changes. When they combined to blast this heretic. We would clamber into our three-decker beds as the night wore on and leave the place to the rats. There were nights when we were out judging Beautiful Leg Competitions,

I came unstuck through training a team to act *Christmas Carol*. We rehearsed in a wash-house, a posse of guards turned up and winkled me out, for subversion, and I found that the others had been collected by the exasperated Germans who thought all the troubles stemmed from our — to them quite unknown — friendship with mere troops. We were returned to the Stammlager only to find three more chaplains under rejection.

Soon we were all on a train bound for Austria. It was crowded beyond words, with the corridors crammed full of civilians, soldiery and children. We were in the custody of a very nervous corporal who was nice enough to us, indeed we spent much time in protecting him. This was possible because our khaki uniforms resembled SS uniforms and we had many salutes from German military. At Leipzig there was an air-raid signal and we were herded with everyone else into a deep shelter under the station. We got four levels below ground before our corporal lodged us in a group of civilians. Under the leadership of a fine old Padre from New Zealand we helped old ladies with their baggage. While doing this a young girl came alongside us and whispered 'Are you really British?' I told her we were and she turned out to be a stranded American student. When she finally disappeared I put my hand in my greatcoat pocket and she had left behind in it a packet of cigarettes. Two had gone from the packet and Padre Coates said, 'They smell of perfume'. Handling the prams and baggage up the four flights later two of us received tips!

Our journey ended in Eichstatt at an officers' camp named VIIB. It was in a very smart Light Infantry barracks. We were searched and I nearly lost all my diaries and notes. The Commandant addressed us later and told us we were in disgrace, forbidden to hold services, our work permits withdrawn and we must live quietly and without talking to any other prisoners, in a room over the hospital. We protested vigorously and demanded an enquiry by the Protecting Power.

It was as different from what we were used to as could be. The mass of the officers in the place were Highland Division officers taken at St Valery. They had a whole storehouse of Red Cross food, from which they drew rations each day, parole walks each day, even a visit to the cinema at times. At first we were suspect by the British administration because we knew no one in camp. 'How could that be?' Two chaplains baled us out, one Padre McInnis, of the 51st Highland Division — at home Canon of the Isles — and a French-Canadian Padre, Roman Catholic priest, who was captured on the high seas bound for a mission station and now permitted to serve with the prisoners.

The whole place ticked like a clock. On Sunday mornings the whole camp turned out to a Scottish Presbyterian Morning Prayer dressed in their ceremonial uniforms which had been sent out to them. The camp was very highly organised by the Scots officers in counter-espionage. It was also organised in classes and meetings. Toc H wanted me to speak to them on Chinese Reconstruction and they ensured that I did, in spite of the ban on me from any association with them. One officer had taught himself to read Chinese although he couldn't speak a word of it, he had also learned Russian, and we spent hours together, studying Pushkin and Mencius.

In this way I gradually built up a connection with this camp and could feel its true pulse. The seeming luxury screened a deep moral courage. There was no difference with the rougher men's camps. They lived so terribly close that having done so for month after month they knew each other too well. There were abiding loves and hates to cope with every day and in public. So deeply were they in Axis territory, escape was out of the question. Their daily veneer of respect and serenity could not but be admired.

One awful experience demonstrated this. We were subject to the first American air-raid seeking Regensburg, the planes flying over us. These officers saw for the first time what they had dreamed a thousand times. One young Australian officer broke out from the guarded hut to see clearly. We watched from our hospital window and a corporal knelt, took very careful aim and shot the young Australian in the throat. There was a howl from a hundred voices, one man ran out to drag the lad in, he too went down under the same rifle. One round into the wall near him would have sent him skipping back. It was murder.

The camp broke off all relationships with the Germans. The Senior British Officer refused to accept the wreath that they offered. He broke of all black market activities, one German was said to be losing thousands of marks a week. A Swiss commission came down and the corporal was taken for court martial.

After seven weeks of this three of our companions were taken back to Stalag IVb but not Padre Coates and I. We lodged another appeal to the Swiss. After a while we were ordered to move. 'To Stalags?' we demanded, they said it was.

Paired once more we moved in civilian trains across Germany. One whole night we had a carriage to ourselves and at seven in the morning two 10- or 12-year-old schoolboys got into it, one German and the other Jewish. Like many an English lad they used the time to do their homework. I squinted over one, he was doing English geography. I invited him to sit with me and do the geography with me. He was only too willing. 'You know England?', he asked. 'It is my Motherland', I said. 'Nein, nein', he replied, 'Auslander you should say "Vaterland".' Then it dawned on him. 'You are truly English?', he asked. 'Ein verdammte Feindliche Hauptman', I said, 'a damned enemy Captain.' He roared with laughter.

Having crossed the width of Germany we at last arrived at

Sagan, Silesia, on the great flat plains which cover that part of
Europe and among the great pinewood forests which give the
area such a solemn landscape. The camp was about fifty miles
from Breslau. Why on earth it should be called a 'Stalag' defeated
me, it was clearly an 'Offlag', being full of flying personnel of the
American, British and other Allied forces. It was designed by and
run by the Luftwaffe as Stalag LUFT 3. We were 'screened' in with
the greatest care and lectured by the Commanding Officer very
politely and very sternly. 'Nothing concerns me more than the
spiritual and moral life of my Officers', was his declaration. There
were ten thousand prisoners in the place, neatly divided off into
camps of two thousand each. The Middle Camp was American,
North Camp the heart of the whole and East Camp was supposed
by the British Officers to be for the people who didn't classify for
inclusion in the North Camp. Another camp which I never saw
had on it a Methodist Paratroop chaplain whom I never saw.

We were both dumped in North Camp to begin with and
vetted there by the counter-espionage team of British prisoners.
There was a chaplain from Australia there who had a wounded
leg and supposed I was to take his place on his repatriation. I took
a poor view of this. I had asked for a men's camp and his job was
very clearly among officers. Wilfred Coates was put among the
Americans. I was soon taken off and put among the also rans of
East Camp. Here I found another chaplain who was very sick, a
Congregational chaplain who had arrived in Crete just in time to
be marched as a prisoner through Europe into various prisons. He
too was an Army man of the RAChD. RAF chaplains did not fly
with the 'missions' and so there were none to take prisoner.

He and I, at first, occupied a tiny little room tacked on the
end of one of the long huts. It faced right out on the hut which
contained the famous Wooden Horse of the escape story. My first
task was obviously to look after and comfort the Congregational
chaplain. We ate together and shared this little room, while he
simply lay glum and silent smoking his pipe which a few devoted
lads kept filled.

When he finally was persuaded to go on repatriation — he was very difficult to persuade — I joined a mess of seven terrific young fellows down the corridor for meals and friendship while retaining the little room.

I soon discovered how wrong I had been to think I would be out of work in an Offlag. It was sheer nonsense. It was just a matter of changing one's service to meet new problems. Whereas in the men's camps there were all sorts of physical problems, in the LUFT 3 situation the problems were inside of the men's own selves. That little bit extra which the Forces look for in leaders made the difference.

My salvation as far as work and worship were concerned was Group Captain John Barratt, who has become a world-known ornithologist. He was a man whose faith was a steady determination unshaken by anything. He had round him a team of lads who were noting the passage of birds across the Silesian wastes. He had them so involved that the honk of geese flying over the camp in the dead of night would awaken them to log the birds. He was as keen about his church. Services in the camp had fallen to a faithful few.

He saw that the coming of a new and fit chaplain was an opportunity and got his faithful friends round canvassing every group of the men. His argument was that every man deserves one chance and in this case a new chaplain should have a new chance. The whole thing went off without my knowledge. I simply accepted the congregations which turned up in the theatre as being what did come to church, but it grew and grew. Then he had me asked out to the evening cocoa sessions which were the chief activity of the social life of the camp and my suspicions were alerted when in these he led the conversation round to China, rural reconstruction and the Sino-Japanese War. 'Are you wangling all this John?', I asked him. 'Sure', he replied, 'You ain't seen nothing yet.'

From the Senior British Officer — a Group Captain Kellett — right down through the serried ranks of officers they all began to turn up at morning service. One young officer joined us who had organised choirs and he saw to the music. In the end about five of us intimates were mapping out each service and chaps were beginning to drop into my little cell for private sessions.

Then I was asked to do lectures in the camp school-hut and began with talks on Chinese affairs and the war before our war: then on Eastern philosophies and religions and finally, as someone said, 'We don't really know our own religion', I began a series of lectures every Wednesday evening on the Christian Faith which ran to 24 sessions. I have called these 'The Wisdom of the Way'. The school-room was packed to suffocation. Classes sprouted out of these, which took place in my little cell in which one of the chaps had made me an ingenious arm chair constructed from a Red Cross crate. Group members sat on the bed and the floor. We went on to verse by verse commentaries on St Mark and St John's Gospels. Once more the 'Church in the Camp' was born. Our free and easy setting, piled on top of each other in that little room, aided the atmosphere of the 'Jesus story' and made it all like the first days of the Gospel. People got more and more excited as the tale rose to the Cross and crisis.

Work piled up. One morning a rangy six-foot Canadian officer — Donald Browne — dropped in to tell me he had thought of entering the Ministry of the Canadian United Church. Could I help him? He brought a friend along and we began a new theological class before the Gospel sessions began. He has now for years been a Minister in Saskachewan and been over here to visit.

The evening hours then followed the morning into the work chart when a group of men interested in the profession came to me and asked for help in the ground-work of psychology. What paens of thanks I put up then to Dr W. F. Lofthouse of Handsworth who had steered us as students through Jung and the other great men of our times. How thankful I was too to idle hours at VIIb where I had gone through the library list of psychological works in that precious camp's equipment. Truly, 'All things work together for good to those who love the Lord'.

The nett result of all this teaching was a stream of men who came in with personal problems. I still have two whole files of case histories of chaps with problems. This was the greatest opportunity of this camp which heaped opportunities on a padre. They were devastated by just being PoWs; they had qualms of conscience about whether they should have baled out of their planes. They had questions about the RAF standards of 'moral fibre'. The gay cavalier idea of the RAF screened bitter internal battles. They had nagging problems from before the war. Their dealings with girls, their broken marriages, anything can nag the mind of an incarcerated young fellow. One by one I fitted them into the crowded days. I assembled from the Germans charts of the planes from which these men had fallen. I collected pretty pictures of popsies, 'which one is she really like?'. I assembled lists of words, rude and good, to create Association Charts. Every now and again there was a reward of fierce joy as some spiritual problem burst in release, a torn relationship healed or a distressing habit disappeared.

This life of teaching, preaching and counselling went on from 9.00 a.m. until well after midnight. It was simply my own life embedded in the life of the camp routine which contained all sorts of things. It was a lonely life in a strange sort of way; none could help me but the Lord God himself. Sometimes I felt as Jesus must have felt among his slow disciples.

One thing helped me in a way that was remarkable. A bunch of chaps discovered that there was an increase in salary for anyone who did the First Year examination in Chinese of the London School of African and Oriental Studies. I fitted them into the programme and found a real rest from other work in the cool philological problems of language which did not rake the heart as other teaching did. From no books at all I finally had one copy of Bailer — the missionary textbook — and we struggled through to examination standards for six of these men and got their papers home. That meant that half the men who tried succeeded.

This was not true of the activity which has made LUFT 3 famous, the business of escaping. To be included in an escape was a very *élite* affair. Hundreds laboured on tunnelling and counter-espionage to get out the men with very long service records of flying. Hundreds of Flying Officers, and Pilot Officers spent days underground digging to get out a couple of senior parsons. For the juniors it was a gruesome job. It cropped up in their dreams, their moods, their thinking. It compelled them to tear off the coverings over their captivity, it hurt. The padre's chief service was to keep men alive and healthy for their ultimate return to Britain and when, after the big break, 'The Great Escape', we had back the urns containing the ashes of those killed on the escape, the Germans closed down on the idea that escaping was a sport. One could really be glad. To the padre it was not luring the German' ferrets' away from a tunnel which was victory but was the work of such men as Colin Dilly, ex-teacher at the Slade, who took men and trained them from drawing a matchbox to beautiful pictures of horses which dragged the sewage cart; or a budding Member of Parliament who discussed the shape of tomorrow's homeland; or young Taylor, grandson of the great missionary, who played with verve in a presentation of 'Our town' or 'St Joan'.

Triumph was when some men found a vocation to medicine, teaching, the Ministry or politics. To me every single prisondom was a desert 'exile', like those of the prophets or Jesus himself. To make men whole, to make them see; that is what it was all about. A group of three or four wrote to me after the war to tell me they were all in McGill University in Canada doing medicine. Another two found a vocation in Forestry and Husbandry. Another became a psychological worker, and others went teaching. One chap whose life was to follow his father as a bookmaker turned right round and went out to Australia sheep farming. Another turned from the London Stockbroking world to become an Anglican parson. These were the victories in this camp with its strong educational system through which men could win Oxford Scholarships.

After two years of this busy life the camp broke up. The victorious Russian advance killed it. As the Russian forces pounced across the land the German command decided that they must move us, the flying men were too valuable to have recaptured. In the depths of winter the order went out to prepare for a move further west.

We got our gear together and made sledges to transport it. Donald Browne offered me a space on a door which he had removed from its hole and I joined his team of three of us pulling this wretched thing out to the roads in such a cavalcade as was never seen before — thousands of us from all the sections of LUFT 3 dragging the most amazing selection of sledges or humping massive kitbags out through the snows. We went this way across Eastern Germany; one night we slept in a school, another in a church and another in a glass factory. The snow gave out and pulling became too much and we abandoned our makeshift vehicles, though some bribed women to part with prams for gifts of chocolate. One night we were all turned out by the guards to do some more walking, this time with no vehicles of any sort and we straggled 12 kilometres through the night to meet up at dawn with a string of long iron wagons and were popped into them forty-five to a truck. Two more days were exhausted by this easier passage across Germany, north-eastwards. Two days later, on a Saturday morning, we were winkled out and did twelve more kilometres to a long row of barbed wire which made everyone say we must surely have arrived. The gates were locked and we all stood outside them, a lot of people shouting to bobbing lights they saw in the dawn, 'Let us in'. It was surely the most extraordinary cry ever put up. At last we were drafted in in fifties by a sullen guard and found the most awful camp I ever saw. It was the 'Milag' that is the camp in which captured merchant seamen had been kept. It was a shambles of decaying huts, with flapping windows, leaky floors, lit by hurricane lamps. Instead of beds there were piles of woodwool. Filth and rubbish were everywhere. The internees must have lived a very undisciplined

life and then decided to wreck the place before leaving it. Over
the wire from us was the 'Marlag' containing the captives of the
Royal Navy and the contrast between their neat and tidy world
and ours only served to make the RAF put out place to rights.
With an almost contemptuous diligence the RAF broke up into
groups and had the place sorted out within the week.

By the Sunday the Church in Camp was also on its feet again
with a mixed choir containing both North and East Campers in
its ranks. The Canadian theologue, a young New Zealand lad, an
English boy and I formed a team in one little corner. Our beds
of wool we put against the three walls and we cobbled up a table
in the centre of the room while Donald built a most respectable
brick stove at the end of the room. Here we could entertain guests
and start our classes once more.

It turned out that we were at Tarmstaat near Hamburg and
so in the Western Front area which gave everybody a cheerful,
participatory sense of being in circulation again. I was talking to
about a hundred men in the marriage class I ran when the first
raid went over us. This was too much for the class. They emptied
out of the place in seconds and stood cheering the fleet of aircraft
as it whirled across us, empty cartons floated down on the camp
from the men above who must have been having their lunch.
We cheered again. Such raids became very regular and the men
argued about the new types of aircraft they had never flown.
Strength had obviously come to the Allies since their day. When a
Mosquito shot up our one and only truck — the ration wagon —
nobody complained.

German morale was steadily falling and trading on the wire
with the guards became an almost open affair until one man
paid the bill for it all. One guard tempted him to the wire with
eggs and the guard on the next tower shot him through the liver.
The campers raved about this until the Command had the guard
tried, when it appeared that the man could see RN men with
equanimity but his wife and child having been killed in Hamburg
by our bombing, the sight of RAF men was too much for him.

Our men fell quiet at this. The lad killed was one of my best Chinese students born in Hong Kong and planning after the war to return to China. Life lost all simple Limes for many men with this instance. The 'Flyer' sees war as in an aerial picture, the hard personal encounter known to the soldier is not his lot. Only the infantryman who stands on the ruins with a fixed bayonet knows the whole of the cost.

Church life increased as the last days ran their course, unlike many activities which folded up. Our night parties became more searching. We sat in that tiny room by the light of a Chinese type of lamp which I used, which would burn just about anything with fat in it, the air already dark with cooking smoke, clouded right out as so many men smoked, and the bombs thumped down outside the camp. It was a picture for Hogarth. We talked on until well after midnight.

Spring broke across storm-ridden Europe and on 24th March, my mother's birthday of all days, we heard through our camp, illegal, radio that 'Monty' was across the Rhine. The old arguments all broke out again. Sweepstakes were lost and won. On Easter Day, 1st April, hosts of people turned out for Morning Service and we received Members into the Church by the Anglican Order of Confirmation and the Presbyterian Order of the Church of Scotland, so bridging the gap in between. Easter Tuesday we all called 'Black Tuesday', for rumours were circling that we were to be moved out of Monty's path, Royal Navy and RAF. We were cast for the role of hostages to be taken up into Denmark. We wondered how.

I had my own problems for the Chinese examination papers arrived from London and not to use them meant the waste of men's time for a whole year. In all the confusion we held the examination and I packed the papers into my valise to carry them home — someday. Low Sunday passed and we all laughed at our panic. On the Monday night we were ordered to march. The Senior British Officer, Canadian Group Captain Wray, spoke to us all. He had resisted the march until he could resist no more. It

was now up to us to go as slowly as we possibly could on the road.
Every man was to present as much passive resistance as he could.

Nothing could have suited these veteran German baiters
more. The weather was glorious springtime, carts and barrows
hung together as by magic. The long procession looked quite
incredible as men wandered about the road. Halts, according
to the Germans were ten minutes in the hour, they became half
hours. Wheels came off prams and barrows, men had broken
straps in their gear. What should have been a twenty kilometre
march finished with ten. A Senior Officer's check showed two
men had been slightly wounded by a raving Nazi-type Major who
walked behind us. The men were cheered by news of this officer,
to bait a spiritless guard was all right, to have a man behind who
had some fight left meant more. We sank to sleep the first night in
a field.

The next morning no one could get the marchers going before
9.30. The day accounted for ten more kilometres. The next day
the Group Captain by some alchemy persuaded the Germans
that under the Geneva Convention we were due for a rest day. We
never walked a mile, except to a nearby stream to bathe, wash our
socks and play with village children who thought we were great
fun. The following day we logged seven kilometres.

Timing now began to make us anxious, we were drawing near
to the Elbe and Hamburg. We hoped never to cross that river.
In the morning our guard was reinforced. Local police were out
with drawn swords as we passed through devastated country
near towns which had been bombed. When we passed through
town streets the cobble-stones played havoc with the barrows. We
were pushed around as we tried to stay on the pavements and at
the end of the day we were ashamed that we had covered fifteen
kilometres. We were at Granz on the Elbe just above Hamburg.
The river would have to be crossed.

It was Sunday and we gathered among the reeds on the river
bank for a morning service ringed in by interested citizens. We cut
osiers and made booths and might have been an ancient Jewish

Festival, as one of my students observed.

We crossed on the Monday in little boats named after great German composers. I was in *Mozart*. An old German trumpeter who must have taken thousands of tourists across in his boat played us over, trumpeting Mozart's music until one Australian told him he'd better play *Lili Marlene* or be thrown overboard. He played it magnificently.

We landed at Blankenese, a place much loved pre-war by English tourists and while we waited for others crossing the river we explored its shops and some men even bought picture postcards. The people said they had never been bombed because of the tourist links. At night we slept in a field four kilometres out of town.

So far we had been blessed with wonderful spring weather and the camping and strolling had been a delightful experience. The skies clouded as we marched the next fifteen kilometres and reached a hamlet where we slept out comfortably for the last time.

Our leader had a difficult decision to make every day. He had to balance slow march against men's health and so far he had, rightly, plumped for slow march. Now he changed his tactics; we were to march hard and get to some sort of accommodation. We brisked up to eighteen kilometres which is just two short of the Convention-permitted twenty. It was the guard who moaned. The next day we did another eighteen and as we constructed our booths at night the rain came and soaked everything and with the rain the crump of bombs. We scattered and found shelter in barns and lofts of the village. The next day we did not march at all. We then did another eighteen kilometres and came to a splendid farm with a beautiful herd of cows which the men milked into Klim tins. They helped themselves from a pile of wood lying near and the German farm owner came to me and asked if I could keep the men from another pile of wood there was nearby. This he said covered his only remaining tractor which a Major billeted on him would certainly snaffle if he saw it.

As we moved on from this good find things began to

deteriorate. There was constant aerial strafing of the roads. We
saw Allied aircraft several times a day and lost some men to their
attentions. The Royal Navy column lost far more. We were now
nearing Lilbeck almost out of Germany, from which we were to
be transshipped to Denmark and the Group Captain dug his heels
in.

We moved on to a large co-operative farm operated by forced
labour, mostly Russian. It had plenty of concrete barns and lofts
and could accommodate us all. Here the Senior British Officer
stood fast. We would go on no more. We all squatted round
the place and supported him. The battle of wits took two days
and was finally settled by the German Authorities removing
our Luftwaffe guard and replacing it with veterans of the
Marine. They only wanted the peace. Meanwhile some prisoners
discovered two barns filled with grain and with farming clothes
which they frankly stole and dished out among the forced labour.

On the 28th April 1945 the guards who did not surrender to
the RAF began to disappear and the Group Captain promised
those who gave up their arms that he would speak for them to the
oncoming army.

Those last days were not our best. We had been geared to
resistance too long. We were lost for a role. I held a service in
a machine shop and another in a barn some distance away for
another section of our column but some people were wandering
the area, some dug out old cars and went for joy rides.

The next day a battle was joined over our heads and around
us. The air was alive with fighter bombers diving and wheeling
over us. Some of the later prisoners spent hours identifying the
aircraft over their heads and trying to gauge the outcome of the
combat. This was especially so when two German Jets — perhaps
the first used in war — wheeled overhead making mayhem among
the Allied aircraft for an hour or so. We learned that two young
German flyers had driven these craft without orders and when
the fuel was exhausted grounded them on the *autobahn* and given
themselves up.

There followed a day of quiet, people were going around swapping addresses as though they were finishing a holiday at Brighton. At one o'clock a single armoured vehicle in British colours sped down the main farm road and an army corporal stuck his head out of the turret and waved at us with a grin. It was our freedom, come like a Chinese cracker in an artillery barrage, but come. Folk clambered on the car for his signature, until his intercom cursed him for wasting time and he drove off with apologies. In the evening RASC men ran trucks up to us. They were fresh from the relief of Belsen and it took all our ingenuity to protect our aged guards from them. At night we slept in the old German barracks of Luneberg.

What a forgathering it was as I moved from one barrack to another finding old companions and swapping news of others. Some things quite scandalised us. There were non-fraternisation notices everywhere and Germans were being used as servants. German girls were cleaning British boots. Others were doing all the chores. I wandered into an Officers' Mess and drank coffee with men and women officers but I could feel glances being thrust at me in a strange way. Everyone was high with excitement, they were visitors and I felt it a different world. It was a relief to turn back to a PoW billet, arrange my torn blanket and talk with people I could understand.

One English girl bridged the gap. As we waited in a queue for food outside a NAAFI she played a concertina and sang to us. It was wet and muddy and she stuck in a pool of mud. A prisoner stepped across and lifted her out. As he did so her shoe came off and revealed her torn and tattered sock and her cold toes sticking out. I found myself staring at it and said, 'sorry'. She looked right at me and said 'That's all right, Vicar, we poor ones can't buy new stockings. It's the poor what helps the poor.'

We were interrogated by the Security and then shipped off to an airfield to sleep and wait for planes to take us to Britain. We flew to Brussels and were served coffee by the WAAF and then loaded into Lancasters. I was sitting on the gun rack of the plane

sucking a boiled sweet when the skipper handed back a piece
of paper to us which said the armistice had been signed back at
Luneberg.

As we landed in the heart of Buckinghamshire I was seized
by a WAAF sergeant who grabbed my kit, threw her arms around
me and kissed me saying, 'I've been waiting for an old 'un'. 'And
you got an old Geordie', I said as I recognised her dialect. She
showered me with DDT and thrust me into a hangar where an
enormous tea-party was in progress, entertained by an RAF band.
A Salvationist had got into the party and every man was handed
a tract, of which dozens were given me as 'parting presents' by
unwilling recipients.

There were only two of us who were Army and we got
swift treatment at 'The Jordans'. New battle dress was given us,
mine sewn with the Desert Ribbon. I humped my kit to the
Underground and reached my mother's home at Richmond. She
looked up and said, 'Hello. It's you. Where's your wife?' I said
'Hello. I don't know.' She was, had I known, on the train coming
down from Hunmanby in Yorkshire to greet me. I greeted her
instead. From King's Cross we joined the throngs celebrating
VE Day in London. Drenched in my own language, pressed on
every side by rejoicing people, only one thing stamped itself on
my mind. A young woman, quite drunk, was stretched on the
steps of a public house, out to the world and not a friend in sight.
Dumped.

My world slipped back into perspective. Truly 'There is no
discharge in this war'. I knew the world a battleground and every
place one which the padre cannot desert.

At Handsworth College , Birmingham

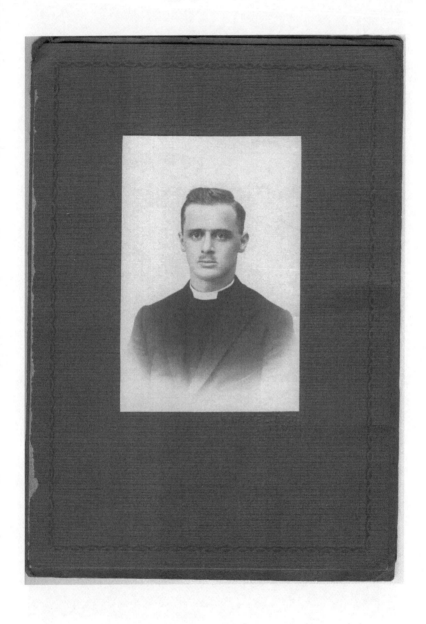

Rev. Douglas Weddell Thompson in 1923

With parents. Florence and Nathan

As a missionary in China

As a missionary in China

School at Yiyang, Chinak

Douglas (top left) with RAF Colleages, unknown date

Douglas, unknown date

Army Chaplain

Army Chaplain

At Gaza in 1941, with Major C.A.Brooks

Outdoor preaching at Portsmouth

With his daughter, Margaret, at the Nigerian Independence Ceremony, 1960 (Above)

With Gladys and Margaret (Left)

Inauguration as President of the Methodist Conference

During the Presidential Year - Greeting the King and Queen of Tonga (King Tupou IV), 1966

As President of the Methodist Conference, Gladys and Margaret, 1966

Presidential Year - talking with the Vice President and
overseas representatives

During the Presidential Year- visiting HM Forces, Aden,
arriving at Khormaksar

Looking at the Deed of Foundation of
The Methodist Church, Nigeria

Wedding to Margret Forrest, 1973
(Left to Right) Charles Geoffrey Ridgway, Victoria Wyatt,
Douglas W. Thompson, Margret Forrest, Stephen Ridgway

With past Missionary Society colleagues after the wedding,
July 1973

Peak 6 - THE LONDON PEAK

England's problems

If you go to Archway Underground Station in north London and climb the great hill which runs up from it, at the top you turn to look on one of the great panoramas of London. The city lies at your feet, in the distance can be seen the dome of St Paul's and the towers of Westminster — the heart of the tourists' London. In between there and your viewpoint, however, lie miles of roof-tops covering thousands of homes carved up by penetrating streets, dotted with tower blocks and here and there a spire pointing to heaven. The tower blocks do not seem to be pointing to heaven, they simply assert themselves against the sky, their rooftop service — plumbing and lift-engine houses, which seem like afterthoughts stuck on post-architect, send the mind bouncing back downwards through the innumerable floors to the sewers beneath.

You will see the hurrying traffic of the roads, you will see men, women and children hurrying in between the vehicles as though the vehicles mattered more than the people. It may remind you of the old days when the poor people passing by doffed their caps to the great people. Here the great people are the bonnets of proud lorries. They keep the people in their place.

All those roofs cover cramped houses, nestling together as though in fear. They are the nests of thousand upon thousand of ordinary hard-working men, their wives and children. Broken up into their neighbourhoods they know each other, like each other perhaps, hate each other perhaps; help each other or prey on each other. 'Pubs' or churches stand on street corners — there people meet. What people? Doing what? Loving what? They are the folk who helped and cared for each other in the War, sometimes seeing visions, sometimes seeing cash and a rake-off. Now angels, now rats.

This hill where Whittington heard the bells calling him back in more spacious days (his memorial hospital lies at our feet) reveals to our minds the modern masses of humanity. It is but the largest example of what covers our land. So it spoke to me on my journeys to the Archway Central Hall to which I went for District meetings. I heard the voice of Jesus saying, 'I have compassion on the multitude'. There with the roar of the northern traffic crashing into London in my ears I could hear the voice from long ago. It was Chiang Kai Shek's voice saying, 'Tao ming chien' — 'Go to the people'.

Coming out of Central China to meet Gladys and Margaret at Hong Kong had not been easy for any one of us. One life stopped and another began while the overtones of the first still rang in our heads.

The return from Italy, Germany and five years of war was much more difficult. This time the daughter involved had sprung from a childish ten to the dawning young womanhood of fifteen years. Gladys had been out at work in a community of four hundred girls and their staff. She had been a goddess to the girls, as the only non-teaching member of staff who really was interested in their personal lives, at a time in life when their own physical selves were tremendously interesting to them.

We met again in our own homeland but hardly belonged to it. We had no home in it. Margaret in her holidays for five years had simply removed to her mother's quarters in another school, billeted in a hospital. Our reunion was three people meeting in a new phase of development which had to begin from the beginning, with our Chinese life a remote image in the back of the mind which seemed more like someone else's life observed rather than lived.

Teaching the men in the Marriage Class in camp about going

home we had always assumed there would be a home to go back
to, it was a return. Not for us. Ours was a new effort to find each
other which had to begin by absorbing what the others had done
and become. For Gladys the girls at school were nearer than I.
For me the herd of purely masculine company, now dissolved and
gone, was more real than she. For Margaret it was the permanent
addition to her life of a male presence in a female world.

This was all part of the process which the 'pundits' called
'settling down after the war'. One sometimes wondered whether
they knew that it was a matter of exercising the will rather than
cosying in on the environment.

After the briefest of stays in one cramped room in my
mother's crowded house at Richmond we journeyed up to
Southport to present her father to Margaret. She was splendid.
She and some of her companions in school were looking out for
us from an upstairs window in the school, they spotted us coming
up the drive and rushed downstairs to meet us at the door. The
Head Mistress intercepted them half way down and said, very
primly, 'Opening the door to guests is work for the maids, dear'.
Our meeting was therefore in the tiny Visitors' room, as though
we were the Tax Inspector and his secretary. This was no trouble
to Margaret. She said after a few moments, 'Do you swim?'. I did.
'Let's get off to the baths, I've just done my "bronze", then you can
take me out to lunch in the town.' Could there have been a better
way of getting to know a grown daughter? We went, we swam, she
in all her growing shapeliness, me out of khaki. Then we all had a
large meal of fish and chips at Rowntrees, Southport, the favourite
pastime of Trinity Hall girls. You could hear the cracking of ice all
round us.

Gladys had arranged rooms for us with a lady at Ilkley
where the Hunmanby Hall School had recently been evacuated.
This lady was a sister to one of our China staff and had often
befriended Gladys during her stay in the town. She gave us her
best room and a bedroom and herself camped in the back room.
It was a very generous action indeed. Here we settled down for a

couple of weeks and between walks on the Moor, which Gladys
knew very well, we began to get to know each other again. It was
not easy. I was receiving an enormous amount of congratulatory
mail on being home again but this was not home. One began to
find the 'circular' type of congratulation in communications from
The Chaplain General, the Secretary of the Methodist Army and
Navy Board and Chairman of Methodist Districts. There were the
very down-to-earth letters on the subject of demobilisation. I was
granted a permanent honorary Commission, ninety days' leave
and told which batch I came out with. There was tedious financial
correspondence from the Finance Department of the Army
largely about money which I never saw.

I was posted, theoretically, to the London Garrison as a
Chaplain to the Tower to eke out my leave. This posting amused
Margaret tremendously. The Mission House asked me when I
would sail again for China — leaving the family in England. The
Army asked if I wanted a Regular Commission in the post-war
Army.

A few old PoW contacts came to see me, which embarrassed
our hostess greatly in the matter of where I could talk privately
with them, the questions they raised, the meals at unsociable
hours. One man who had shared the organ loft with me on the
march in Germany, was so overcome with the propriety of my
home that I have never heard a word from him since.

Gladys had very many acquaintances in Ilkley and they all had
to be seen and visited. They included the local Minister, who had
been in China and was in the throes of leaving our Ministry for
education. He was one of the chaps with whom I first sailed to
China but we had drifted so far apart we could not communicate.

That whole holiday was for me a kind of limbo enlightened
only by one flash of insight when I was asked to preach in Ilkley
on the Sunday which followed the dropping of 'The Bomb'. Its
nature fascinated me. Mankind had, as I saw it, taken the very
stuff of the universe and managed to convert it into a means of
destruction. War had entered a new dimension. It was not so

much the defeat of Japan which the moment marked but our entanglement of God and his creation in our human wars. Was it for this that He had endowed us with the power to read his thoughts after him?

We left Ilkley and made a visit to Slingsby in the Vale of York, Gladys's old homeland, where we stayed with a married sister on a farm which she and her husband owned. This was in many ways another postponement of the day of reckoning with life. Life there was always an entry into the farm's life. One either took to their way of doing things or did nothing. The war had left them all untouched. All the brothers in the family being farm owners and workers but me, were exempt from military service.

Then as the summer drifted away there came one day a letter from the member of the Stationing Committee of the Church to ask what sort of Circuit I would like to enter when, in September, the new Church year began. The Stationing Officer responsible for putting returning chaplains back into the system was of the Home Mission Division of the Church. Naturally he was very interested in putting men into the Missions of our total Church. He asked if I would be interested in going into the Edmonton Central Hall in north London.

This interested me and I began to ask questions about the appointment. The Hall stood on the High Street of Edmonton, was the classical type of Hall in which I had first begun. It was included, however, in a Circuit of normal churches — the Enfield Circuit. The Minister then stationed there had broken down. He was a fiery Welshman who had done more than this health would stand and was to have a 'year without pastoral charge' in which it was hoped he would recover. The Hall was frankly difficult. Its future lay in the balance.

Gladys and I went to see it and the house, which was three miles from the Hall, in Tottenham, in Landsdowne Road, just behind Tottenham Football Ground. We learned a great deal about the work by talking to the outgoing man, whose view of it was far from exhilarating. His wife was a dear little lady carrying

him and his work day by day. The house was old, decrepit, too far
from the work, a large double-fronted structure. Yet, to Gladys, it
was a house, somewhere she could call her own and which could
be our home together — our first manse in Britain. We agreed to
go.

September, the new church year, found us in the Team of
London Missioners by being in charge of the Edmonton Hall.
We arrived to a warm, welcoming tea party arranged in the manse
by the local stewards, and a whole run of Welcome Meetings
arranged by various groups both in the Hall and in its sister
churches. I got out of khaki.

I now faced my own problems. In China I had had a definite
scheme of attack on the problems of evangelism which included
many social elements, which to me made evangelism relevant to
the people's lives. None of that would do in this new work. Here
people could read and write. Here when sick they had the hospital
service to help them. Their style of life did not need my help in
sanitation, hygiene and disease prevention.

The problem was, therefore, to find the things in these
London lives which, to use an old Chinese phrase, 'tickled or hurt'
in their lives. I searched back over the war years to find clues there.
Rich, uninhibited friendship stood out immediately. Classes
in life's daily puzzle — subjects like the marriage class and the
psychological class clearly had a place. Counselling had been a big
feature. Slowly I began to build up the skeleton of a programme.
I knew that there would be other things to add, there were hosts
of children and teenagers; there were the old. These had not been
part of the world gone. There was also the part in the work which
Gladys would shoulder, she was keen to have her share.

The first quarter through to the new year showed me where
the difficulties lay. My first Leaders' Meeting was engulfed in
finance, a special feature being that the Hall was a licensed
premises for music and public concerts. This meant bookings,
hirings, fee collections and would have to be done. It also involved
keeping to the structural demands of the licensing authority. Part

of the premises had been taken by the local council as a rest centre which should have been the very place for Youth Clubs and Older Persons fellowship. It was cluttered up with the partitions and quite unusable. It was into January before this was cleared. In my diary is the succinct entry 'Learned a lot'.

Some things nicer than these soon began to pop up. First I discovered that the Borough, a Labour Borough for years, ran a rota of Ministers for the burials of people with no church connections. One had Cemetery Duty which must be observed. This is a Minister's gift. The very first to which I was called out was the funeral of a young man who had taken his own life. It was a large turn-out and I could talk to a host of people with no church links. One gained an entry into their homes.

I found there was a fine elder lady who had for years run a joint Preparation Class for all the departments of the Sunday School. She had a general session of all the teachers and then they hived off into their own sections. This was a real power house in the Hall. I was able to team with her and do general biblical introduction to the lesson for the week.

In such a densely populated area men and women were streaming back from the services. It was for them that I put into action the first bit of my new plan. We founded the Wesley Club, which became one more power centre in the Hall. It was designed for the ex-service types, men and women, and people of their age group and it took off from the first.

In this way we grew round us a younger set of leaders, married people in the first ten years or so of their married life who could feel the meaning of what we were up to. They were aware that the world had changed and demanded new ways of expressing the old Gospel. I needed them badly as it turned out for there was an older element which wished to use their membership of the Hall simply as a home for their own little church-group life and resented any additions or changes. They were not to be lost but to be enlarged. In their sheer presence at the Hall they were necessary. If that sounds a bit cynical, it is also true. Their own personal development into the fullness of Christ demanded that they took the full shock of seeking others in ways in which others could be sought naturally. Thirdly, the things they believed were part of the wider concept of Christianity. They lost nothing but a few weeks' interior comfort and the Hall and they gained much by trying to retain them.

In the upshot, with the exception of one middle-aged couple who desired to marry, we lost none and those who stayed found that they had a new lease of spiritual life. They in turn kept me nearer to the basic personally religious side of our faith.

Usually a Central Hall minister is in charge of his Hall and that is that. In the Edmonton case, the Hall being set in a circuit this was not so. I preached on Sundays at several other chapels of the Circuit. This complicated what I call 'series preaching', working through wide themes over several Sundays. It meant missing talks with casual worshippers who dropped into the Hall — a growing number. They, if they needed counselling, did not find the minister of the Hall. I sometimes missed old PoW companions in this way. I, personally, had the care of one little country chapel at Goff's Oak, now a centre for a new-grown estate. It was, in my days, a struggling little cause dependent on two families.

Preaching at Enfield, the Circuit chapel, was always a pleasure. Everything was so much in order, with carefully trained stewards and an upper middle-class congregation who intelligently came for some spiritual food. Ministry here was straight down the mid-riff of Methodist worship. At Bush Hill Park, where the junior minister was in charge, it was a case of ministering to the people of a new private estate with all that that involves in caution. 'Bungaloid' life has its own problems and one had to prepare specially to meet them. Then, there was Ponder's End, a struggling new cause of the London Outspill Estate type which was different again. These were the people who had come out of the centre of Edmonton and such down town areas on their way up via Bush Hill life to Enfield life. It will be clear that there could be no such luxury as taking the sermon round the circuit. Each was each.

I managed some sort of continuity at the Hall on Sundays by making every Sunday a triple-deck day. I would be at Goff's Oak in the morning and Enfield at night but would put in a session at the Hall about 3 p.m. and of ten stay to tea. There arose a question of leadership for an inner group of young people around the 16-year-old range and this I filled in by having their own meeting in those afternoon visits. This group grew into a well-formed unity and became the Christian Centre group of our wide-open Youth Club which went up in numbers to over the 100 mark. Two or three couples in the Sunday afternoon group I married and they are now in the main leadership positions in the ongoing work.

To balance the Wesley Club, which was supposed to be an open door for the non-churched people, I instituted the School of Prayer for the older and more conventional types which went through whole books of the Bible verse by verse and also tackled the problems of personal prayer life.

The Boys' Brigade and Girl Guides were an important part of the Hall programme. The Brigade I knew well and took a lot of care in the staffing. I found it led, when I arrived, by a man outside the Hall fellowship and when he left I had three of our own young fellows come in who proved to be towers of strength. We were short of a Brownie leader until one younger woman offered her services to the young girls.

I have never believed that the youth club age-group is the only source of recruitment into membership of the church, people can be awakened at any age right up to pensioners, but this welter of young life at Edmonton did interest me deeply. I imagined my own life-training as a lad and its paucity until H. Taylor Cape took me in hand. These kids were already in the church and their life was a daily expression of the Faith. If they went off the rails at their work it would stand out in their factories and shops far more obviously than the errors of their contemporaries. I could remember my own Manager saying, 'We don't expect this sort of thing from you', when I had blotted my copy. There were also moments in which they would have to defend their beliefs in the places where they worked. I was determined that they would be equipped well to deal with such moments.

Consequently I arranged two other classes for them, one on the lines of the talks I had given on the Christian Way in Camp (which was published during my time at Edmonton), one on the preparation for marriage (which was also published by Epworth Press) extending it to the problems of youngsters below the age for marriage.

With the standard business meetings of the church such as Leaders' Meetings, Trustees' Meetings, Mission Committees, Overseas Missions Committees and Home Mission Committees and the local extras such as Repairs Committees, Lettings and Finance, life was pretty full.

Believing that a church cannot grow without intimate religious education I had to think of my little country cause at Goff's Oak and inaugurated a class meeting there.

Day after day in my diaries of the time there are records of whole days, morning, noon and night, taken up by the work and ending after 10p.m. Very rarely is there a record of time taken off for an outing to a theatre or place of interest. This was the cause of the greatest strain of all. Gladys became more and more depressed by her loneliness. The tension at times between home and work became intolerable and only her tremendous stability of character and sheer determination saved us from shipwreck. The women of the Hall Sisterhood loved her dearly and made her their President. The folk at the School of Prayer, which she attended very regularly, also took her to their hearts but she was not accustomed to their style of living.

Her home church was in a Yorkshire village, a robust church where people's lives were grown into one another and her family was the mainstay of the cause. Her professional life in England had been in great hospitals, such as Manchester Royal Infirmary, in the rich fellowship of Sisters and nurses. There times on and off

duty were as the laws of the Medes and Persians. It was her job to
see that they were. We were halfway through our time at the Hall
before one or two women of an older age-group really found their
way to her heart and understood her loneliness. Margaret was
away up in the North at school revelling in girl friendships, such
as fill the life of boarding school children, but her holidays back
with us made the only relief periods.

The London Christian Commando Campaign fell within
the years at Edmonton. In the Eveready canteen one day there
were hosts of women with fewer men. Our Team Leader, the
Rev. Maurice Watts of the Congregational Union, decided that
the best attack was to put up the Wesley Deaconess Probationer
who was on his team. She got up on a table to talk to this sea of
women and began by saying, 'The best thing that ever happened
to me occurred in a London taxi'. This highly spiced audience of
women thought they knew what she meant and dissolved into
laughter and cries of 'you should be more careful', and the men
whooped into whistles. Unabashed the Deaconess repeated her
statement with colossal results. Maurice Watts said, 'get her down',
and pulled on the hem of her frock. One of the men asked her
privately to come and speak to the night-shift but the Salvation
Army Captain on the team said he would do that one. Just a few
years later Margaret was on her first teaching appointment in
the suburbs of Manchester and this same lady, now an ordained
Deaconess, stationed in the Manchester Mission, became her
friend and was doing splendid work in the Mission. One wonders
whether if she had been allowed to ride out the laughter she
would not have made a serious impression on those women. Had
she gone on to say 'I know what you are thinking, it was greater
even than that', she would have won.

The Campaign was a limited success in our area. It was
probably the last kick of the older evangelical technique which
was then falling out of fashion wherein the evangelist speaks to
large crowds. Speaking was not the attraction it had been. Some
men and women were moved by it to turn to listen to the church

and at the Hall we got more than our share, being one step nearer
the public than an orthodox church.

There was more to be gained by the long, patient programme
of visitation in the homes of people round the Borough. This took
up a great many hours. From a small proportion of homes in the
suburbs, where sin and problem are as common as anywhere else,
to the masses of terraced houses round the doors of the Hall, this
exercise paid dividends. There was, for instance, the little home
whence the young wife turned up at the Wesley Club, always
alone. She was a pretty girl and I wondered why. I went round one
evening to find out. I met there a robust, good-looking husband. I
asked him why he never came himself but consented to his wife's
regular coming. He said that Club night was his Pools night. I
asked him if he would mind if I dropped round to pick up his
wife in my sidecar and take her. He said, 'Well, you're getting on a
bit'. I countered, 'others aren't'. That did it, he came.

In another home lived two elderly single ladies on whom I
was wont to call. One was sick and mostly in bed. I would pray
with her, holding her hand or with one hand on her forehead.
She would stir, rise and sometimes put on a dressing gown and sit
out saying, 'Your hands have healing power, you always make me
better'. I knew my hands none other than ordinary — I wished
they were — but remembering the mad women of China I never
contradicted her, for her they were different. Why? Who knows
but God.

When we came to Edmonton Dr A. T. M. Wilson of
the Army Psychiatrical Service suggested that I go to the
Clinic which was then a general psychiatrical venture staffed by
a very good staff and I accepted Dr Wilson's offer. I sat in with
the psychiatrists in their group study of individual cases which
they had in their lists and also with Psychiatrical Social Workers
in training. It was a very refreshing process. I was there because of
personal interview work I had done among sick men in camp and,
teaming up with Dr David Mace's new movement the Marriage
Guidance Council, added this to the work of the Hall. I could see

around the place things happening to lives which were the very
things which had caused distress to the men at war. There were
actual wartime persons available for help. There were marriages
in jeopardy. It all made me keen to begin a Church Counselling
Centre, which we did begin but it faltered out of life for lack
of clergy support. Meanwhile I saw person after person alone.
People just turned up and sought help. The trouble was that each
individual required numerous hours, which had to be carved out
in times available to them and to me. That meant more late night
hours very often and stretched out the days inordinately.

There were simple cases, such as the couple who were in
contention about money which they spent almost without
knowing they had done so. I sat down in their home and
budgeted their total income penny by penny. They simply lacked
the arithmetical knowledge to do so. It made a great difference in
their total life together. There were other cases which needed far
more radical cures than this, helpless young men caught in black
depression who blamed their condition on their lack of faith
when the true reasons lay elsewhere.

After three years of this life we thought the time had come
for a change. Much had been done at the Hall, much at Goff's
Oak and in the community life of the Borough. I persuaded
another Handsworth man to follow me, knowing that he would
administer the same treatment to the whole enterprise and we
accepted a call to the Watford Circuit at Bushey, King's Langley
and a London Outspill Estate at Carpenders Park where a new
church was being pioneered. I suppose it was the likeness of
the estate work to the Hall work that induced the Stationing
committee to place me there. I was convinced that the life of the
stately Bushey church would suit Gladys better and so we said our
goodbyes to the Hall.

I followed a fine old minister, Mr Leonard Webb, at Bushey
who left the whole concern in fine fettle and all the handover
material superbly done. The house was tidy, well cared for and a
total contrast to the manse we left, which they sold as soon as I

had left it.

Our transplantation from Edmonton to Bushey was not half so difficult as had been our ingoing to Edmonton. It was no more than the moves made by numerous Ministers from one Circuit to another. The Ministerial Team was a good one. Mervyn Blow (ex-Burma) was the Superintendent Minister, I was the second minister, Cyril Davey (ex-India) was third and Morley Rattenbury (born in China) was the junior man. All four of us were on Mission House Committees and this meant frequent meetings in London as well as our own staff meetings and made for good policy making in the circuit. Our work was similar in our sections of the Circuit and one did not feel that sense of isolation which dogged me as a Central Hall man in a circuit at Edmonton. I was no longer that 'poor relation'.

Greatest of all the changes, however, was the soundness of the judgement that Gladys would find more work to her hand and take a living share in the life of my churches. She made an immediate hit at Carpenders Park and the contiguous Oxhey Estate, where they put her in charge of the Women's Meeting which at first met in a barn, later in a work's canteen, where she often presided over the meeting sitting on a beer barrel. She really transformed this group of fifteen or twenty women. She had a genius for cultivating the gifts of women, training them into articulacy and leadership. She soon got others on to the beer barrel and into the secretaryship of the meeting.

With her nursing training she was also soon in demand at Bushey as well as Oxhey to care for sick women and some of them worshipped her for her common sense care of their physical deficiencies. So that at Bushey, where the number of gifted women was high, she had no need to preside over them but became a well-regarded person among them.

The third thing which made a difference to her was that the manse, being among our people, she could have people in who appreciated her counsel as well as her good Yorkshire cooking. Margaret's school friends and their people could stay with us when they ventured up to London. My full life did not press on her so fiercely, she had her own interests. They were in the province of our joint life in a circuit. Now and again she would be off with the wives of my colleagues, baby sitting for Rattenbury or nursing the Super's wife, who became very ill.

In the modern scene she would have been out at work in the local or London hospitals, I have no doubt, but to her in that generation she would have thought this a dereliction of duty. Her life was given to the Church and in it she must find her role. Had she not left Manchester Royal Infirmary to serve the Church in China? Circumstance now put her at the service of the British church and that was that. At long last this particular circuit found her a role. Her steadfast character fitted her to play it well.

It was very good that it was so for the work at Bushey was just as demanding as it had been in the Central Hall. There were three places to care for and they were all as different from each other as they could be.

Bushey was a well grounded church with a roll of some 200 members. Many of them were old families who had been in the church for years and were distinctly old Hertfordshire families with the county in their blood. Others were business executives in London commuting to the city every day.

King's Langley was historically the royal offset to Abbots Langley just a mile or two away which had a history of defending the ecclesiastical power in the old days. King's Langley was a beautiful village. Our very lovely little church sitting in the middle of it was very conscious of its rural dignity even though Ovaltine had established its great farm-factory between the two villages and one of the great oil firms had put its research laboratories down in it. Here the old historical world and the new industries combined to make one community. Moreover both had their people in the one congregation.

Carpenders Park with Oxhey was our new venture, which for good or ill tried to harmonise the life of a private estate of bungalows on one side of the railway with the London Outspill

Estate major development on the other side of the railway — an almost impossible task. Moreover the work began, years before the coming of the London Outspill, on the bungalow estate and was the child of Bushey people who took their membership out to their homes and laboured at it. The leadership was all on the Carpenders Park side.

The Carpenders Park people were one thing, the Estate another. The Estate people were mostly the people of Paddington's crowded streets down in London. They were used to 'Mum's house' being just down the street and to a 'Fish and Chip' shop just round the corner. On the Estate, at its beginning, they were a good three miles from the shopping centre in Watford and even the nearest pillar-box. Bushey was inside two miles but not a place with many shops. On the Estate they had good housing, better than they had ever had, but facilities were the later part of the building programme. It was clear that the construction plan was politically dominated to a 'dwelling unit' objective.

From the minister's point of view there was the sheer task of getting around the three centres. The King's Langley church was a good ten miles from the manse, Carpenders Park was three miles and the Oxhey estate at its nearest point was two miles away and it stretched another two in its width. When to these distances have been added the visitation to outlying homes of people in all three places it will be seen that there was a generous amount of roadwork to be done. I had invested my War Gratuity payment in an ex-WD motor cycle combination BSA 500 cc (this was long before there were motor grants from the Church). It had the full quota of faults natural to an old cycle and gave me lots of repair work but it was our salvation in matters of communication. One can learn.

Flying round the area this machine got the title of 'The Red Demon' from the people who saw it frequently and I must have looked the most unconventional parson in the Connexion swathed from head to foot in protective clothing. In wet weather it was a chilly business. It did a wonderful job for seven long years.

We even drove, three of us, into North Yorkshire on holiday and back again.

Bushey was the main church with its thriving Sunday School, its talented Young People's Clubs, its Guides and complete Scout Group of Rovers, Scouts and Cubs. There was a Guild, which in this environment could be so operated as to be what the Wesley Club at Edmonton had been to younger ex-service people. There were two women's groups, a Sisterhood type of gathering and a Ladies' Circle which concentrated on sewing for the church's bazaars. In addition there were all the usual committees on overseas and home mission work and the statutory meetings for governing and planning the total life of the church. There was the 'pulpit', the minister's constant burden.

The outstanding feature in this church was that the Methodist Class Meeting had survived in it and was a tremendous asset. There were at least six classes in homes meeting regularly and the people in them, either neighbourhood groups or age-groups or sex-discriminated, met regularly. These the minister visited on a quarterly basis.

Under these conditions it was possible to meet and know people very quickly, one was always meeting people in some group or another and the making of friendships was easy. It was the sort of church wherein one could get out results exactly in proportion to the time and attention one put in. There was, for example, the case of a young ex-serviceman who had an Army Scholarship to an Oxford College who became depressed and in trouble in Oxford. He joined the younger end of the fellowship in Bushey and came to the manse one day to tell me that his tutors had discovered a very distinct improvement in his work and health after he joined us. They had his scholarship moved to London University so that he might enjoy more of the friendship which helped him.

The younger end of the church became a haven of developing people. There were in it at one time nine young folk in higher education at the same stage of their education. One, a nursing student at St Bartholemew's, was a Swiss who sailed through

the nursing training to come out at the top of her year and then
transferred to the Medical Course to become a doctor. She and
another girl began a branch Sunday School in the Pine Ridge
estate on which she lived. Her living witness to the faith in the
hospital and daily life were such as might have graced Jesus'
own band of wanderers in Palestine. Another, the daughter of a
solicitor's chief clerk, who was Treasurer of the church, gave up a
job in the same office as her Dad after 17 years of work there to fill
a secretarial vacancy in the Mission House.

The widow of an RAF sergeant shot down over Germany who
was struggling along at work caring for her only son joined us and
became the leader of a most extraordinary class in her own home
and radiated joy. To go to that class was a benediction, smiling
happy faces all round and a deep analysis of life in its discussions.

In the upper ranges of age there was the same devotion to the
tasks to which people laid their hands. Mr Evans led the Youth
Fellowship and devoted his whole time at church to that one
thing. The Choirmaster-Organist did the same with the choir,
giving his time to it. So it was right through the organisation. The
minister was the coordinator of a dozen enterprises and friend
and adviser to all the members.

It was in itself enough but there were the other two to think
of. King's Langley was at first quite stuck in a rut. It needed
careful attention and the resolution of some of the strains within
its life. I resolved to give it one week-day to itself every week and
this became only a base line. As time went on we organised a
Sisterhood and a Youth Night out of which I got a membership
training class of young people. A Guild grew up. I visited round
the village and neighbouring Chipperfield assiduously and began
to know families outside of our regular church orbit. People
began to dribble in. Others remembered, when we remembered,
that they once used to go to church and began again.

One couple with two children who had been married in a
Registry Office ten years before came to ask if they could have a
Church Wedding. I explained to them the limitations there were

on this and agreed, to their great joy, to perform the ceremony for
them in our little church. Another unchurched pair of lovers came
to see me and in the end I married them at the church. I called
on them after the marriage one day and the girl was in difficulties
with some gynaecological trouble and could not go to the doctor,
she said, because she did not know the terminology with which
to describe her complaint. I sat down there and then and gave
her the proper medical terms she needed. I was the cat's whiskers
throughout her village family unit for ever after! Here was one
medical fruit of my China ministry.

There were corners of the old church life into which I had to
enter very cautiously, they were folk with an extreme Calvinist
fundamental faith and they suspected I was not. On the other
hand, next door to the chapel was a couple of people whose door
was ever open when I wanted a rest or a cup of tea at any hour —
and there were some quaint hours. He was a civil servant fairly
well up the ladder therein. He really lived, however, for his hobby
of radio — he was Radio Ham Number 1 . He and his wife were
of inestimable help to the life of the church. A Mr Harvey, his
wife and their charming daughter and sons were the backbone of
the cause and had been in it for a lifetime. On such people's work
it is possible to build up anything. The village-wide reputation of a
family is of the most importance to our work in villages. A church
may be 'Mr so-and-so's' church and people stay away; or they may
come just because it is his.

The Carpenders Park situation was entirely different from
the other two. This was Christianity in the raw. It was a constant
demand for ingenuity and work done at subsistence levels. Mr
Webb had acquired the use of a barn on the road side as the
private estate development grew and with it the promise of a site
on the Carpenders Park side for the building of an estate church,
which no doubt the developer would have helped to erect. Bushey
members had transferred to this cause in a gallant attempt to
create an offshoot of the Bushey work. When I followed Mr
Webb, however, the whole situation was changing and put the

whole plan into flux. London had begun to put its estate down
across the railway and the Home Mission Department of the
Connexion had plans to give it a church under the Plan for
developing great new areas . Carpenders Park was to become a
mere fleabite in comparison with the new thing which began.

Nevertheless our only base was the Barn Church and in it
we had a thriving Sunday School and a small congregation. As
transfers came in of people taking up residence in the new Oxhey
estate one could only invite them to cross the railway, walk right
through the Carpenders Park estate and join themselves to a
group which was socially different from themselves. Some made
this sacrificial journey but it was not a recipe for growing a new
church to serve the two estates. Everybody tried to make it work.
A few women from Oxhey joined in the life of the Sisterhood but
getting children or young folk to come proved impossible. One
cannot speak too highly of the patient work of the Carpenders
Park Society as it struggled with this intractable policy.

Then a catastrophe occurred which looked, at close range, like
the end of the process. A gang of youths burned down the barn!
It is hard to know why they did it. Was it protest from the new
estate at the seemly life of the Carpenders Park, anti-Christian
protest or sheer vandalism?

We hired room in the Day School for both the worship and
the Sunday School on the private estate. Leaders Meetings and the
only Fellowship class were already meeting in private rooms. We,
with many groans, gave up thinking of the site for the church on
this estate and transferred our thinking to the site on a main road
in the Oxhey estate which had been allotted to us by the London
Council. We began to hold an open air Sunday School on the
Oxhey estate. It grew and grew. We then got it into the Oxhey
estate Day School — in a word emphasis began to lie on that side
of the railway.

In my third year in the Circuit the London Mission Extension
Fund came to our aid and we had built the first stage of our
premises on the site allocated by the London County Council.

It was a School-Hall type of general service premise and into it we transferred the Sunday Worship, the Sunday School and the Sisterhood. This meant harder work for the Carpenders Park segment of the people — they had now to make the journey through the tunnel under the railway. On the other hand our presence on the Estate, with a visible presence, caused an upsurge of interest on their side. We began to get Stewards and helpers from among the Estate people who worked really well at various sections of the work.

Contrary to the expectations of some we only made one bad bargain among our new contacts. He was a man who offered to run a Scout troop in our premises, which he did very well, but he proved to be a 'ringer', absconded from home after being tracked down for things he had done in his last place of residence and left his wife and family behind in a council house to face all the consequences.

The Women's work grew and grew; the congregation held together. The Sunday School also grew. The membership, however, still remained split by cultural differences. We were up against deep social differences to which the planning had not given sufficient weight. In addition we were confronted with differences in religious attitudes between suburban concepts and the newly awakened attitudes to religion which came to us from among the new people.

To meet this I tried bringing in the Bushey connection to soften the struggle but only at one or two points did this make any improvement. In one I had the idea that the Estate people needed roots in their new area and I used to talk to the parents of newly born children about having their babies baptised at Bushey and entered their names in the same register as the children of old Hertfordshire families in the Bushey baptismal roll. 'Give your child the mark of this new place', was the argument, 'and the child will grow up to feel he is of the soil'.

The other was by using the junior end of Bushey in their social life within the Guild system. Week by week we had younger people, especially young married people, in the Guild at Bushey where they made local friendships which helped them to settle into life.

In my fifth and final year in the Circuit we had the building project completed by building the Church, joining it on in an 'L' shape to the school hall. It was a lovely church of the modern style and was made possible by the transportation of a War Damage grant from a London area in which it was not necessary to rebuild. Some of the members of that church came to our opening. This meant, of course, that the Carpenders Park people gained a church which they had longed for by merit of the London Council having put this estate on their doorstep. It also was a demonstration of the value of the national Connexion which is the Methodist Church, for without the central planning of a national Connexion the building would have not arisen. People felt greatly supported by the totality of the Church.

It was in that year that when I was preaching one morning at our Bushey church a little group arrived in the church at nearly the end of worship. They had missed the Bushey and Oxhey railway station and been carried on into the train sheds at Watford. There they had to be bailed out by the train cleaners. Gladys and I took them back to the manse as a kind of compensation for their misfortune.

At the manse the truth of the matter came out. They were a 'listening party' from the Portsmouth Central Mission, which was changing ministers. They had been told to see if I was their man to replace him. Their 'listening' had come unstuck but they had talked with some of the Stewards at the church and meeting us in the manse they decided to go ahead as though they had enjoyed the whole service.

I got in touch with the Home Mission Department who had initiated the approach and found the whole thing dated back to Edmonton being in my records. We both said we would give the proposal serious consideration, see if Bushey could be well staffed and let Portsmouth and the Stationing Committee decide the matter. They left satisfied — probably by the lunch which Gladys put together for them.

Portsmouth is a great city but it is peculiarly itself. On an island, dominated by the dockyards with their low but regular wages and the Royal Navy establishments. It has become a centrifugal entity which fascinates its people into staying in Portsmouth for a lifetime. There is no hiving off to London of its young folk seeking work, the work must be in Portsmouth. An invitation to go there is to go to a community of artisans, content with their position, loyal to their city, which they consider is no mean one. Its football team is its and no other, its City Hall is the centre of the Portsmouth organism, its Southsea Front, twinned with the harbour views of the life of the Royal Navy going about its business, makes a unique combination. Seven sea-front miles bedecked with massive Naval movements is the tops in the tourist trade. Portsmouth simply is Portsmouth.

To go there meant going as Superintendent of the Portsmouth Methodist Mission which was led from the Wesley Central Hall in the famous Fratton Road made notable by Kipling. The second Hall which fell to the second minister for care was on the front door of the Royal Marine Barracks in Eastney. There was a third Hall deep in slum property in Queen Street at the very gates of the dockyard itself. There were some lively churches spread across the city but they were not the Mission's concern, they belonged to the Portsmouth and Southsea Circuit which had its own administration and staff. It often seemed that the only connection was that as Mission men got on in the world and moved out to the suburbs they became leaders in the local churches.

It was to this that we said we would go. It summarised a very great deal of what we had done in our previous years in the ministry. Half the old ladies and still existent husbands had served in dockyard work in Hong Kong and Singapore and other corners of the world. The work had similarities to Edmonton, its likeness to the outspill estate was obvious. The linking of the little Queens Road cause to the great Central Hall was similar to the link with

Goff's Oak and the experience at King's Langley. The shore line and the Royal Navy neutralised the sense of 'containment' we often felt. Finally, I was to follow a most active and successful minister whom it was a privilege to follow. We wrapped up our Watford work and went to Portsmouth, in September 1953.

There is something of kinship between Portsmouth and Newcastle. They share the work of ship-building and ship husbandry, people from the commercial yards in the Tyne find their way into the dockyard at Portsmouth in such numbers that the town has something of their mark on it. The low standard of living in Portsmouth gives it a touch of the hard times of the northern 'Special Area' — or it did in 1953.

It was a place that we could be happy in with the one great snag of the manse being in Southsea, down by the Cricket Ground on the Front and a good three miles from the Central Hall. (It was so because one of my predecessors had bought a house inside of the banned area during the war when property near the Front had been at a very cheap price through war risks.)

This brought back our old Edmonton problem for Gladys who felt herself cut off and out of the swim of the Hall's life during her first six months. This was especially so as I had to give a lot of time to the Office at the Hall because of 'lets' and repair contracts, getting the Hall back into shape after the war years. There was when I first arrived a Secretary to the Hall who coped with office chores and took an active part in the younger end of the work. She was completely carried away with the policies of the man whom I replaced and resented the fact that he had left and consequently made life difficult for me. She resigned from the job after I had been around for three months saying that I did not need her, as I did so much of the chores myself. She stayed in the life of the hall and subsequently married a young man she had herself brought to the youth club movement and he became a minister himself under her hand.

This worked out to our good, and the young man's too. Gladys began to come up to the Hall and have tea there with

some of the women, she would help in the office work and in time
she took over the leadership of the Queen's Street women and
organised their life so well that the Women's Meeting got up to
35 or 40 women every week. The fact that the manse was near the
sea attracted guests to our home and Glady's life blossomed out in
such a way that we had in it some of our happiest years.

Sunday evenings were the high spot of the Hall's life. A
congregation of 500 was common then though the morning
services averaged out round 50-80 adults and a mass of boys
and girls. The evening Communion services could average over
the 100 mark and got up to 180 on great Sundays. By 1954 I
arranged to have a film service once a month in the evenings.
These could pretty well fill the Hall with all kinds of people. We
had everything, Hymns, Lessons, Prayers and the feature film
all on celluloid, except for a tiny section in which I spoke to the
people. Men especially were attracted by this, unchurched men
did not like standing up with a hymn book in hand to sing and
this system helped them a lot. The Scripture readings done by
great actors also set the Bible alight for them. The great difficulties
lay in getting suitable feature films. Much of the religious output
was maudlin and inturned on Church life. We did far better on
secular films such as 'Sanders of the River'.

On Sunday afternoon I began a Young People's Class which
took in the firmer end of the enormous Youth Club — an open
club which refused nobody, even the police who had to come
in on occasions to cool it off. I roped in one of the older young
people as co-leader of this class and it went very, very well. In it
we discussed every aspect of life round the Bible and out of this
discussion there came a life-pattern for many youngsters. Linked
with it I instituted a 'Middle Hour' in the open youth club which
handled some life situation from the Christian point of view.
Some of the kids would leave when it took place but by far the
majority stayed for it and took part.

On Monday evenings Mr Tom Parsons and some of his
friends ran a city-wide meeting for older people which they had

called the Comradeship. It was an evangelical meeting which Tom
led, together with a Queen's Street old gentleman who led chorus
singing. This was a roaring success. It often filled the Lower Hall
with older folk. For them it was fellowship, song and the Bible. It
was, as they sang, 'Oil in the lamp' and kept them burning. I loved
going in to them once in the month to talk to them and would
often go on other occasions just to be with them.

Tom was a great chap. He had not always seen eye to eye with
the minister before me, who was keenest on modern ideas and
some of the younger folk. Consequently, Tom was determined
that the old gospel should remain as the witness of the Hall.
My 'China' point of view that there is no rift between a modern
witness and the old appealed to him greatly and we did all kinds
of things together. The Secretary to this Comradeship was a
woman who was the chief seamstress at the Cooperative Store just
across the road from the Hall. She did the difficult sewing, such as
wedding dresses, etc. Her life was the Hall and the Comrades. She
worshipped Tom and on his death she took over the meeting and
kept it alive.

The Comrades meeting on the Monday of each week, I
organised on Thursdays a social get-together of the same sort of
people which, under the name of 'The Good Neighbours', was a
haven for anyone in that age bracket. Of this Gladys became the
mother and champion. We played party games, had quizzes with
prizes and had groups in to entertain. One or two elderly couples
gave their service to this club and made it thrive.

The Billy Graham period in London came in our second year
at the Hall and I took the Relay into the Hall. It was packed out
with people, over 1,200, and some of our folk said 'Why can't we
be this full every Sunday?' I had to tell them that people from
every church in the city were in the place and such a congregation
every Sunday would empty the churches. We were there for the
unchurched, to make a bridge from non-church to church for
people estranged from their faith. I soon learned that it was more
than the sermon Dr Graham preached that changed people.

The music, the atmosphere, the singing to mass-voice aid all had their part in the getting of responses. The tough job was in the counselling after the services when people got down to life. Later, when I arranged to have the Graham Organisation films in our nearby cinema on a Sunday this factor was very evident. People came forward simply moved, their problems still unearthed. It was the careful personal research into their own particular condition which opened the gates for Christ to enter their consciousness.

Aldrich the Eastney man, and I found this so in other circumstances. We had the habit of preaching in the open-air on the Southsea Front in the special public debate reservation there. We would start in about seven o'clock and gathered a crowd as did the other speakers on the spot. There was one atheist speaker there who gave me a boost he never intended. He told his crowd not to listen to that little man on the Mission platform because he would change their lives. That was just what I was there to do.

It was a thrilling experience to have the crowd round on a fine evening and talk to them until the lights came on along the Front and to deal with their questions, serious and frivolous.

Soon it became apparent that the personal questions came as the darkness fell about ten o'clock. As one got down from the rostrum men and couples would seek for a private talk. Then it all came out, a marriage in jeopardy, a habit that could not be conquered, nagging doubts that had never been dealt with. Many a friendly conversation that began on the Front was continued at the Fratton Road Central Hall. One couple picked up in this way joined the Hall choir, for instance, and became thoroughly involved. The man was sent to Malta dockyard to work and there they were leaders in the music and life of Floriana Methodist Church. The process gave city-wide width to the work of the two Halls. Many a sailor found newness of life style not in the Hall or a church but on the Front.

This 'fishing' technique impressed me at Portsmouth. We had just over 12,000 people hear Billy Graham in the total campaign, which we based on other churches in the city as well as the Central Hall and the total effort brought 110 people in for counselling. Although the counselling was the moment of crisis in every case the mass effort had brought them to the point at which we could deal with them.

As Portsmouth at that time had no public performances of the usual kind on Good Fridays we stepped in and took cinemas over that day, owing to the pressure of Arthur Rank at the top of the industry. We started with one of his places in the first year and took two cinemas the second and subsequent years. These could easily be filled with people and we could get suitable films.

This type of city-wide appeal was always against the solid background of the office work of the Hall as far as I was concerned. The hours of every morning were taken up by the sheer weight of financial and other work at the desk and this meant that very often the direct evangelical evening work found one too tired to be on the best form. But I reflected that the people who came to the meetings had themselves been hard at work all day and so one was on all fours with them.

It is a method suited to people who are used to the great events of a big city's life and not to people whose reactions to life are in the quieter modes of country life. Gladys who attended the session at the Eastney Hall disapproved of the whole procedure.

By the Anniversary meetings of the second year, 1955, the evening congregation had crept up to 600 people and the week night anniversary meeting logged 800.I began to feel that we were, at least, becoming a city mission in a real sense. With the youth work now developed by the addition of a Junior Youth Club, work among the children was covered. The Boys' Brigade was recast, the Sunday School thronged with children and not only the children of the membership. One little fellow coming to the morning Harvest Festival was heard by Gladys to say, 'This bloody marrow weighs a ton' as he carried it into the premises. Young adults were catered for in the 'Over 20s Club', and older middle-aged in the Guild, and the old in the Comrades and the

Good Neighbours Club. There was work for anyone who felt
they would like a share and there were the outside contacts into
the life of the city. Devotional life was attended to by the Bible
Class and the Prayer Meeting and there was the attention given to
counselling for individuals.

A Central Mission station gets all kinds of calls to service
from near and far. One of the quaintest at Portsmouth was a
telephone call one morning from Wilfred Pickles, whose heart
really lay with the Roman Catholic Communion. As a result of
one of his broadcast programmes he had received an appeal for
counsel and help from a Portsmouth woman with two or three
children. Would I see her? I went round to her tiny little home
and found her to be the wife of a Presbyterian sailor in the Royal
Navy. He was just ending a two-year commission in the Far East
and his ship was coming home to pay off. She, however, had living
with her another man and had had one child by him. Could I
sort out this situation for her? The Royal Navy is very cautious
about allowing any interference in the affairs of its sailors outside
of the Royal Naval welfare structure. She was too uncertain of
his attitude to write and confess the situation to her man. Being
a chaplain in the Army opened the Navy doors to me and I
wrote the man and got permission to see him on his arrival at
Portsmouth. She for her part got rid of the second man right out
of her life. I found the man to be a real Scot with a well-developed
Presbyterian mind.

With one tremendous effort he came back to the woman and
took on the whole bunch of children, including that not his own.
He did better, he came out of the Navy and took the whole family
north where he retrained as a coal miner in the Midlands.

When I called round at the house before they left the woman
said she had to show me her gratitude for the help we had given. I
asked her how? She said, 'I've had the children confirmed'. I asked
her where? She replied, 'In the Catholic Cathedral'! Fortunately
Wilfred Pickles himself had remarked on the phone before I
began, 'I know Methodism is bigger than a denomination'.

The years simply scudded by in this work as one crisis or
another had to be dealt with in the context of the daily round.
Aldrich departed to take charge of the Walsall Mission for which
Portsmouth had fitted him. In his place came Wesley Peacock.
There arrived a Wesley Deaconess to help in the Wesley Central
Hall, Sister Edna, who made her contribution chiefly among
the youth and younger adults. Her presence made it more
possible to take a share in the wider Connexional life of the
Methodist Church and I served on two of the Mission House
Committees, and with the British Lessons Council Committee
on Youth material. I could also do more writing, though often
in the small hours. My PoW story came out at that time and my
book on marriage was also published. I was commissioned to do
two volumes for the Edinburgh House Press of the Missionary
Societies of Great Britain. One I did on the rural work of the
mission and one was a volume of portraits of Chinese Christian
Leaders who when the missionary force left China carried on the
work alone.

There were some outstanding special days at the Hall. One
was the occasion when as President of the Conference Dr
Leslie Weatherhead came to us and for the first time we had the
embarrassing problem of an overflow congregation, having to set
up extra radio connection into our lower Hall in order to cope
with those who wanted to hear him. Another was the occasion of
the first BBC Broadcast Service at the Hall. We subsequently did
two further broadcasts of the ten-minute type.

In 1957 I began to receive invitations to other Circuits and
we began to feel that five years at the Hall would be enough.
There was an invitation to Barnes which would have taken us
from Portsmouth after four years and we reluctantly turned
it down, although going there would have put us very near to
my own people living at Richmond. Indeed I did conduct the
marriage ceremony of my nephew and his bride at that church
shortly afterwards.

In October 1957 we were asked to consider going to South

Norwood Circuit and went up to see it. It was our sort of church and we felt we could deal with it. Some of my old PoW contacts lived near it, another attraction. Finally we agreed to go there in 1958, subject to the Stationing Committee's decision.

There are moments in a life when the whole world seems to collapse on one's head leaving dazed amazement as the only sensation. They are terrible moments these, they usually signal a complete change of life and a man has to sort out all his values to deal with them.

March 7th and 8th were such a moment in our life at the manse. I first had a telephone call from Basil Clutterbuck, who was then senior secretary at the Mission House, who said he wanted to come and see me. I thought he was coming to ask us to return to China or some other Chinese project somewhere else.

The following day he came and presented me with a copy of a document prepared by an Enquiry Commission on the life of the Missionary Society which proposed great changes in its methods of work and direction. It stated that the Society was at the turning point in relations with the churches overseas which were nearing independence under the pressure of the political changes in their various countries. Where would the missionaries themselves stand in these changed circumstances? What would be the financial position of the Society's funds in this situation? How is the home church to be educated in a new concept of its mission to the world?

The existent management of the Society provided a Field Service Secretary for each corner of the world and one for Home Affairs. The work covered by these Officers left no room for the thinking needed to meet the changing situation. The proposals of the Commission demanded a Secretary who would be a Chairman of the Officers without a field responsibility to try to recast the administration into such forms as would deal with a changing world. My name was proposed as this new Officer of the Society. It was suggested that I go to the Mission House for one year while Basil was still in the service and use this year as a time for collecting data and then take over the direction in the following year.

Basil Clutterbuck laboured long to persuade me that this really was my work. I don't know to this day how they came to select me to do it. He had to work even harder to persuade Gladys that this was right for us. She could sense the long days of separation that the job involved. The world is a big place and our Church is all over it. I think she knew that her sacrifice in accepting would be greater than my own. Margaret was all for it from the beginning — anything which put her Dad on the world map to work was OK by her.

There was the problem of the verbal commitment to the South Norwood Circuit but this they had thought of before Clutterbuck came to see me; the Society would take all responsibility for that in the Stationing Committee. So we said yes I would do the job if the General Committee of the Society agreed to this Executive proposal. The next problem was for the Home Mission Department to find my successor; this they did by inviting Leslie Timmins to take over. He was a much younger man whose ministry had been in missions from its beginning. I was content.

Peak 7 - 'THE WORLD IS MY PARISH'

The Overseas Division

The headquarters of the Methodist Missionary Society, now known as the Methodist Church, Overseas Division, is an imposing building standing on the corner of Marylebone Road, near the Baker Street Station and nearly opposite Madame Tussaud's wax works. (This has been a little joke in the church for years.) The counter-part joke is that when the building was erected ancient bones were discovered in the digging and when the London Bible College was built later on the opposite corner everyone prayed that similar bones would be found in its foundations, but weren't.

The building stands eight storeys high and is blazoned with a symbol of mission on its imposing entrance.

One day I stood on the eighth floor, which is graced by a lovely chapel in which daily prayers are said, and from the chapel verandah I looked out over London. There the city lay all around me. It was, I knew, filled with great business houses whose profits came from a world-wide trade. The House itself had, when I began my service, been in the setting of Bishopsgate cheek by jowl with Leadenhall Street and near the Royal Exchange and the Bank of England. It had moved to get more room. At the beginning of World War II the Marylebone Road House had been taken over by the BBC — its bits and pieces were still with us when I first got there. Here had been the greatest Communication Centre of the world. From here Britain had rebutted Count Haw Haw and sounded the 'V' signal to the nations. From here the voice of Vera Lynn had countered the voice of Lili Marlene in the hearts of soldiers all round the world. It stood surrounded by the centres of all the trade and enterprise of the British nation round the world.

Beneath my feet in all the lower floors was a staff of more than a hundred people who were all struggling to find the way to bring the way of Jesus to a hungry, tired and baffled world of nations in the changing times which had engulfed us all. They had been the servants of an Empire of churches which ranged across Europe, Asia, Africa, the Caribbean and the Islands of the Sea. Millions of people looked to this House as the centre of their religion and the medical, educational and agricultural work, which expressed it. Other centres in America, Australia and other spots carrying the same burden looked here at this London House for leadership and advice. On our doorstep in this very city of London other Societies, Anglican and ethers, existed for the same purposes as us and they all looked to the Methodist Society for The Word, The Message, as the largest missionary society in Europe. We were so because the Methodist Church in Great Britain puts the task of world mission directly on the shoulders of every member in the Church. Our thousands of churches up and down the country are each and every one committed to world evangelism, as they are to local church life. So that every District and every Circuit looked to the House for guidance in its work for world mission too. There was not a church hall or Sunday School without propaganda in posters on its walls. Most of them depended on us for their decorations!

As I contemplated London from the height of the House's eighth floor I knew how the high vision of mountains dwarfs the spectator. I had engaged myself to lead this team down there to this task. In competition with the Kingdoms of this World I had to find the way to deal with a dying imperialism, the subtle temptations of modern neo-capitalism which is worse than imperialism, Communism which was the great alternative to the way we taught, and nationalism which is the easy solution to the immediate perils in the eyes of so many. Out of this battle I had to forge a family of equal churches which would hang together as one group in the world, yet be at the same time 'friends of all and enemies of none' and to carry the Home Church with us in all we did.

From this mountain top I would have to go below and meet and befriend every soul in the House itself; I must venture out to the ends of the earth and talk with our colleagues in churches there, talk with them in the language of confidence, freedom and collaboration. I must circulate through the churches in Britain and set their minds on new ways. 'Who is sufficient for these things'. Others had confidence in me or I would not have been elected by Conference to do it, but where lay my own confidence in me? It had to be in the chapel behind my back, in the Lord worshipped there. It was He who must conquer not I. So I went to the task; a little man with a great Lord.

———————————————

I entered on this remarkable task in September 1958 and my reception among the staff emphasised the sense of inadequacy. The house I was to live in was due for very necessary repairs and sat by a wide busy road unrepaired. I could count the number of cars which swished passed it in the rush hour through a wide crack in the study wall. The whole place was so decrepit that Gladys hated it. There had been no redistribution of rooms at the House and I was tucked away into a corner room and only Miss Compton — the senior assistant secretary — as my spare time help when she was not busy with her other work. There was a general story round the place that Mr Thompson had come to the House not to work but to think for a year before beginning to work. Most of the staff thought this quite hilarious. Strangely it chimed with my own mood and opinion of myself and helped me; the little man thinking in the corner was me.

Within a day or two I was introduced to my first Officers' Meeting. This was the heart of the Society. The Field Officers with the Society Treasurers met in regular conclaves to deal with all the affairs of the Mission. One man and one woman Secretary for each Field: Asia, India, Africa, Europe, the Caribbean and Home affairs were their several responsibilities and the India Secretary, Basil Clutterbuck took the Chair. Nothing was decided, however, without the whole meeting agreeing and each member was responsible to the Connexion for every decision. It was a 'Cabinet' structure. It had been so since the early 1900s when my distinguished namesake E. W. Thompson had laid it down as a counter-blast to an ancient dictatorship. Indeed, this cabinet principle was so deeply regarded that it was said by Conference that I was to enter the House as 'Chairman of the Officers' and not as General Secretary as was the habit in other Departments of the Church.

My first experience of this formidable team in counsel was as they dealt with the question of Lay missionaries' Pensions. No one was responsible for this subject, it had to come out of the immediate thinking of the group aided by the advice of the Finance Department leader Cyril J. Bennett. Only the pensions of Wesley Deaconesses came under the personal knowledge of all Field Secretaries. Laymen were in the Society's employ in other corners of the world, Ghana and South India containing the bulk of such personnel. Among them were educationalists, doctors and administrators. Did one buy a doctor a practice in this country when he left our employ? If so what is the equivalent compensation for a teacher or lecturer? By how much could a layman differ from the mass of ministers who simply came home to circuits and the tiny pensions they had paid for under the Methodist Ministers' Retirement Scheme?

It was, in a way, a very good debate to start with for me. It contained all the issues which now create strikes in industry and public service today. 'Differentials', categories, mass decisions and basic norms. Could it be handled in the peace of God; in three sessions of keen debate it finally was. It was, however, a debate right outside of the life of the churches overseas who got all the aid of foreign staff quite freely. This emphasised for me the difficulty they had been having in turning the mind to new ways of handling the life of the overseas churches. Where was the time and personnel to do this? Running on in the old way cost so much time and thought.

Of daily work of a routine pattern I found there was nothing for me to cope with which was very depressing for me. I found a corner in the House and got ahead with British Lessons Council work, writing for the *Methodist Recorder*, jobs which had been peripheral in circuit. I looked up a lot of paper on the scheme which had introduced me to the House and realised that some of those who promoted the idea were simply after a sixth secretary. The exception to this was Thomas A. Beetham, the Secretary for African Affairs. He was deeply concerned with the ebullient life of Ghana and Nigeria and he shared his ideas about changes there with me. Indeed the first autonomy for an overseas church, in Ghana, was his work. On the Women's side, Miss Alice Walton was the person deeply interested in the future. She, however, was just retiring from the work. I attended all the sectional committees and picked up the problem areas in each of them. I was launched into House Prayers and House Communion and so began to know the staff — a great experience.

In the work of Deputation everybody agreed that I should be launched from the beginning. In the first quarter — the last months of 1958 — I was thrust into deputation at Whickham, then I went and did the York District, three days of meetings and preaching, just getting home for the London Medical Meeting. Then the following week to Birmingham with another Central Hall thrown in and the Handsworth students of the period. Then back to London for a supper club and on to Liverpool for a one-day Conference. Within the next two weeks I went off to see if the church in Tiger Bay, China Town, at Cardiff, was suitable for the implanting of the Group Project of Geoffrey Ainger which the Mission House was to launch. It proved narrower in opportunity than the present Notting Hill location.

Just before Christmas in 1958 there arose the serious question of the retirement of Wilfred Easton, who was responsible for Caribbean affairs and the added problem of the request of the

Conference of British Missionary Societies for the services of
Tom Beetham. This constituted a real problem in my eyes for Tom
was the best mind in the team for the big issues such as devolution
and Wilfred knew the Caribbean area like the back of his hand.
He had done much to create that great community of churches.
With Basil Clutterbuck's departure we were to lose three of the
Officers in one fell swoop.

The team of advisers composed of outside folk and the
Officers appointed by Conference gathered and welcomed
the idea of Philip Potter, now General Secretary of the World
Council, as a Secretary in the House. It received a very warm
welcome. Both Wilfrid Pile and I were new to the work and the
general picture became practically a new start. Philip's friend
Harry O. Morton was suggested as the man to follow Wilfred
Easton. They both came and our new team was complete; Donald
Childe of the China world was the reliable and hard-working
back stop to a team of new people; for meticulous care of detail
and careful, home produced memoranda he had no rival. Philip
Potter, Wilfrid Pile, Harry Morton, Ralph Bolton, our gallant
Medical Officer and I made up the men's side. Muriel Stennett,
Tom Beetham's loyal colleague, Mrs Edith Ladlay, Mrs Margaret
Bingle, Betty Hares represented the Women's Work. Money was
represented by Mr Carey — who had been High Commissioner
governing Austria after the War — and Ralph Treadgold, a tough
business man, with Mrs Crawford Walters, an ex-President's wife,
representing women's finance. It was a strong and happy team
which spoke its mind fearlessly but never quarrelled in doing so.

Behind us in the second echelon were some remarkable
people who carried the burden of working out the execution of
things which the Officers decided. Prime among them was C.
J. Bennett, the man in charge of the financial day-to-day life,
Pauline Webb who looked after Youth and Literary work, and
the phalanx of Personal Secretaries headed at the beginning by
Marjorie Compton, an indefatigable secretary, and later Margaret
Forrest who knew the African world so well and the life stories

of all the male candidates for service. John Beech, who left us for the North London Central Mission, Fred Pearson who assisted the Home Secretary and looked after internal affairs in the House itself. It was this team which saw to our deputation wanderings, our overseas tours and all the chores for committees — I myself became a member of sixty-eight — and the long string of interviews and meetings with people.

Each New Year began with a meeting of the whole Connexional Staff, including all the departments of Methodism and all grades of service in Wesley's Chapel, City Road, as the year dawned. We all were John Wesley's devoted servants anyway and we thus went back to our roots. The service, unique for its rendering of Wesley's hymns, was followed by a get-together which was wonderfully helpful in sorting out our ideas of service over the wide range of interest the Church covers. My first experience of one certainly did much for me. Life had been so many bits in my first quarter in the House that it had become difficult to see the wood for the trees. Deputation in Birmingham, York and Wales had been individual sorties into the unknown, committee had followed committee ranging from Counsel's Chambers in Lincoln's Inn to domestic matters of staffing. Somehow Wesley's Chapel harnessed it all and the meeting of all the staffs tied things together. One was in a real team doing one thing after all. We finished the day by having a conference on the way the Youth Department's work fitted into our own.

The year 1959 saw the beginnings of our attempts to change the position of the Mission in relationship to the churches which had already sprung from its own work — preparing for the changes I had been appointed to ensure happened in that year. We sent out across the world the framework for getting some localised answers to the questions we were asking ourselves. Each District overseas was asked to tell us the answers they saw in their area to the questions of Nationalism, changes of work and opportunity, the use of Mission strength and Mission personnel. From fifteen countries the voluminous reports came back and occupied Officers' Meeting time for hours. Each was considered carefully, comparisons were made, likenesses and odd ones were carefully combed through.

The result of this survey by correspondence is summarised in the Annual Report of 1960 which was edited by Pauline Webb. This was the first report to contain such articles, which were collected and retained by many of the Ministers who made them the heart of their information.

Broadly the guidelines of the survey revealed the following factors in the new overseas situation. In every place there was a new duality in the nations' reactions to the West, they cast off political tutelage. It was pointed out that Eastern films had replaced Western in cinemas in Africa as well as in their homes. Each of the nations was undergoing the emergence of a new social class — broadly speaking a Middle Class — as old tribal grouping faded. This was disguised behind the world dread of the spread of Communism, when in fact the great issue was that the new technologies were creating a world change which was the real revolution. A third factor was the rise of affluence in all classes everywhere. Affluence has to be gauged by the point from which folk come and not by a two-car American standard. In the fourth place it was apparent that the changes involved changes in religious belief. Both Islam and Buddhism had become potent revolutionary forces. Our Faith carried the burden of its imperialist origins in the West. On the other hand 'secularisation' was rampant. People had become 'stimulus-drunk'. We faced new material bidders for the hearts of people. In the fifth place new race-tensions were left to deal with after the tension between the East or South and us Westerners was gone, such as the strain between the Indian, Malay and Chinese in Malaysia. A sixth fact was that each state, however tiny, must catch up with the new technological age if it was to signify. In doing so they have all had to resort to State control of industry and economic planning. The final note gained from the survey was that the revolutionary movement throughout the world had given rise to a crop of

appalling fears. Fear is always the concomitant of change and
the greatest fear is that you are afraid of showing that you fear.
Mao-Mao in Kenya was perhaps the chief example of this drag on
progress.

It became clear that the life of the Church in the widest
sense was affected by these changes. Its life is conditioned by its
past. It is evident that an old local faith which has survived into
the new day is more appealing than an imported faith such as
Christianity. Yet it is as true that the pioneer work of the Church
was often there before the area in which it existed was named and
given frontiers. Methodism loved and worked with slaves while
slavery was still a world-accepted reality. This means both that the
Church can be seen as part of an old imperial world, coming from
the West, and also that it was the only early protest.

The criticism of missionaries to be heard in the smoke rooms
of liners on their way across the world that 'we spoil the natives'
was in fact grotesquely true. Those who came through our
educational processes and had real contact with us did cease to be
'natives' and became people. They frequently became the middle
class leaders whose lives triggered the revolutionary movements.
Yet that movement could condemn Christianity as the religion of
Imperial Nations which oppressed the peoples. In the days, now
gone, when the World Council of Churches was dominated by
Western votes the case was proved every time the Council met.
(Today the boot is on the other foot and a 'coloured' majority in
the Council sometimes irritates the Western world.)

In the new world of free nations, world wide, it was time for
the Church to change too. We had, broadly speaking, founded
the Church from the lowest levels of society but we had changed
these people into self-conscious citizens of the middle-classes.
John Wesley's remark that he could tell the Methodist homes by
the cleanliness of the curtains at the house windows had acquired
worldwide verification. We had washed or removed many mental
'curtains'.

Much of the great work done in the pioneering days was

through the service of individual missionaries who had carved out
for themselves little kingdoms of influence in medicine, education
or agricultural change. They became little gods in their areas. This
was very satisfying for them and also helpful to the areas in which
they gave life-service. The Home Church loved them. Their day
was, however, gone in the new post-war world.

After this mental bath in the deep waters of the new nations
I began to realise that my being chosen to lead this move into
the future had some real sense in it. I had served my missionary
training and work in China, a land outside of the British Empire,
in a land where foreigners had been suspected for two hundred
years, where the official Minutes of the Church's synods had been
in the Chinese language, where foreign titles like 'The Reverend'
had been banned and where the debate on the things done was
dominated by Chinese thinking. I had been one simple teacher
on the staff of a Chinese schoolmaster. I had held responsibility
in a team of workers in a Chinese Health Station not a simple
missionary hospital. In a word, I had been groomed to make
Chinese changes in an Imperially structured church world. I had
also seen the type of Indian life under the Raj in which foreign
leadership was a fore-ordained foreign ascendancy. The Chinese
proverb 'T'ien sha wei kung' (the world is everyman's) was part of
my life.

It was decided that I should go and see Africa for myself. I
had already fallen in love with Sierra Leone, the baby colony,
what of the rest? Accompanied by the Treasurer, Mr Treadgold,
we set out and journeyed first to Kenya. There with Elliot Kendal
and Frank Bedford as guides we saw the teeming life of the cities
such as Nairobi and met some of the leading personalities of the
country, found a site on which to build a new church for middle-
class folk. Then we blasted off over Mount Kenya to see our
wonderful agricultural work and religious work up round Meru,
while billeted in the steel-wire protected manse of its missionary
family. Here we were in direct touch with Mao-Mao. Treadgold
discovered that the local church had put its African ministers on

mopeds to get round the wide district they served. The original
coffee plant of Kenya sat covered in berries in the mission front
garden. The school-girls slept in our school armed with machetes
to defend themselves. We visited a National, government-owned
Teacher Training College which had a missionary head and
learned much from him.

We then winged our way into Rhodesia and stayed with our
Chairman of the District, Harry Lawrence (who was to prove
to be the last White Chairman). We interviewed people like
the Head of the Educational Department of the country who
cheerfully admitted that he was frightened of the efficiency of
our Ministers out in the 'bush' because they found his mistakes
more often than he found theirs, in the records of the schools they
managed. We went off with one of these redoubtable Ministers,
Andrew Ndhlela, then the superintendent of the Pakame Circuit
out in the African reservations, as guests of his family. He showed
us everything in his very wide area and whenever we had a massed
congregation out in the open air we discovered a motorcycle
police sergeant of the rulers on our tail. I spoke with some of these
chaps, for I didn't care for their attention, but always they were
apologetic and said it was just routine. They were entertained by
the African leaders in just the same way as ourselves. Schools and
chapels; the world was sown down with them. The congregations
were enormous and the women's movement named the 'Red
Blouse Movement' was everywhere in strength. We attended
the District Synod of the Rhodesian Church and found it full
of bright and competent African leadership. Andrew told me
in quiet and personal conversation, 'We do our best to keep the
peace and get progress but if it comes to bloodshed you know
which side I shall be on'.

We left Rhodesia for the north, into North Rhodesia, now
Zambia. As I passed through the formalities of Airport Customs
a grizzly White official said 'You're bound for Lusaka; you can't
get there too quickly, we don't want you here!'. To which I replied,
'Are you wanted here?'. It was pleasant to be associated in one's

mind with the struggle.

Zambia is indescribable: on the one hand, wide open land hardly tilled since the Fall, ready in two hundred acre parcels to any lad who had been trained to farm it; on the other hand, the roaring industrial life of the Coper Belt pounding out its copper. There we met for the first time Colin Morris and his peculiar congregation of both colours. We examined his Course of Study for White overseers of Black labour which the nation had adopted as essential. By his courtesy we lunched with Kenneth Kaunda in his home on the Kafue River. His first activity was to order the white man who had been in charge of preparations to clear off the table all intoxicants. 'I'm not entertaining Politicians.' I sat with his wife at table and she occupied much time in telling me her problems in rearing her numerous family. She did this in connection with our project to educate young women who were to be the brides of educated trained husbands. 'They must match their man.' It was a simple 'people's' home.

We went out to our great schools and down into the Zambesi valley, sampling all the variety of opportunity for work from primitive people just breaking into civilization to the sophisticated industrial peoples at the Copper Belt. Any high-spirited young Englishman might be proud of being offered a share in building this nation.

How serve? That is the question which arose in my mind when we were taken on to a remote rural area and to the home of the Chief. There was there a little boy about eight years old, with brilliant ginger hair, clothed in African style, with flies buzzing round his head, unkempt and dirty. As we watched the Chief playing the African organ — a series of reed pipes on a gourd — I learned that the boy was the bastard son of a Scotsman who had retained the Chief's daughter as his housekeeper in Lusaka. He had gone back to the Scottish hills and the deserted girl had brought her Scots son home. What service is this? What would be his adolescent opinion of Scotland? Which good man would marry the deserted girl? In our church in that area a whole row of men sat, outcast, for marrying several wives. One said to me, 'Double wife, double trouble!'.

In a neighbouring village was another Big Chief who himself was not a Christian and he had only one wife, who was a Christian. She would serve meals for all the two hundred clients who came to the Chief for judgements and who must by custom be entertained by the wife or daughters of their Chief. Service by servants would be insulting. He provided her with every modern machine which would help her serve them but she was quite worn out and ill with the constant labour. As I pondered the church law which forbade duplicate marriage, I realised that only a sovereign African Church could properly handle such a problem.

It was now time to turn attention to West Africa and in order to get there Ken Johnson, surely the gentlest soul that ever served North Rhodesia, drove us up through the north to the Zairian frontier. The extraordinary comment on life in general in this trip was that we came to the Zambian border and were passed over it by examination of one lonely African soldier. We crossed the bit of no-man's-land in between and a second African soldier — now in Belgian uniform — graciously counter-signed our papers and let us in. Both were the agents of European powers. If both had the lonely power of admittance or rejection, why were they European troops?

We hastened through Zaire as it was under the American section of responsibility in our Mission life, simply stopping to visit and confer with the Bishop in old Elizabethville and to see the Press of the joint missionary societies in Leopoldville.

Then, Ghana with its colourful and exciting press of city life. We stayed with and consulted with the Rev. Thackray Eddy, the local Chairman of the District, who had direct access to Mr Nkruma and was often consulted by him. There were tremendous talks with African leaders, led primarily by Mr Sam Amissah, who later became the first General Secretary of the All-African Council of Churches.

Here Methodism was clearly very firmly grounded. This could

be seen by the enormous congregations we met at the central
Wesley Church, where I was, all five feet six of me, helped in a
service by a six-feet-plus probationer who told me he was also a
Thompson. At Winnebar and Cape Coast it was the same. In the
latter we talked with the staff, led by an African, at our influential
Mfantsipim School which seemed to have produced a large
number of the principal men in the state. They gloried in the list
of names carved out on a plaque under the pulpit recording the
long list of Englishmen who had come and died for Ghana in its
Gold Coast days. This was a nation which had fought through
anti-westernism.

I went up to Kumasi — head of the old Ashanti nation —
where I met the Asantehini (King) of the old dynasty whose only
comment on our Mission's intentions was that I had to remember
that 'New trees always grow off old stock'. This adage off the lips
of the last representative of an ancient Royal House has helped me
again and again since.

On the other side of life I went with our missionary
up-country to a village where the headman demanded that
Christianity should be taken out of his village because he
reckoned that edible snails had deserted the village ever since
the church arrived. The missionary minister talked him out of
his grim decision. We saw the thriving Bookshop which proved
bigger than our London one and all the other institutions of the
Church and felt that this Church was lively and great enough to
manage its own affairs.

Then on to the 'plum' of the tour, Nigeria. Here was the
greatest Black nation in the world with its seventy million people
and its thriving Federal life. The structure of government was the
very air of Nigeria at the time of our visit. We were there long
before the great civil war which began in the Eastern of the, then,
Three Regions and it is remarkable that the Nigerian Methodist
Conference was the only Federal Structure never to disappear
before the onslaught on all types of structure then being born.

Rolfe Treadgold's time had run out on us and he had

returned to England from Ghana, consequently I missed his companionship very greatly. Alone in the Western Region I went up to the Ibadan area and fortunately stayed with the famous Owolowo who was Governor of that region. This man, so ebullient and powerful, himself a Methodist, was married to the most winsome little lady who contrasted with him in every particular. She even ran a Methodist Class Meeting for the ladies of the government party.

I saw the great University of Ibadan in which we had a stake, numerous institutions which we ran, or had share in, and everywhere were intelligent and devoted leaders capable of any governing function. Our central church in Lagos was of terrific calibre. Churches on the new town estates growing up round the capital were wide expansive buildings. I flew down to Port Harcourt in the Eastern Region and met Azikwe, one more Nigerian politician produced by our Church. I saw in the port our work among girls picked up in the streets, and personally went into the Drum Clubs which thundered out the night club life of the town and was quite amazed at the number of ex-Methodist men I met in them in the small hours of the night who had been purged from the Church under the rules on polygamy. Most of them were still keen Christians at heart and very willing to talk. It was easy to see where the indigenous churches like the Cherubim and Seraphim got their worshippers, churches which accommodate such men.

Although the Eastern Region and its Iboe people were definitely the poor relations of the Federation the men were keen and good businessmen. It was their incursion through commerce and civil service action in the Northern Islamic Region which precipitated the civil war. Their educational standards gave them such advantages.

I penetrated through the forest regions of the East up to stay with the Rev. James Jackson, Chairman of the District, at Umuahia, a characteristic market town. One rally in the forest up there surprised me. The West was supposed to be the most

numerous Christian community but in that rally in the forest
I saw the greatest assembly of Christians of the whole tour. It
contained a whole battalion of Boys' Brigade among hundreds of
adults.

The District proliferated in institutions ranging from
the Trinity College, then run by Dr Igwe, to the scene of Dr
Frank Davey's world-famous Leprosy Colony at Uzuakoli,
which matched the Ilesha Hospital in the Western Region, so
famous for its wonderful work for children and for which the
government paid large grants. Schools were everywhere right
over to the boarding schools for boys and girls in the Calabar
under its African headmaster on the site of Mary Slessor's famous
adventures. Down there I went on circuit with African judges and
barristers judging cases.

Time was now pressing. I had been away for weeks and going
up to Kano in the Northern Region I caught a plane which
brought me home. The Ivory coast and Gambia Districts had
been left for later treatment. It was time. Gladys was frantic with
loneliness. The House was without a head. Such is an executive
life.

It was in May and June of 1961 that this long process of
survey and journeying came to its climax. In that period we
called the 'Connexional Overseas Consultation of the Methodist
Church'.

This Consultation was an historic event, nothing like it
had ever happened. It was unique. Its body was made up of four
categories of people. First and foremost, there were the national
leaders and missionary servants of every place in the world
which contained the Methodist Church, most of them meeting
each other for the first time. Secondly, there was a group of
international leaders, not necessarily Methodist, which served the
fellowship of churches in all the world. Examples were Dr Daniel
T. Niles of Ceylon and Dr Donald M'Timkulu of the All-Africa
Church Conference. Thirdly, there was a panel of women drawn
from different parts of the world. Fourthly, there was a group

who bore responsibility for the various types of work the whole
Church does in Britain. The administrative team which saw to all
the detail contained sub-committee chairmen and the secretarial
staff of the House itself, and hard they worked.

Twenty-eight nations were represented, ranging from the
British Isles to Hong Kong eastward and India, westward to the
Americas and southward to Central Africa. It was significant
that eleven Republics were in the team. In earlier years it would
have been a Commonwealth conference. Now after 200 years
of Methodism it was a world conference. Wesley's note of a
comment by a West Indian woman in the eighteenth century had
come true, 'You have many children', the old lady had written,
'whom you will never see'.

The Consultation began in Wesley's Chapel, City Road.
There in the early centre of Methodism we made our promises to
each other to do the business we were committed to with heart
and head. We drove in coaches to the YMCA (a force known in
some way to every member) at Skegness which had welcomed us
to meet there; we went via Epworth, the homeland of the Wesley
family. We were received like princes by the Town Council of
Skegness, which laid on a wonderful civic welcome mixing old
England, a Chinese juggler, old songs and new in the Town Hall.

In the preparatory letter it was written, 'In such a Council
we shall hope to reach a common knowledge of the whole of our
resources and the whole of our opportunity; to plan our line of
progress; to facilitate exchanges between parts of the Church; to
devise means of continued service, mutually organised, through
autonomous Churches; to make the resources of the Missionary
Society an evangelical tool of each and all the Churches'.

These four objectives ruled the Consultation, but life and
vigour were given by the interchange of emotion and ideas
aroused by the presence together of so many living examples of
the problems we encountered. Many conferences record their
work merely by a list of resolutions agreed in them. This was not
our way. The best shorthand writers in the Society made it their

business to record every word verbatim and the speeds ran up to 200 words a minute. Miss Compton and Miss Forrest bore the burden of this work.

After taking the chair of the conference through the long days it was a most revealing business to go on into the night preparing the next day's edition of the whole proceedings of the day before. We certainly worked like slaves, but one by-product of the work was the firm friendships emerging between the members of staff of all the Society.

We only fell into one trap in organisation and for that history was more responsible than us. The Rev. da Silva Cunha reported for Portugal, he a real representative of all that is forward-looking in Portugal. Dr Fred S. da Silva reported for Ceylon, the oldest Methodist Church in Asia, and the staff put them both in the same bed! Who in the YMCA staff of Skegness could know that Portugal centuries ago had ruled Ceylon and left her names with her blood in that gorgeous island? Like brothers the two da Silva clansmen sorted this out with mutual courtesy. It was typical of the whole Consultation that they both got beds of equal comfort by a friendly discussion of their several pasts. In the life of Angola and Mozambique there was recently evidence that it is not so common to work things out this way. The great Wesleyan principle of Connexional family life conquered where the 'world' would have botched it. What was it the old gentleman said, 'One family in all the world'?

The extended reports of the Consultation were speeding across the world by air mail within three weeks and reached the Churches before the representatives arrived in their homes. They laid before the leaders the total of facts concerning us all — right down to the last penny in the coffers of the Society — a complete review of all the difficulties, prospects and hopes of us all.

A new life began which took years to follow up. It stretched from the massive Church of South India to the tiny work in Gambia and the beleaguered lone church in Paris. Today's great family of Independent Methodist Conferences started in the

Lincolnshire town of Skegness.

In November of the same year I met the Chairmen of all the British Districts and relayed to them the thought and ambitions of all the Overseas Districts, nobly backed by the District Chairmen who had been part of the Consultation; and so we opened the floodgates of new plans upon the British Church, which received them with enthusiasm.

That same month, on 18th November, the World Council was due to meet in New Delhi, India, and I took this as the trigger for an Eastern journey to match the African trip. The weeks between the Consultation and the World Assembly passed in a frantic series of committees and Connexional meetings: the Transfer of Authority Group of the Conference had to be dealt with as only Conference could actuate changes. The Stationing Committee of the Conference, for I represented in it all the ministers returning from overseas, our own domestic committees of the Society, Eastern, Western, Finance and Pastoral took their place. So did Lawyers committees and the Youth and Advisory Committee, with The Care of Students Committee and Care of Immigrants Committee. This activity was matched with weekend appointments up and down the land to enlist the support the Society expected from the Home Church. It was no wonder that Gladys would ask me why I didn't take my bed down to the Mission House. Her salvation was the work we did for overseas students at the Methodist International House under the care of Miss Hilda Porter, MBE.

Hilda and she got on well together and Gladys largely became her confidante and friend. There were things — like bedding — there which Gladys thoroughly understood, and there was nursing to be done and counselling. In my wild life of travel and absence from home I owed a very great debt to the MIH. Its committees were one place where Gladys and I were together and on the job together. She was a very loved person there, one of the very elite band which could influence Miss Porter.

A party of us from our Church moved off for New Delhi

on a BO AC plane on 16th November. We were a Conference
designated bunch including representatives of the whole of
Methodism in these islands, the Society's three representing
overseas interests.

In Delhi we stayed at Wesley Manse, the house of our joint
church with the Baptist Mission which catered for English
speaking worshippers in the city. This was a thriving church with
people, mostly Indian, who found the English tongue their only
means of communal worship. The church thus expressed one of
the good things which British Imperialism had given a polyglot
country. It, strangely enough, had arisen out of the work we did
among the men of the British Army! Swords beaten into plough
shares.

Only a few things remain to me of the debates in the vast,
crowded meetings of the Assembly. One was the way in which
Archbishop Ramsey was awakened to the 'world Christian
themes' by men like Philip Potter and one or two others. I have
always thought that it was the rebirth of an Archbishop we
witnessed. He really woke to the worldwide relevance of the Faith
as compared with the parochial British world. The second was
the exposition by the Orthodox Church theologian of his own
communion's 'spiritual bond' type of unity. It was a rich comment
on our own Methodist way of doing things Connexionally. It
reinforced my sense of the way we were fashioning our Church
into a new local independence. The third was the way in which
the Church of South India had opened up a new way of living
through its union of Anglican, Methodist and other units in one
Church.

The life of Delhi was a sight to see in our changing world. Its
poverty made our youngest delegate ill; its retention of all the
trappings of the old Raj shocked me; the splendour of its New
Delhi filled with *élite* persons from all over India — it seemed to
be dominated by southerners — contrasted strangely with the
squalor of slums in the old Delhi. It encapsulated all the problems
of our modern world. Concrete and glass; pomp; material gains;

sheer hunger and homelessness; made up the general picture of
he-who-has gets.

I was glad to leave it, alone, for Lucknow in spite of the
fellowship of the Wesley Manse days. In Lucknow I entered a
world where the British, Australian and American Methodist
Churches were together struggling with one of the most daunting
tasks that could be imagined for a missionary team; wrestling
to give the Christian witness at the very heart of Hindu faith.
Proclaiming the Gospel on the burning ghats of Benaras is no
sinecure. You don't expect mass-movements there. Ones and twos
are your victories. I heard of the struggle to create the United
Church of North India, which it was dreamed would complement
the southern structure. I met ministers and missionaries of all
the negotiating Churches and saw their educational and medical
institutions before leaving them for my old haunt, Calcutta and
the Bengal District.

Bengal was one District in which I did not lack information,
having worked on its staff and attended its Synods. I refreshed
my acquaintance with its Leprosy work and attended my old
church to find it changed by the absence of the Army but thriving.
I departed from it at the end of a week and made, by plane, for
Rangoon and our work in Burma.

I found in Rangoon the work of the Bible Society still in the
hands of a Methodist minister, Mr Vincent. There never was a
man with more fluent Burmese than he and we made a good pair
of companions. I had a session with the multi-denominational
Ministers' Training College and then flew up to Mandalay, the
centre of our Church, for we left Lower Burma to our American
staff. Our English Chairman then lived in Mandalay and a great
city it is. The work based on its stretches away to the frontiers of
Burma both on the Chinese and the Indian sides.

It sprang out of the work of the Army in the Burma War. It
has a tremendous hold on the Burmese Army today who come
to church in truck-loads. In Mandalay we had a Leprosy Colony
operated by a Burmese man with a missionary wife, and a school

for preachers to augment the work done in Rangoon. The splendid Wesley Church is there too.

Burma at that time was undergoing strained political conditions and I found my movements checked and controlled by the military secret service. This gave no trouble except when I visited the homes of Chinese residents. They quickly got to know of my Chinese language capability and I was invited by them to parties in their homes. I flew off to Tahan away in the hill tribal country and from there up to the frontier town of Tamu by Land-Rover. On that journey it was most moving to see the well tended graves of lonely British soldiers who had died there, carefully fenced in in the forest by bamboo and decked daily with flowers. The road leading down from India had been constructed by the Royal Engineers who had built culverts and bridges and laid down expanded steel road-sections into it at all the difficult places. In remaking their homes after the war the population had ripped up all these fancy bits and put them into the construction of their houses. The side plates of a deceased tank made a wonderful Church bell at our church in Tamu!

I stayed in the campus at Tahan which is three weeks' journey from Mandalay by road — I had fortunately been flown in by the Burmese Air Force. The station was in the charge of Leslie Cowell, who had done a wonderful job in translating the Burmese and English literature into a local Tahan script. He and his wife, Margaret, made a wonderful team for forward missionary work. She was then expecting their second child and was quite happy three long weeks away from professional aid. One early morning she was seeing Cowell off on a journey and tripped on the verandah steps. This event she only celebrated by saying, 'Don't worry, Tahan children are tough'. I was not so tough and decided that Leslie should not go with me to the extreme points of our work up under the frown of the Himalayas. Dennis Reed and I (Dennis was the man in charge at Mandalay of all the work in the north) went off with a group of tribesmen to visit the hill villages and the frontier town. School choirs, open air classes and dancing teams marked our path all the way. Joy was everywhere. One of the churches we visited was half way up a great mountain and there was another still further up. At night in the cottage where we lodged there came an influx of men and women which filled the place. 'We thought we would come down to meet you', their leader said, 'our legs are so much better than yours'! It was the congregation of the upper church.

Song, joy and discussion were the ingredients of Hill worship in Burma. Cowell had indigenised the forms of worship. The singing was terrific. It was accompanied on the gong which struck a million notes in my Chinese mind and it was pure harmony. Material like 'Love Divine all loves excelling' was matched with Hill folksong into a perfect amalgam. Everyone was beaming with the emotion of the singing. Then after worship the whole group sat down to chew over and extend the doctrine in the sermon. The whole thing could occupy three hours. It was hard to realise that Church Order is more severely interpreted here than anywhere else in the world.

Up in Tamu — a frontier town indeed with wood-board footways — I met a Chinese who invited me to his home and told me in Chinese that he lived there as a dentist but had other interests such as the trade across the Indian border.

I went to the actual crossing point on one occasion as we had work which lay on the Indian territory and I wanted to see it. A Burmese Army sergeant very politely told me I could not go through as my passport was British. He was quite unmoved by the Delhi Visa from the Burmese Consulate there. I looked disappointed, I suppose, for he told my guide to take me up the road a few miles and into the forest and there we could stroll through. 'He is a Chief Pastor after all', was his comment. My guide and friend on this trip was Vulchuka, a Burmese minister, trained and ordained in the Tahan area. The first of many.

I got back into Mandalay at 6 a.m. on the 22nd and plunged into a gathering at Wesley School at 9 a.m. for their Christmas Concert and breakfast which was a big outdoor event. From there we went to a Nativity play at the Leprosy Home and Hospital; what a day!

On the following Sunday I began to go out to the other parts of the District, the Burmese area, and the hill country leading to the Chinese frontier. We visited up to Maymyo on that side. We had a conference about new work in the Somra Tract but strangely perhaps my last memory of upper Burma was a Buddhist one. Vincent had taken me up to a great concentration of Buddhist life and on the plinth there were rows of images of the Buddha circling the area. I noticed a middle-aged woman going from image to image and bathing the head of the Buddha with water then laying bunches of flowers in each lap. I asked Vincent to speak to her, which he did with a supreme courtesy. She welcomed our advances and calling her husband, the pair of them told us their little story. It was, it appeared, her birthday and her husband's gift to her was the money to buy the flowers and enough of his time to accompany her in a round of worship. Blessed pair, I felt, love stemming from sincere religion.

It was the 14th January in 1962 before I arrived back in Rangoon. There I found that Mr Vincent had one more task for me to do. He had received a request from the Minister of Culture and Religion that I should pick a team of three missionary theologians and lead them in a discussion with three of the Minister's own choice of experts in Buddhist lore. This ended in an all-day conference in a Rangoon Hotel where we shared food and talked over the two religions' points of view. It ended with a request that we provide a New English Bible to put in the magnificent Buddhist Library — a national monument in Rangoon. I flew back to Britain in the long haul of nineteen hours, leaving Burma on the 18th of January.

The day after I returned I was plunged into the committee of all the Connexional Secretaries and spent it in the review of our activities which such a committee represents. This was typical of the weeks that followed. Committee followed committee in endless procession dotted with interviews with individual people,

like the American Bishops, Continental Mission personalities and
the domestic staff of the House. This was against the background
of weekend appointments in the British churches which in the
period took me to Kingswood School, Bristol, Manchester and
Leeds. Many of the London churches claimed deputations and
free Sundays were very rare phenomena.

Days and nights were thus gobbled up completely until
in June 1962 the Methodist Conference was heralded in that
year by a meeting of the World Methodist Council's Executive
Committee meeting in London. This brought in people from
all over the world and the Mission House was their anchor in
London. I attended their sessions as far as I was able, as the
General Committee of the Society and a One-Day Conference of
all the partners on the British Missionary Conference intervened
in the period, and then it was time to go to Stoke-on-Trent where
the Methodist Conference, my master, was due to begin.

Only those who are Methodist People can appreciate what
the Conference means to the Church. It is the Episcopate of
Methodism in its corporate wholeness; it stands between the
church and the nation as the regulative body. Its word is Law for
all Methodist people. It embodies all the functions of the Church,
pastoral, doctrine, legal and administrative. All departments
of church life are subservient to it. It is the total master. Nearly
six hundred and fifty persons, ministerial and lay, constitute its
formidable strength and all share equally in its debates. Its Leader,
the President of the Conference, is chosen without previous
nominations by the total body and is designated the year before
in open Conference. He, during the year represents its authority.
As a governmental system the Conference is unique. It combines
the strict authoritarianism of its Founder, John Wesley, and the
democracy the years have forced upon it. Once upon a time it
was exclusively a ministerial gathering, and now for part of its
function still is; gradually it opened to the laity and it successfully
combines both strains. The new General Synod of the national
church is modelled on it.

Its business is done by introduction from the Departments, now termed Divisions, of the Church. Conference so, can support, correct, prune and criticise any and every activity of the Church as one by one they come before it. When the Senior Secretary of a Division has presented his Division's report, written in the Agenda, and spoken to it, the 'floor' of the Conference has its freedom to deal with it as it sees wise. In the debates anything can come up and it never yet has happened that there are none to criticise and correct before the Conference makes the report its own — as it was presented or as it has been revised.

It follows, therefore, that the report to Conference is indeed a great responsibility for the person who has it to make. The whole authority for the entire committee work of the Missionary General Committee lay squarely with the Conference. Such adventurous policies as conferring autonomy on a foreign Synod of the Church need the backing of the great assembly or nothing could be done but stay put.

I laboured at this task; the appeal, to move, to foresee the difficult factors, to answer innumerable questions. Gallantly backed by one or other of the Women's Work Secretaries we for the most part had the Conference with us on the policies which we had worked over so carefully in the Officers' Meetings. They were great days and great debates.

The President of Conference in 1962 was the Rev. Dr Leslie Davison, Secretary of the Home Mission Department. He and I, as responsible for two wings of the Church's work, were good friends and we frequently had common interests in the work. In the years leading up to the Conference he had grown a real interest in the origins and development of the world's religions. As the Conference drew nearer that year he told me of his deep desire to meet and make friends with Pope John XXIII and we arranged for him that he should do so. It would be the first official approach from us to the ruler of the Roman Catholic Church.

Accordingly the visit was arranged through Cardinal Bea's office in Rome, with the assistance of Father Stransky of the

American representation to the Vatican. The Second Vatican
Council was in progress and our visit was connected to it. The
Rev. Rex Kissack of our church in Rome assisted greatly. Leslie
arranged that he should call in Rome on a visit to our church in
Malta and I arranged a visit to the Methodist Synod in Italy.

On the morning of the visit to the Pope we were all together
in the manse in Rome. Very early in the morning Leslie had
confided in me that an image his dying wife used to have on her
bedroom mantelpiece had been broken in accident by her nurse,
he wished to replace it and have it blessed by the Pope. It would
have to be identical with the ruined one. It was before eight in
the morning. I took him out to search for one and after looking
round several great shops in Rome we did find one little one with
the identical model of the Mother and Child. He was over the
moon. People at breakfast chaffed him about it but he stuck it in
its pristine tissue paper into his trouser pocket and when we robed
for the visit it went with us.

Kissack dressed simply in Guernsey sweater and corduroys
went to drive us over to the Vatican. The President, The Rev. A.
Douglas Spear, who represented the Royal Navy, Army and Air
Force Board, and I walked through ranks of Swiss Guard and
Gentlemen Ushers of the Vatican for what seemed miles, leaving
Rex Kissack behind in an ante-room. We walked right through
the Audience Chamber and arrived at last in a tiny little study,
lined with calf-bound volumes in which Pope John XXIII waited
to meet us.

He rose to greet us, a tiny little man with ageing face, who
might have been some venerable Methodist supernumerary
minister. In fragments of Latin, English, French and Italian
he managed to converse with us. Where his language failed
him — we were completely ignorant of the Slavonic tongues
which he commanded — a Monsignor with him helped. He was
extraordinarily well briefed; he told Dr Davison that he, Jesus and
Leslie shared farming fathers — a great blessing. He told me that,
as I travelled very far very often in my work, I must never hope to

become a saint. I answered that St Paul had done so. 'I knew you
would say that', he said. 'Have hope! Many have done so, Ireland's
St Columba for instance, but be careful.'

We chatted until he suddenly asked where was his friend
Mr Kissack. 'He who lives just across the square from me', he
commented. Kissack was brought in in his casual clothes. He
immediately told the Pope that he must see what the President
had in his pocket. Tenderly the Pope took the tissue parcel from
Leslie's pocket, opened it and then said, 'I will not bless it, she is
of a different communion and would not understand. Tell her
I kissed it.' Which he did on the spot. It was one of the most
Christian moments in my life and I think the same for Leslie
Davison. We talked on about the life of his Church and the life
of ours, deep, understanding talk. We offered him a copy of the
Methodist Hymn Book which we had brought for him. This
moved him deeply and he explored it for Catholic hymns, of
which it has many. We told him of Charles Wesley's six thousand
hymns — a mine of devotion. He compared this with Faber the
Catholic Hymn writer. We went through a Faber hymn in the
book and ranged it alongside one of the Wesley tradition. He
lamented that his work in Eastern Europe had delayed his study
of our language, saying that it contained so very much of beautiful
devotional material. The whole visit ran on far beyond its allotted
time as he invested us with the 'Order of Mother and Teacher'
recently created by him in the Church's life. He sent the hymn
book up to his bedside and came with us through the long series
of chambers and corridors to say farewell, passing *en route* the
Italian Legate who was very impatiently waiting his summons to
the presence. We could not but feel that here was a very weary
minister, surrounded by people who criticised and very glad to
talk to non-controversial fellow Christians for a while. We did
him good, prayed together, sang Wesley together, and clasped the
hand of friendship. Within a year or so he was gone; one day we
shall meet again and sing to our hearts' content.

We called upon Cardinal Bea, that doughty champion of the

reunion of Christendom, and were generously received. I was
approached by the Cardinal in charge of the Vatican staff. He
wanted me to provide a copy of the book, *Constitutional Practice
and Discipline of the Methodist Church*. I was surprised that he
knew it. He explained that he had worn out one copy in his
research on the amount of primitive church law still to be found
in the Christian world. We sent him a new copy.

The President went journeying on to Malta, where there were
serious property difficulties, and I stayed on among the members
of our Italian Church talking with Mr Sbaffi, its Chairman, on
autonomy and its relationships with the Waldensian Church
— which is the oldest form of protestantism in the world. At
that time it was politic in view of the state of Italian life that the
two remain separate and yet good friends, one representing a
nationalism seven hundred years old and the other being a world
church with influence in more than ninety countries. Today the
situation has moved on toward a union of the two.

In the years which followed the Independencies of the various
overseas Districts of what had been British Methodism took
place one after another. With the Anglican Societies we gladly
conferred it upon region after region. There were times when
Archbishop Fisher and I set out across the world at the same times
to negotiate the change with our various churches. Once he said
to me, 'I'm one ahead of you'. It was not for long.

Each area had to have a Constitution peculiarly its own.
We hammered them out in committee at both ends of the
negotiation. A local group dealing with a Mission House group.
There was one general meeting in Freetown, Sierra Leone, of all
the Churches down the African West Coast which I attended
and in it some general sections of the Constitutions were agreed.
The Overseas Conferences and the British Conference have, for
instance, common representation in each other's Conferences.
We agreed that expatriate ministers and laymen in the work of
a particular Conference would be in the total command of the
Conference in which they served. We also agreed that a local

Conference should plan its own work even when that work was
paid for by funds from Britain. The Sierra Leone consultation,
however, did not accept what the Anglican Communion did
accept, that there should be an overarching Diocese of West
Africa. Our people feared that the enormous differences between,
for instance, Nigeria with its many millions, would outweigh
little Gambia in such an arrangement. We also agreed that Unions
of Churches should be at the local Conference's decision and
that no union should cut us off from each other. This was but
to universalise the principle we had adopted over the Church of
South India.

The orbit of Churches linked into the American Methodist
Mission Board had a harder time passing through this phase of
change. It caused great agonising of spirit in the American home
church and men like Eugene Smith, with whom one often spoke,
had greater difficulties to overcome than we had in Britain. After
all, we had the experience of change in the old imperial days to go
on. South Africa and Ireland had gone before it into Connexional
freedom then.

In a way, within the councils of the World Methodist Council
we had a wonderful forum in which the new President of the
Ghana Conference became a well-loved and deeply respected
colleague. As he, Mr Francis G. Grant, was joined by the others
coming through, like Mr Sbaffi of Italy and the newly-appointed
President of the Nigerian Church, it became more easy for them
to frame the American orbit pattern as they saw the system in
operation. Their solution differed from ours, they created a system
of Central Conferences which netted the work.

The old British world Methodism today presents a number
of independent Conferences, all equal in status, linked to each
other in one great world family. In the religious sphere it stands
shoulder to shoulder with the Commonwealth. We all benefit.
The old charge of religious imperialism which still dogs the steps
of some groups is irrelevant in our life. Within the World Council
of Churches there is no Methodist overseas church which speaks

in Council through a British voice.

There have been one or two irregular situations to cope with. The church in Paris using the English language, after all the French speaking Methodist churches had long gone into French organisations, is a case in point. It was treated as an English Church, subject to the British Conference. Rhodesia was another. It was thought unwise to free it in the '60s' though in this decade it is an Independent Church.

There were correlates of this constitution-making period in both the ecumenical field and the field of Faith and Order, not to mention relationships with emerging new Governments within the nations concerned. In Ghana great crowds of people filled the streets singing Wesley's great hymn 'Omnipotent Redeemer our ransomed souls adore Thee'. I was asked to the National Independence Celebrations of the Nigerian Government. Gladys was also invited to this occasion but did not wish to go and our daughter Margaret went instead of her. It was a truly great occasion when the Princess Alexandra representing the Queen — and looking like a fairy princess — handed over the Documents of Inauguration to the then Prime Minister in the Government House, a replica of Westminster. To be with the enormous crowds at midnight when the new national flag went up was a marvellous experience. The amount of goodwill for British people there at the time was most touching.

An equal joy was to be in Zambia when our Church and the other non-episcopal Churches united into the Church of Zambia thus attaining their independence. The President of Zambia preached the first sermon and, in the open air, Colin Morris preached the second. This occasion was phenomenal in joining the fruits of both the British and the French missions among others.

I found a new spirit too in ecumenical gatherings which I had to attend. It was remarkable enough to travel via Paris to Mexico in the company of Russian Priests of the Orthodox Church, bright young men with a command of English. On transshipment

at New York to an aircraft going down to Mexico via Houston I
was locked up in a steel room with them for an hour or more, I
presume on the principle that 'evil communications corrupt good
manners'. My passport and visa from London showed plainly
enough that I was no Soviet citizen! Instead of wandering New
York I sat with my rejected companions and drank coffee while
one of them phoned his embassy from behind the locked door
and told the Ambassador of our situation.

It was greater joy, however, on entering the concourse of
people at the girls' school which was our venue to find that Philip
Potter had had me share a billet with Francis Grant of Ghana.
For days we shared this four-bedroom — minus girls — and I had
to form a new habit. He was in the habit of singing to himself
Wesley hymns just before dawn, and we did all our favourites.
There are worse ways of starting the day. Mr Grant, incidentally,
when visiting Britain had asked me to get him a rail ticket to
Scotland as he said he wanted to go up to the village churchyard
where lay the remains of the Mr Grant who, as a slave owner, had
founded his family in Ghana. 'I would like to pay my respects', he
said. No man's forgiveness can cross the centuries better than that.

Younger nationals had other ways of reacting to the Western
world. On another trip to America I attended a conference away
down in the south in Gatlinburg in the Smoky Mountains. Dr
Daniel T. Niles of Ceylon and the South East Asian Churches
was there. One night, very late, we both felt we wanted a change
from the conference attitudes and he invited me out to a Soda
Fountain in the town. Before accepting his order the girl behind
the counter demanded his nationality — was he African? He
played with her, 'You tell me', he said. She hesitated and then
said she would get the manager. He arrived and asked the same
question. I joined in and asked him if he had ever encountered an
Englishman. That stalled him as I was the first he had seen and
he said so. I told him it was strange he and the girl had not asked
my origins. 'What about those drinks?' Daniel then enlightened
him on his Ceylonese-Tamil beginnings and entered into far

more detail than was essential. We got our drinks. 'You're not the worst people in the world after all', he said as we drank. We said, 'Tomorrow we will come here again and bring an African, how's that?'. We did, a strapping Negroid type, and we got three drinks.

Others had this 'colour' difficulty at that conference; it does complicate international Christian conferences. The Liberian Ambassador to Washington was involved in an incident in the airport. He wanted food in the café there and was segregated before he got it. The scene backfired on the manager for the Ambassador flourished his papers, to the manager's great distress, but the Ambassador insisted on sending a report in to the Federal Government. He said it was his duty as not all Liberians carry such devastating documents. It was not the documents which gave human dignity but God. Down in South Carolina there were Liberian students at the university; he had been visiting them and they must be protected.

In the mid-sixties one of the most fascinating activities I had to share was in residential conferences, not only of the missionary society but other sections of the Church and sometimes the conferences of other organisations in Britain. Big ones often met at Swanwick and could last more than a week. There were other centres dotted all round the country. Some of them met in university grounds. Wherever they met there were young folk and older people all anxious to use the days together in getting to know themselves and their world more fully.

There was never an easy option for the speakers. Anything could come up in the discussions. Theories of life far apart from the Christian Way could pop up in them. The framework of living together, eating and playing together could stimulate all kinds of personal questions not in the formal agenda. Consequently there were personal sessions to add to the planned ones and in them folk could take decisions they would never have made under other conditions. All the missionary ladies together is one group; all the students of Methodist loyalty from our universities is quite another. A conference of business men up near Manchester is a different matter; a conference of Youth Club members still another.

I grew more and more convinced that this part of our worship life within the Church is terrifically important and should be one of the activities of every circuit and every district. There must be times when people actually live together, not just meet for an hour or two.

I was contentedly living out this extraordinary life in the Missionary Society's life, in and out of England, up and down Britain, when suddenly and without warning the blow fell upon me which disturbed it all and made life even more complicated. The main thing for which I had been sent to the House was accomplished, the Independence of the Overseas Churches, and we were living out the new arrangements. I was in the full stream of all the activities of the complicated life of the Churches here and overseas when the Conference produced other thoughts.

Peak 8 - IN WESLEY'S CHAIR

The unexpected

Near the end of the seventeenth century no one who saw John Wesley alone on horseback tracking his way across the Northumberland fells could have imagined that his head was full of plans not only for the fell villages but was filled with plans for all Britain. Not a miner or a miner's child in the villages but had a place in that pulsing brain; not a parliamentarian in that age of slavery but had a place beside the humblest miner within that Wesleyan heart. Wilberforce, and his colleagues, in the highest circles of the realm had their share in that transformed Oxford Don's thinking. Something which mastered Wesley's mind had the will and the charm to weave a universal pattern in terms of people and their eternal destinies. Were not all one in the Divine Eye, the worn miner's wife, the child and the Caribbean slave? There is a mountain experience in marking the trail of that tireless, fastidious little man as he journeyed from spot to spot across Great Britain in contact with all the soiling of this sin-struck world. He was cleanliness in contact with filth. He was sweet reasonableness in contact with violent passion. A mountain of a man set in five feet of human body dogged by illness.

The first months of 1965 were gladly spent in the service which filled his life. There was a rush trip to Zambia accompanied by Dr Donald Soper, who was scheduled to speak to the tough white folk of that world. That was in the January of the year and was straight-away followed by a visit to the Chaplain's Depot in Aldershot to speak to the forces there on Rhodesian affairs. Then a dinner of the Methodist Association of Youth Clubs in London at which Mr Howell, then Minister of Sport, was the principal

guest. In the February came a Ministers' Conference for the
Wolverhampton and Shrewsbury District. March disappeared in a
welter of committees and weekend deputations and the rush went
on round to the Furlough Conference of missionary staff and key
members of the British Church at Swanwick, at which the chief
lecturer was to be Mr Annan of the Ghana Church. In the June
the Conference of British Missionary Societies met at Dunblane
in Scotland. From there we went to Plymouth to prepare for
Conference, which was meeting there that year.

There it happened. I began to feel my colleagues in the
Stationing Committee, which allocates all the men to their
circuits and is composed largely of District Chairmen, very
warmly welcomed me and were particularly careful about my
health, which had nothing wrong with it. My only anxiety was
their solicitude. I mentioned this to my secretary and she told
me that it had been the same at her desk. With characteristic
kindliness she let me in on the act. There was a move among the
Chairmen to nominate me for the presidency. I gasped.

When three days later the Representative Session of
Conference met, her guess came true and I was designated for
the Presidency to the following year by an enormous vote. I
can remember going back to the team of Mission House staff
completely shot down and how kind they were. Congratulations
rolled in from all kinds of folk but I could not congratulate
myself. From home Gladys wrote that good wishes were rolling
in from all over the country but she asked what does this mean
for us. What indeed? The President's itinerary on top of the
Mission House one! Long days of separation and a mass of new
responsibilities. After forty years of hard work done for the
Methodist Community this was the end.

It was then that I turned back to contemplate the life of
our 'Reverend Father', John Wesley, and mused on his tireless
journeys. I turned back to the book which was given to me with
the Bible at my Ordination. In the flyleaf there were subscribed
the words 'So long as you abide by our rules we shall account you

as a brother among us'. I realised that this admonition was but a
paraphrase of Jesus' own words. 'You are my friends so long as you
do whatever I command you'. Obedience and fellowship correlate
one with the other. I bent my mind to obey.

Presidency of the Methodist Conference is for the year in
which he presides over the annual sessions but, though little
known, the work involved laps over into the pre-presidential year
and the year afterwards. In the pre-presidential year there are
churches which want your presence, there is the tremendous task
of making the itinerary of presidential visits, which will fill the
year with travel from District to District. This includes agreeing
with the Chairmen of Districts the type of occasion they have in
mind for the visit to their particular Districts. There are numerous
discourses to prepare, sermons to create, enough for the busy
days to come. An overseas tour to visit the Armed Forces of the
Crown in some theatre of activity to arrange and visits to other
Churches than ours and to ecumenical and national events. This
must all be done while carrying on the work which is normally
one's function.

I can remember Mrs Maldwyn Edwards telling me how she
did it all for her husband in the drawing room of their home. I
suppose I was fortunate, the Mission House staff rallied round
and did most of the routine work and fashioned out my itineraries
and visits until by the end of the year it was all codified and in my
diaries. I can never be too grateful for the love and service given to
me in this period by the secretarial staff of the House.

As soon as Conference ended I left for Portugal with the
Rev. Frederic Greeves, a Past President, for the unique business
of ordaining two part-time Ministers into the full ministry of the
Methodist Connexion. This had never happened in Britain and
was indeed pioneered in Portugal.

Ordination Services in the Conference town in Britain have
always been packed out — our people seem to feel for the men
ordained — but there never was such a crowd as that at Mirante
Church in Oporto. It filled the church to standing capacity and

there was a whole square outside filled with people to such a
degree that the gendarmerie sent a posse of men down to control
the crowd. The Roman Catholic Hierarchy sent bishops to
take part. The Oporto newspaper the next day headlined the
occasion with a banner notice emphasising this ecumenical and
Anglo-Portuguese event. It took more than an hour for the two
Ordinands to receive the kisses and good wishes of the vast crowd
outside the building.

Dr Greeves behaved most meticulously. An old Portuguese
gentleman named da Silva who entertained us with every courtesy
took it on himself to coach Dr Greeves through the intricate
formula of Ordination in the Portuguese language which
contained several of their difficult diphthongs, which the doctor
had to rehearse interminably before his host was satisfied. When
it came to the moment they slipped off his tongue with ease.

I was left with the solemn task of persuading the Conference
that we had not compromised the case for part-time ministers
in the ranks of the British Ministry in Ordaining two men so
in Portugal. It was necessary to point to the old law passed by
a Conference in the past which gave the Society permission to
adapt our laws to overseas conditions. The names of the two men,
Alberto P. N. da Silva and David D. de Almeida, still appear in the
universal list of our Ministers.

I got home after visiting Monte Pedral, Lordello and Aveiro
churches with their lively congregations of younger people and
seeing the site on which Dr Salazar had given us permission to
erect a village church. Gladys, Margaret and I went off for a brief
holiday on Lindisfarne Island, the place where so much began.

Then it was time to go to Stockholm in Sweden for the
meeting of the World Methodist Council's Executive. The
Executive is not in great numbers but the Swedish people made a
big event of our presence and we had some crowded meetings in
between sessions of the conference.

In September 1965 the Church of Scotland held its own
Church 'Skegness' and I went up to guide them in the ways we

had used in our own event and was with them at St Andrews
for ten days. On the Sunday morning I preached at the Great
Church of St Andrews and found this most moving as it echoed
my father's own religious history within the Presbyterian
communion. Our consultations together followed much the line
we had followed at Skegness.

October brought the British Council of Churches meeting at
Aberdeen and a party of us from the Mission House staff went up
there in the night and back from there the following night with
one great day's debate on the intervening day.

It was at the beginning of the long drawn out quarrel about
the future of Rhodesia and the British Council had before it a
proposition to advise Her Majesty's Government to reinforce
Her Majesty's Forces in Rhodesia by simply adding new units
to the British South African Police Force in Rhodesia, a process
which it was thought would terminate the rush to Independent
Self-Government. In the debate I found myself arguing with a
woman whom I did not know who was the chief opponent of
this idea. When the meeting broke for lunch I discovered that the
woman was the first lady of the Scottish Peerage. The proposition
was carried and through the Chairman, Dr Ramsey, and the
usual channels, was conveyed to the Government. It was never
implemented. The Stand-by Formation of the British Army at
that time was the Scottish Lowland Division. In the February of
1966 I was invited to go down and talk to that Division about
Rhodesian Affairs and found many NCOs and Officers very
sympathetic to the British Council of Churches' point of view.

In all the turmoil of committees and deputations which
filled the Autumn of 1965, including the re-opening of Victoria
Central Hall at Sheffield and the great North Western Laymen's
Conference at Abbots Hall, one little pool of quiet stands out to
this day as a time of peace and refreshment. It was in the Quiet
Day proceedings of Selly Oak for which I was tremendously
grateful. In it one had time to recollect the greatness and goodness
of God over and above the toil of committee work in the field of

service.

As the 1966 Conference drew nearer there were issues looming up which would have to be dealt with there. One of the outstanding was Women and the Ordained Ministry. There was a dilemma here for our Church. We were in close and world observed negotiations towards union with the Established Church, while at the same time discussing the ordaining of women which had a very divided position in the counsels of that Church. Moreover, both Churches were due to make definitive statements in the year 1966. Discussions had already rumbled on for years, our Conference had made a statement as far back as 1961, repeated in 1962. The longer the debate, the more impatient people were apt to become. It had in all been on the Conference Agenda thirty-four times.

Two subjects, the Ordination of Women and Union with the Anglican Communion, had become linked together in treatment and it was to prevent Methodist action from upsetting the union arrangements which the 1966 Conference had to address its mind to. It requested the Archbishops to set up a team to join us in an exploration of the difficulty. This became one of the headaches of my post-presidential year. In the end, the Methodist Church went its own way. With Wesley Deaconesses enjoying Lay Dispensation to celebrate Holy Communion in sparsely served circuits and the Diaconal pastoral ministry in many circuits with complete acceptance, it would have been wrong for us to do otherwise. We felt that terms of mutual acceptance could embrace this peculiarity in any union church worthy of the name.

As each President in his turn is expected to point to some particular angle of the general church life of Methodism, I had in early 1966 to address myself to this question. I first determined that I would not take the life of the Missionary Society as my theme but look to the general life of the church in every village and town.

I determined to speak to the Conference about the nobility of and value of what it already possessed in our nationwide, universe-wide, Connexional system, which finds its sticking point in little chapels and great town churches. To make the Church conscious of its own weapons was what I was after.

'The Circuit is a noble institution. It is the national mission in its regional presence. It is the whole of Methodism at its sticking point. It is the Connexion embodied in the territory. It is the strategical deployment of our strength set to meet the needs of all who live in the territory. A circuit is a social phenomenon. It is demarcated to do a special function. It is the mode of mission.

'The real business of which the chapel worship is symbol and part is with the shops, canteens, places of leisure, home, welfare agencies and every other feature which makes the pattern of British local life.'

This stepping out into the life of the local community seemed to me so vital to our whole mission as I had learned it in my own ministry that I was not ashamed of making it then, and now, the theme which really concerns the whole Connexion. It is part of my own technique to this day.

For the sessions of the Wolverhampton Conference, when once it began, I was lodged in an hotel on the outskirts of the town. Gladys came up and we had a good room in the hotel, which alas proved to be over the band when the place had special parties and the noise was terrific. We very soon departed into a back room of the hotel and gave up the glory of the first room.

Unfortunately the Secretary of Conference, Dr Eric Baker, who normally piloted the President through the laborious business in the night before each session, was far from well and could not do so in that year. 'You know the business procedure as well as I do', he told me, 'At least you should do with the Mission House General Committee under your belt. I'll leave you to it. If you want help at any point just call on me.'

The moments of installation were, as John Drew, the *Recorder* general impression writer, said, quite 'bewildering' to me. He wrote, 'He listened to the affectionate compliments of the retiring President as one who is listening to a speech about someone else

and then turned to address the crowded Hall. It was a speech
which was a curious mixture of profundity and homeliness;
thoughtful and constructive. Holy worldliness at its best.' It is a
general experience of past presidents of Conference that things
are going on inside themselves which do not originate in their
own thinking or feeling. A period arrives in which the man is
greater than his routine self. I speak of all of us who have tackled
this task.

In the business sessions of Conference as debate follows
debate one desires to take part in each great debate but has to
guard the neutrality of the Chair, and keep the Conference
alive during some very routine discussions. This is where caustic
comment and a little spiked humour come in useful, a gentle
rebuke to some very wordy brother or sister. One has to get into
the Tribune dozens of ordinary members of the House anxious
to say their say and some very shy people for whom to speak is an
ordeal and to wait hell. The business runs on from 10.00 in the
morning to 7.00 in the evening, if it is not extended beyond that
time. It is a tiring process.

One of the earlier debates which roused great interest was
whether Conference should be televised. It had within it all the
objections raised in Parliament and Lord Soper outlined them.
Who edits the tape? Who makes the cuts? Will there be those
who speak for television effect? Conference gave the matter to its
television committee to hammer out an actual scheme before the
next meeting of Conference.

Lay Training produced the next big debate. It sought to stem
the drop in listed membership. To do this by the solid policy of
training every member to be an effective advocate of the Faith —
a task often left to the minister alone was the general response.
The Conference set aside with great joy Miss Pauline Webb to be
the Director of a new organ — The Lay Training Board — which
would co-ordinate all the training done now in bits and pieces
into one structure.

We encountered one of those moments where the real

motives of a Motion were not those obvious to the eye but
underground behind all the discussion. Dr Baker proposed that
as the meetings of the World Methodist Council were to be held
in Uppsala on the dates that were set for the next Conference, the
date of the Conference should be moved to an earlier one. Some
of us knew that Dr Baker had wished for an earlier Conference for
years in order to get nearer to the Church of England, somewhere
round May each year. This suggestion was barred from the overt
discussion by the existence of the anti-union groups in our
Church.

Dr Baker's change was immediately challenged by the
representatives of the Irish Church which always had its
Conference presided over by the President of our Conference just
before the meeting in England. What would happen to them?
Others, led by Dr Strawson, then a College professor, raised
difficulties. Dr Baker replied by uncovering some of his real
reasons. Now the fat was in the fire. Asked the number of those
we should send to Uppsala Dr Baker told us the number was
eight. From a Conference of 600. This looked shaky. The eight,
however, had always contained the President and Secretary of
Conference. Throughout this heated debate one had to be aware
of the underlying issues and be fair to all sides. In the end his
resolution survived and a new date for Conference was accepted
but for one year only — the major battle would be fought after
the Union Negotiations with the Church of England had been
determined.

My own department came under the Conference eye next.
Wilfrid Pile took my place in moving the Report. He paid a
more than adequate tribute to my sitting in 'Wesley's Chair'. He
used this as the key thought in his presentation of the Society's
work of the year. He brilliantly made his survey of a changing
world and our response to it in men, money and in thought.
He presented the resolution for the Independence of the Sierra
Leone Conference. Harry Morton did the same for the Kenya
Conference and the Rev. Hugh Sherlock of Jamaica did the

same for the Conference of the Caribbean and the Americas.
Conference gave its permission by a standing vote in each case.
The Rev. Akinumi Pratt gave thanks on behalf of his own Sierra
Leonian Church. The President Elect of the Kenya Conference
capped it all by saying 'Perhaps your maturity can still strengthen
our youthfulness. Perhaps our youthfulness and flexibility may be
able to challenge your mature and staid ways.' It seemed possible,
for the Kenya Church has grown ten times in fifteen years.

Dr Soper intervened in the debate to draw attention to the
religious needs of the Communist European Countries. It is only
in these years that the fulfilment of his prophecies is coming true.
We had better take heed of those he is making now.

One of the great highlights of Conference is the Reception
into Full Connexion of the men who have finished their
probationary period and are due for Ordination. The Visitors'
Gallery is packed out and the membership in full attendance.

The Conference by a Standing Vote receives the candidates
into Full Connexion as Ministers in the Church and remits
them to the Pastoral Session for The Ordination Ceremony.
It is the President's privilege to say a few words of thanks and
encouragement to the candidates and to the Wesley Deaconesses
who have been received in Convocation and are to be Ordained
to that Office in the Church.

I reminded the men of the long road down which they had
travelled to get to where they stood. That the road by which
they had come and the status to be conferred on them were alike
the gifts of God to his Church. I said that the older ministers
in particular envied them the new world in which they in their
turn were to work out the forty years of service. I asked them to
encourage and train the generation which would come after them.

We then turned to the seven Probationary Deaconesses and
I told them that I knew their work very well and that part of my
own early training had been given me by one of their number —
Sarah Page in the Newcastle Mission — and others had shared my
life overseas and one was to be my new colleague in the Mission

House — Sister Dora Dixon of the Caribbean. I told them of
the many Sisters they had overseas, in ministries of the Word,
of healing and of education; that their Order was unique in the
Churches; that personally it came right under John Wesley's own
word, 'Expect no thanks'.

There followed after this magnificent moment a wrangle on
Union with the Church of England. It arose over the frequently
asked question in the Methodist Press and some national papers.
Could a Methodist Society which did not believe in the Union
resign its part in it and take with it the property in which it
worshipped? What is their legal position? The debate grew hot
and I had to intervene several times to avoid a general discussion
of outside problems. Dr Baker, called upon by Dr Roberts, who
had given his ministry to this problem of our Union, answered
that the whole question was hypothetical and dealt with things
that none should discuss before the Union was consummated.
Would there be such a Church anywhere? We could not know,
he said. Many of us thought we knew already, but the Memorial
making the enquiry was thrown out and Conference got back to
non-hypothetical matters.

The Youth Department people, led by the Rev. Douglas
Hubery whom the Conference always listens to very carefully,
got us back on course with a report concerning The Methodist
Association of Youth Clubs, which lives out its own particularly
difficult life in between the State Youth policy, which regards the
MAYC with great respect, and the inner life of our Church. He
defended this position. One denomination's internal Club Life
could not succeed in the present age alone.

On the problems of teenage life, Reg Bedford, on behalf of
the Teen-Age Committee wanted to go to the Department of
Education and Science for aid (as one of the bodies they aided),
not as a Churchy Cinderella but as a vital section of the nation's
youth life. His report was commended to be studied throughout
our church meetings.

The Rev. Len Barnett then rose to commend the report and

in doing so introduced a very long amendment to it, of which
Mr Hubery said he was in general agreement. The resolution
demanded a more active reply than the resolution. Debate became
more active, people called to have the lengthy amendment read
again and Len read it again. Mr Douglas Brown mounted the
Tribune to say he thought the original more useful. I intervened
a second time to tell him that if he disliked the amendment he
would know what to do. The amendment was lost by a large
majority.

In his speech in this debate Reg Bedford gave Conference
a tonic (non-alcoholic) in his attack on an article in the
Sunday Telegraph which he would like to see more informed.
It concerned the modernity of modern Youth services. He
referred to the basement Youth Club in Darlington Street in
the Conference town. I had visited this lovely club and seen
how it gave day-long hospitality to youth in enormous numbers
in a really 'modern' setting. I found one of my old Youth Club
team, of whom I had once despaired, leading it. On average, Mr
Bedford said, seven out of ten club members were people with no
church connection, three out of ten had never been in one. Yet
twenty-five young people from clubs joined the Church last year.
This two-pronged attack was great stuff.

Dr Davison, an ex-president and leader of the Home Division
team, demonstrated how Conference passes from its own chores
to high theological thinking done in a modern context when he
spoke to us about the changes in atmosphere and belief both in
the churches and in the society which surrounds the churches.
His plea was for more positive criticisms of both times and the
Church. He contrasted the differing climates of opinion in
Continental Europe, Britain and the United States. He found
in Britain a general acknowledgement of God's place in our life
which was not expressed through church going. He saw in the
lively life of USA churches a maximum state of social approval
of church life. In Europe he found the Churches facing far more
anti-churchism than here and a drift away from any religious

attitudes in society. They faced real atheism.

He did not see the answer to our unpopularity coming from one greater leader emerging, still less from the Church indulging in bitter criticism of itself. He saw it rather in entering already open doors in society and in pooled thinking on new ways of expressing our Faith.

It was a moving demonstration of what Conference and the Church is seeking to do. He and I, respectively of mission at home and abroad, were obviously on the same wave-length.

So subject followed subject in debate as the time flew by: the Ministry of Healing, Care of Immigrants, Law and Polity, personal resolutions. In one case a younger minister said the Home Mission Committee proposed, was out of touch with the present world and asked if he could propose new names. Dr Baker replied that if they wished 'they could sack the lot'. They did not, but he got some younger blood on to the list.

The conversations on the Union of Methodism and Anglicanism in this country took up a great deal of time and demanded attention to several points of view: the legal tangles, the question of dual membership, the status of property, the present difficulties of already active local unions among them. They were dominated by the question of a minister's status in any united church. The crux of the matter was that Dr Baker proposed a resolution which would facilitate union to which the members of the Faith and Order Committee moved an amendment urging that what Dr Baker wanted should be looked at by them before Conference accepted it. There were times when I thought that every member of Conference wanted to speak on this one. The queue at the Tribune grew longer and longer. It was very wearing to make certain that every view should be expressed. I laboured at sorting them out. At last the amendment was defeated and the original proposition passed. Personally, if free to have done so, I would have been with the Faith and Order phalanx but I was in charge of the debating procedural aspect only.

Conference perhaps reached its highest point when the

Social Responsibility Department raised, among other things, attitudes to the current discussion on abortion. The Resolution in the first place deplored the rising tide of such crises. It called for more moral education to combat that tide. It then expressed its dissatisfaction with the present Act on the subject and called for its amendment. It wanted more clean and professional treatment of the persons concerned; termination of pregnancy to be controlled by registered medical personnel.

I intervened to say Conference should give precedence to the doctors in the house, of which there were many, and Conference agreed. Dr Frank Davey was the first to take advantage of this preference and spoke of such down-to-earth factors as the fact of rape precluded abortion because of the long legal processes pushing the pregnancy too late. He spoke of the need for a second medical opinion. Dr Backus, a psychiatrist, followed and stressed the need for abortion on behalf of the mother's as well as the infant's mental health. There could be psychological reasons of great weight and he asked Dr Davey to accept an addition to the amendment to that end. Dr Kenneth Leese, a general practitioner, did not want Dr Backus' correction. He, as a general practitioner, saw an average of two cases a week and he thought the second opinion should be of a 'general practice' doctor. Dr Arthur Hill, a veteran doctor, wanted something done about the legal clause which used the age of sixteen as a criterion. A case to him was a case regardless of such legalities. Dr Miller, once of the Newcastle Infirmary, spoke on the danger of getting so close to a position of 'general abortion' for all cases which would put a tremendous strain on the BMA. This he did in opposition to a very wide amendment by Dr Soper.

At one point Dr Baker rose to remind the Conference that the time was rapidly coming for the Devotional Session of Conference. This produced a most surprising resolution that the Devotional Session be postponed, which was carried. The Conference then carried on with the Abortion Act debate. Dr Soper's amendments were then confirmed. The difficult task of

bringing our contribution to the eye of Government was the
business of Rev. Ted Rogers, who took great glee from this job.

There then popped up a 'stranger in the House' problem, for
the first time in any Conference. The Conference Arrangements
Committee Convener had spotted a tape recorder hard at work in
the visitor's gallery. He asked for guidance.

I said 'The Conference may wish to decide whether the
instrument should be removed or not'. Someone in the hubbub
cried, 'I move that it be surrendered to the President'. (I didn't
want it. We had several I could use in the Mission House!)
Mr Kenneth Holdsworth then rose to plead that Conference
had nothing to hide, even though it had not consented to the
machine's presence. Mr Foot Nash, a former vice-President, said
he was responsible for its being used. He had not thought he
needed permission. He apologised, saying he needed for legal
purposes a verbatim report on certain affairs. I thought this was
further reason for getting permission! It was further revealed that
Mr Foot Nash was engaged on a law suit concerning a chapel.
The Conference roared with laughter when I told Mr Foot Nash
that no one would doubt his innocence. He had what he wanted,
one debate's transcript, now would he remove the questionable
instrument.

Women and the Ministry produced one of the great debates
at this Conference. Seven long years before the Conference
had set up a Committee which had served seven years before
making a report. Mr Kingsley Turner, a very active Chairman of
a District, explained that his Committee had been ham-strung by
considerations passed on to it by the Committee on Ecumenical
Relations, which had said it would hamper their work if the
Conference were to adopt a Resolution which promoted the
Ordination of Women.

Here was a situation where, in the opinion of most people,
two good things were set in opposition to one another. The
Committee felt that the situation demanded an official meeting
of representatives of both Churches (Anglican and Methodist)

to confront this issue in the open before the Union proposals went any further. If the issue were raised later after some Union agreement had been made there would be charges of unfair action on our part. Mr Turner's Committee proposed a resolution that this take place as soon as possible.

Speaker after speaker spoke to a desire for both of these good things, the Union and the Ministry of Women. The Faith and Order Convener, the Rev. Rupert Davies, drew attention to the thing we had already done in the 1963 Conference when we declared we believed no theological grounds could be found for debarring women from the Ministry of the Word and Sacraments. He, however, thought that the conclusive vote of actually adopting the practice of ordaining women now would raise difficulties in the Conference as well as in the other church. Members might vote for it to obstruct the Union of the Churches (there was loud dissent at this remark).

Miss Pauline Webb, a past Vice-President, rose to do battle. Her battles usually end in victories. She spoke for the proposition by adding to it her own amendment. She thought the resolution too weak to do what it sought to do. She prefaced it with a statement that Conference was certain that women should be admitted to the Ordained Ministry, that our determination should be discussed in a special committee with the Anglican Church with a view to finding how an accommodation could be secured. Further, the joint committee should discuss and define how such a group of Ordained women would be treated in other Churches should they emerge. Forty churches in the World Council of Churches now had such women. We could push on and Ordain women in our Methodist way; we could refuse to do so, but would have to come to terms with Churches which now do; or we could temporise.

Dr Maldwyn Edwards, Chairman of the Cardiff District, assuring the Conference that he personally desired the Union, said that it seemed to him that we should not modify our convictions on the subject of Ordained women. We must

remember that many in the Anglican Communion desired it
and we could strengthen their hands. The President of the new
Church of Zambia supported this view in truly Colin Morris
terms. The amendment was incorporated into the resolution and
seconded by Geoffrey Litherland of the Wesley Deaconess Order,
and was passed resoundingly by the Conference.

Conference finished its crowded hours of business on the
Friday. Some say it was slow in its early sessions but profound in
its final hours. It is true that in presiding over its sessions my one
great determination was not to get rid of it as soon as possible
but to allow members on the floor of the House to have their say,
regardless of Divisional competition. I think I succeeded in, at
least, that.

The last official business was the Devotional Speech by Rev.
Harry Morton, who himself was not far from becoming President.
He was asked to essay some comment on the relations between
the old and the young and did so with his usual brilliance.

Of course Conference cannot meet without its surround of
off-time meetings. Most of the Divisions stage one rally on their
own field of interest and there are official services outside of the
actual sessions of the Conference.

Pride of place is usually given in these to the Unity Service
of the Conference. At this particular Conference this was held at
the Collegiate Church of St Peter in Wolverhampton. Preaching
at this service I tried to draw some helpful parallels between the
mass of interpretations which are given for our world, in politics,
ideologies and scientific TV programmes and the business of the
Church, which is itself an interpreter of both the world about
us and the setting of our life in the great human programme.
We attach our interpretation to the famous biblical words, 'The
Earth is the Lord's', on one hand and, 'He has made of one blood
all nations under heaven'. My appeal was that the Church should
enter the dialogue of world ideas and draw out the conclusions
for daily living which our posture demands, while asking ourselves
how well we could be seen to be doing this if we do it in division.

Our whole argument rests upon the Unity of God and on the
unities which he has created to demonstrate his own life to us.
Seven hundred million Christians all declaring that God rules,
God judges, God cares, was a witness that the world could not
neglect.

Another of the great moments of Conference outside of the
Conference Hall is the series of Ordination Services. They are
split over three or four services to accommodate the enormous
congregations which wish to participate in them. I presided over
the service at Trinity Methodist Church and the immediate
ex-President gave the charge to the ordinands. Others were held
simultaneously at the Central Hall in Walsall and the church
in Bilston. Each presided over by an ex-President. On these
occasions each Ordinand has the right to have one minister
who has influenced his life laying hands, with the President and
Preacher and other officials, on his head at Ordination. So we
demonstrate the view of Ordination which this Church holds
dear — from the President, symbolically demonstrating the
origins in Wesley, we include Ministers young and old with the
act. At Bilston there was the Italian President assisting. Since that
day the Presidents of many of the overseas Conferences have taken
part.

Dr Baker led the formal Conference Service which is usually
broadcast. There was a fair amount of comment on the form of
the Service which was used, as it has been for years, employing
John Wesley's own recension of Morning Prayer as it appears
in the Anglican Prayer Book. This recension was commonly
used in Methodism in its early years. Some of its critics missed
this point under the pressure of the Conversations, thinking we
had capitulated from the Free Church traditions. I am sure no
Anglican thought so.

I preached on 'witness'. I made the point that every man, if
he knows it or not, is witnessing continually to some thing by
which he lives. The fruits of popular themes for witness can be
seen in the way in which life throws back the image of what we

really believe. We can see the results of the witness to affluence in our world round us. The fruits of a theory of power are to be seen in war. If we don't like what we see in action round us we must witness to another way of doing things. That to which we witness is the Way of Jesus.

Lord Caradon, who was the greatest spokesman Britain ever sent to the United Nations Assembly, gave the Beckly Lecture that year. His theme was the United Nations and he said that people felt that the UN was in trouble. He stoutly affirmed that its business was trouble. He and I were staying in the same hotel and as the night wore on one had to be careful not to be the last person to leave the lounge for Lord Caradon demands audience, conversation is his hobby. Fortunately my own work had made me familiar with the world he cared about and we had long conversations about it.

Within three weeks of the ending of Conference I was out into the grand procession of Presidential Visits round the Districts. In that three weeks, three things really caught my attention and gave me joy. The first was to marry my daughter Margaret to Geoffrey Ridgway, a fellow member of our church at Crawley. To be precise, the local minister conducted the ceremony and I helped him, my brother giving away the bride. The Crawley people were generous beyond a fault, they threw the reception open to whoever wanted to be there and most people did. Over three hundred were fed and entertained by this remarkable Church.

The second was to go down to Bristol to Wesley's old Chapel in the Horse Fair and marry two missionaries, John Stedman and his bride Jill, in that lovely little chapel with a beautiful dog bedecked in ribbons staying firmly by the bride's side all the way through. The couple were on leave from Ghana and went back there; indeed they are still there — up-country in the thick of it.

The third was to open a new church in my mother's old circuit which had been so kind as, for her sake, to send me parcels during my PoW days. She was a member at Kew Road Methodist

Church; the new church was in Kingston, but a circuit is a circuit and with the clergy of the Orthodox Communion to help we had a great time.

By the end of July I was off to the Persian Gulf. There is a standing tradition that the President should visit the British Forces in some place or another, perhaps in Britain, perhaps overseas. Having had the experience of Active Service in several places I felt it my duty to take on an area of Active Service in this tradition. I consequently found myself engaged in a visit to the Middle East Command, which then was based on Aden. I went as the guest of Admiral Michael Lefanu, who at the time was Commander in Chief of Middle East Forces. All three Services co-operated magnificently in my visit.

For most of the time I was accompanied by the Rev. J. A. Fullerton of the Irish Presbyterian Church, Senior Chaplain of the Free Church and Church of Scotland, who was then stationed at Aden. It all began with a journey to Lyneham, the RAF base, where I was guest of the mess and met all the staff. The Commanding Officer told me that he had not a Methodist President on his VIP List and had entered me on it as Archbishop (Methodist). He asked if this seemed right. I was shepherded round the station by the Rev. Sylvanus, who was a Welsh Presbyterian chaplain, and his assistant Sister Kathleen Share of the Wesley Deaconess Order, whose chief concern was the host of Air Stewardesses who flew in and out of the station constantly.

I boarded a Comet next morning and we flew to Cyprus, where I met the group of chaplains stationed on the island and on from there over the deserts I had once lived on and came down at Muharraq near Bahrain town. Muharraq was an inter-service station centre of all our efforts to keep the peace in the Gulf area. Everywhere Commanding Officers stressed their need for chaplains and many of them told me stories of the activities of individual chaplain's work. I also met the representatives of our Government with their tricky job of good relations with the Islamic Bahraini Government. These visits helped me a great deal

because chaplains familiar with the Islamic religion could do so
much in keeping things happy. We must send men for whom
Islam is 'the third religion of the One Book'. This was one of the
things I always mentioned in going round the men in their billets
and posts.

We returned to the RAF's flight-plan and flew off to Sharjah
in the Trucial Oman States. This is a vast expanse of sand
scorching at 116 degrees of heat. There is a beautiful chapel
standing there under the burning sun. In it we had a service
attended by a vast number of Officers and men. Here there was
at the time no chaplain stationed, which gave ample opportunity
to our Methodist Local Preachers, for whom the Services have a
great regard. I went into Dubai, the State Capital, and met there
the British Political Agent on whom good relations so much
depended. He leapt at one point and stuck to it; could there be
five chaplains in the area. 'We need them, both the men and this
town', he said.

One day I took a trip to the desert ranges of the Trucial Oman
Scouts. This was a unit officered by desert-loving British soldiers
but composed of local troops. Here I disgraced myself completely
at breakfast. They served a very highly flavoured goat curry
and it was too much for me in the morning heat — I flopped. I
found myself waking up on the Commanding Officer's bed with
him and a doctor bending over me, anxious that no Methodist
President should die on their patch. They were sure that I had
suffered a heart-attack and would not take 'no'. I was hustled
into a twin-prop little aircraft and sent back to the hospital at
Muharraq, accompanied by a Warrant Officer who told me his
daughter had just been entered at Southlands College to train as a
teacher. I had the pleasure, lying with him bending over me in the
aircraft, of assuring him that Southlands was not a Convent but
part of London University.

They got the Sultan's own private doctor to bring his machine
and he did the usual tests on my heart, passed me as being fit and
gave me the tape to assure the High Command. There had been

nothing but the Gippy Tummy which is the plague of these areas.

One more little aircraft and I was in Aden, where I stayed in the home of the Commander in Chief of the Middle East Forces. He and his crippled wife were courtesy itself. He was a real character and all the men, of each Service, adored him. He told me how he had got his 'polio' wife into the act by telling a group of Navy men to practise lifting a heavy load into a seat in a naval helicopter and when they were proficient he told them the real load was Mrs Lefanu, who they slung up into the craft with ease. One of the Army corporals told me how the Commander had taken over his digging machine on the new military road and insisted on working it. He ended by nosing it into a sand dune. The Commander said, 'I'm not so good at that as you'. 'I could have told you that before you tried', said the lad.

Wherever I went by land I was accompanied by an armoured truck manned by men from the three services, while I rode ahead of them in the Commander's car. On one occasion Sir Michael halted the journey, got down, went to the truck, told the Naval Petty Officer to take his place in my car while he took the place at the machine gun. 'You know which is the most dangerous place?', he said. 'Yes Sir', the man said, as he came to it.

I flew across the bay to Little Aden to see a regiment of tanks which was stationed there behind a ring of barbed wire. Here many of the men had their wives with them and some children. On the way over we startled a host of pink flamingoes, which rose in a gorgeous cloud. Behind that barbed wire I found the same spirit of general friendliness. I went, for example, into the tiny shop run by two devoted old ladies of Middle East Mission group. In the shop was a little lady buying odds and ends. She turned to the Colonel of the regiment, who was with me and said to him, 'You haven't commented on my hair'. He said, 'My dear, how rude of me. It's marvellous! Have you just permed it?'

The high spot of this security operation was on the beaches where the women and children bathed as freely as at any English resort in the late afternoon. In a ring behind them were the

guards, chaps with machine guns at the ready behind any sort
of cover. I wandered round among them and one Commando
opened my eyes by saying, 'Look at all these Arab kids, see how
they play clustered round our guard positions'. There they were,
little brown kiddies at play near each of the guards. So, I said, 'the
guard is not only for our kids down on the beach'. 'You've said it,
Padre. That's what its all about.'

The heart of my Aden visit was the Sunday's work at the
'Church on the Rock', the central church for the Church of
Scotland and all Free churchmen. The morning worship was
packed out with a congregation ranging from the Commander
in Chief to the soldiers, male and female, and wives and soldiers.
Halfway through the service some incident out in the town
blotted out our lights in the church. We just went on. Personally
it seemed as though the great services at Sudder Street, Calcutta,
had come back to me with an armed congregation filling the
church. The singing led by a choir of men was tremendous. I hope
my sermon was as good.

There was to be a Welcome Party in the late afternoon and
so in parties we went off to lunch. Where I stayed for lunch the
news was brought in that an RAF Sergeant and his friend had
gone down to the market. The Sergeant was shot dead and his
companion wounded before they even got home from church.

I went round to his home to speak to his wife, a Scots girl
from Glasgow. I found her very quiet, accompanied by a little
group of wives. This widowed girl said to me, 'I'm on the team
which is running the Party at the Church this evening. Would you
mind if I just carried on with it? The church people are my old
friends.' She was there in the evening handing round refreshments,
comforting and comforted. The next morning she was flown out,
accompanied by a woman Warrant Officer back to Glasgow and
her people. That day I really saw the Church in the world in naked
truth. I knew that the British Army down the years had been the
agent of God by founding the Methodist Church in over ninety
places from Capetown to Mandalay and here in Aden from the

highest ranks to the simple soldier, people had told me that the
Church was utterly necessary to good living. Here was one more
evidence. Where life presses hard folk discover this.

I got back to England on 25th July, the anniversary of my
wedding in Shanghai so many years before. By the 31st I was
at Slingsby in Yorkshire and preaching at an open air service
in the grounds of Castle Howard. For most of August I was on
holiday in Slingsby, the farming home of my in-laws, then the
round began again. I went to open a new church at Luton, then
I went off to preach the New Year sermon at Wesley's Chapel in
London and from there to the Sheffield District for a five-day
visit in which I went to numerous churches in that District, and
among them opened the newly reconditioned Victoria Hall in
the centre of the town. We were given the highest civic treatment
by the Cutler's Livery Company giving us a formal lunch. On
the Tuesday of the next week I was at the Valedictory Service
of the Missionary Society in which it says farewell to outgoing
missionaries. The next week was devoted to the London South
West District, which included the Centenary of the Bayswater
Church, the Springfield Hall in the down-town section of
London, and a great Diamond Jubilee at our Barnes Church. The
week ended presiding over the Christian Citizen Committee.

So the round went on with a visit of a week to the Chester
and Stoke District during which we celebrated the Centenary of
St John's Church in Llandudno. October began with the Cardiff
and Swansea District with big gatherings in the Valleys of Wales.
The Chairman of that District at the time was noted for using
up the available time of Presidents by speaking himself. We had
one Rally at the head of the Rhonda. It was packed with men,
mostly miners. One miner came to meet me who had been in
Camp with me in Italy and he told me he was in charge of the
Rally arrangements. In the meeting he took the Chair and with
real Welsh freedom of speech he recounted our adventures in
that Camp 70 period. My part in his life there was his theme
and he certainly let it go. The audience was moved to tears and

cheers. The Chairman had difficulty to get in a word! That week ended chairing the Youth Committee. There followed the next week the Carlisle District, with no pending Friday Committee. Then the Plymouth and Exeter District, ending the week with the Methodist Association of Scouters.

The following week was given to the East Anglia District, with an extra day for our schools in that District, and ending with the Methodist Education Committee. There followed the London North East District and after it the Connexional General Purposes Committee, which itself was followed by the Home Mission Committee.

This brought us to Remembrance Sunday and an attendance at the Cenotaph. On arrival I was ushered into the room at the Home Office in which the members of the Cabinet were preparing for the ceremony and waiting the arrival of Her Majesty the Queen. Soon the Moderator of the Free Church Council joined me. I wondered at the time why the arrangement was as it was.

On filing out to the ceremony I discovered the reason. The Queen stood at the side of the Cenotaph looking down Whitehall toward the Houses of Parliament. The Anglican clergy were massed with a choir on her left, the foreign ambassadors were on the opposite side to her facing up Whitehall. The Church of Scotland and Free Church representatives stood on her right in one phalanx with the Government and the members of the opposition. It was a parable of the nation's life.

My itinerary went on. I left the Cenotaph Service for the Manchester Mission's Tuesday Service, looked in on the Preston and Blackburn area and then back to London for a meeting at Lambeth with the Archbishop, and then hopped into a train bound for the Scotland District, in which I went to Dundee, Wallacetown, Glasgow and Edinburgh. Back from there I took the Central Finance Board Meeting in London.

There followed the London North West District, the Southampton District, including my old haunt at Portsmouth

Mission. Back from there I spoke to a meeting of the Methodist
MPs in the House of Lords, some sixty of them. The following day
I took the Connexional Education Committee and got off to visit
the Nottingham and Derby District. Two days later I was in the
air again to visit the Kenya Church, which I did in all its length
from Nairobi right up to the Somali frontier and our work in the
heartland of Mao-Mao. There the mission houses and schools
behind barbed wire fences and with constant raids on them took
my mind back to Aden.

I got back from Kenya just in time to spend a blessed
Christmas at home with my wife and daughter, who had
almost ceased to recognise me. Only her work at the Methodist
International House with people she knew and loved had saved
Gladys from being totally browned off.

I finished the year 1966 by going to Cliff College,
Methodism's great Lay Training Centre, for a couple of days
and started 1967 by meetings with the Ministerial Training
Department and the Conference of Chaplains at our RN,
Army and RAF Board. The next week began with the visit
to the London South East District and ended with a visit to
a Conference at Willersley Castle one of our many holiday
resorts. This was followed by the visit to the West Yorkshire
District for four days and then the Liverpool District for five
days. The Birmingham District followed that and ended with
the Committee of the London Extension Fund. Four days in the
York and Hull District were followed by another four days in the
Newcastle District. This was a great refreshment as I stayed with
a cousin on my home ground. On the other visits I had stayed
with the Chairmen of the Districts I was visiting. They were
exceptionally kind and understanding but could not compare
with the home of a relative.

The Newcastle week ended in London to give a dinner to the
King and Queen of Tonga who were visiting England. A special
chair had to be found to seat the King. The Queen sought for
guidance in finding clothes for princesses in London. Shops had

great difficulty in fitting them. 'Don't tell me Marks and Spencer', she said, 'we've tried them'. The King and I found a common interest in the use of the Chinese Abacus on which he is a world authority. Then came the Leeds and Bristol Districts separated by the London Laymen's Dinner of the Missionary Society. After that the Cornwall District and four days in the Lincoln District.

Toward the end of March it was the turn of the Channel Isles to be visited. This was special for they insisted that Gladys came too and had a holiday in the islands. This made the visit quite different and she won their admiration by the way in which she worked a tomato grading machine on Guernsey.

After this refreshment I took the Chair of the RN, Army and RAF Board, followed by a visit to the Wesley Deaconess Convocation, which is the central organ of the deaconess movement, a visit I thoroughly enjoyed. Then I was off again round the churches; the Darlington District, the Wolverhampton District. Then I was back in London for the General Committee of the Missionary Society, in the chair for a change. There followed the Manchester and Stockport District which was followed by the Connexional General Purposes and Policy Committee.

Then came the Methodist Association of Youth Clubs Annual Meeting which crowded the Albert Hall with young faces all in the best of spirits and all sober, an achievement in itself. It was my job to host a principal attraction, a TV star and his children in the Royal Box. He was most desperately nervous and when I wheeled him on to the platform he was ashen grey. On another occasion when Gladys Aylward had been the guest she had been as cheerful and at home as he was miserable.

I nipped up to the Missionaries' One Day Furlough Conference at Swanwick and then went to Heathrow to fly off to the West Indies island of Antigua to inaugurate the West Indies and Americas Conference of our Church. Eleven national flags flew over the Conference's new Headquarters. We had federated the nations if the Government could not. The Irish Methodist

President shared this honour with me and we both stayed with
the first black Governor of Antigua in the State House. We
tossed up for the bedroom in which Princess Margaret had slept
on her honeymoon and he won. The Conference sessions were
wonderful and the worship in town churches was alive with West
Indian music.

From song to song, I came home and went directly to the
assembly of Welsh Methodism accompanied by the Rev. Cyril
Baker, an old Chinese colleague of mine whose home was in
Wales. It was his wicket and I let him do the batting. I followed
this with the visit to the Oxford and Leicester District centred on
our own university church. This was enlivened by the interviewing
of students, some of whom were contemplating service with the
Missionary Society and other overseas organisations. Leicester
was conspicuous for its Youth Overseas group led by two young
fellows now in the Ministry in America.

Two days in the Stationing Committee preparing the draft
of the stations of the Ministers in readiness for the coming
Conference were followed by a flight to Ireland for the meeting of
the Irish Conference. This had for generations been presided over
by the President of the British Conference. This habit had come
to be heavily criticised in Ireland and I reversed the order for
the first time, by letting the Irish President do some of the work.
The Conference governs a Church which ignores the Border and
operates as one Church in the whole island. This pressed heavily
on the Ministry. A Minister could be stationed in southern
Ireland or in the north, with tremendous pressures on his children
due to changing systems of education.

I tried without succeeding to get the young ministers who
had a great desire to visit America to change to visits to the
Italian Conference and study there the real nature of Roman
Catholicism, arguing that this would enhance their usefulness
much better than American visits. The best I could get was
invitations for Portuguese and Italian Ministers to visit Ireland.

In this period an invitation came for me to lunch with Her

Majesty the Queen at Buckingham Palace. This was 'quite outside the engagements of previous Presidents and caused a stir in the Mission House. The day arrived and dressed in frock coat and trimmings I set off on the Tube to the Palace. I had previously attended one of the famous Garden Parties and not been terribly impressed except with a Lyons' waitress who said to me 'I'll be in one of the shops tomorrow away from this shower'. I had briefly shaken hands with the Queen but an intimate lunch was different.

In a tiny little room there were five of us, a renowned Headmistress, an Australian political leader, the Queen, Prince Philip and myself. I sat next to the Queen on her left, with two corgis under the chair. She captivated me with conversation on the subject of Islam. The King of Saudi Arabia had recently criticised the Christian Faith in talking with her, while King Hussein of Jordan had spoken of the links between the two faiths. Between us we sorted out the differences within that great Faith and the nature of its sects. I was more than impressed with her keenness of mind and her grasp of affairs. The way in which our traditions and religion work themselves out in political and state life was as clear to her as it is obscure in so many modern leaders. The way in which she insisted on helping me to get rid of the corgis' hairs on my coat was as impressive as her conversation. It was in direct contrast with the servant's shock when he offered to get my car called on leaving and told him I was walking to the Tube.

There followed the miscellany of engagements which come just before Conference. I spoke to the Valedictory Service at Southlands College and to the London University Methodist Society, a great gathering of students at Hinde Street Church, and then shot off to speak at the Durham Miners' Rally which they call the Big Meetings, accompanied by Pauline Webb and John Vincent. I noticed how the Meetings had shrunk since I had attended as a boy. I fulfilled a lifelong ambition by preaching on this occasion in Durham Cathedral, which for a lifetime had been for me the whole meaning of England. 'Half Church of God; half castle 'gainst the Scot.'

It was with very mixed feelings that I turned my Anglia toward Middlesbrough for the Conference of 1967. It was still my duty to preside over the Ministerial Sessions of that Conference and to give it some idea of my impressions of the Church as seen in my round of it. After that I would have to fulfil the functions of the Past President. I was tired after the strain of preparing all the talks I had given up and down the country. The Chairmen had said, 'You never repeat a talk', and I don't think I did. I had tried, as Wesley commanded, 'to speak to their condition' whether in Kenya or Carlisle. Of what use would have been a well-tried 'score' in Aden with men under fire? There is as much social difference between Cumbria and Cornwall as there is between Ghana and Gateshead. It is precisely that difference which our Church must tackle. Not the visits but the preparation for entering a new situation each visit was the cause of my tiredness.

I found myself billeted in a nice hotel at Redcar by the sea with all the 'platform' end of the Conference. One of the most dignified members hailed me on the morning of Conference, beginning with the salute 'You've had it; it was good, now it's over'. I wondered if he meant my long forty plus years of Ministry or that one brief year, or did he mean honour and great occasions? Certainly, I knew whichever way he meant it while I was in John Wesley's band of preachers nothing would be over except time.

At last the Fathers and Brethren were gathered and I spoke to them on my round of visits in the corners of our Church. The *Methodist Recorder* leader headed its comment with the cross-heading 'Realism from the President'. I kept to my theme, the presence of the Church in the nation and our presentation of our message to it. This Church is the corporate body of Christ in the midst of world affairs and from the appearance of a church building stuck down at a street corner to the bonds which make Methodism a Connexional whole there is not a factor which is not part of the revelation of Christ.

A class meeting in an obscure village or a presence of our

members in a verbal scuffle in a factory are alike deeds of God.
There are thousands of them every day. On the other hand,
pigeon droppings piled up three feet high against the door of
a church (as I saw in one place) are a contradiction of Christ as
much as any popular sin. The presence of our Ministry in towns
and villages is a Christian 'Occupation', their itineracy a social
training of unequalled quality.

As soon as the Ministerial Session was ended I moved myself
out of the Redcar Hotel and went to stay in Middlesbrough
itself with my colleagues from the Mission House and was much
refreshed by their companionship. It was my duty to install
the succeeding President who was Dr Irvonwy Morgan of the
London Mission. Then I took the ex-Presidential chair on his
right on the platform.

My mind this time was ahead on the Overseas Consultation
we had planned at Didsbury College to follow up the initiatives of
the Skegness events. I had fitted in the preparations for this in the
odd moments left by my other duties throughout the presidential
year.

Now it was arrived and had to be dealt with. Packing our files,
etc., into the Anglia I took Margret Forrest and Betty Swinson,
two key assistants on the staff, over the Pennines to Manchester as
buses took the overseas members of the Conference to join others
in Didsbury College, where we would be for two weeks.

At Didsbury we were well under one roof and all on one diet
and I often think this is the ideal way of getting to know other
folk. We found it so. In session after session, in odd moments
over meals and sitting together we went over the needs, personnel
needs, money needs and strategic needs, of our mission across the
world, all done in equal brotherly fashion. If anything can be both
tiring and refreshing this was it. It still echoes round the world.

From 24th July to 5th August Gladys and I went on a much
needed holiday. It was needed if for nothing else than to get
together again. Separation seemed to have been the order of
the day for months and we thoroughly enjoyed ourselves. Great

meetings and receptions were not Gladys' choice of occupation
and this had made our separations longer as it made our reunion
more meaningful.

One of the two burdens which Conference placed on my
shoulders in 1967 was to head the team of Methodists on the
Joint Commission on 'Women in the Ordained Ministry'
demanded by the 1966 Conference. My opposite number on
the Anglican side was the Right Rev. G. A. Ellison, then Bishop
of Chester. There were four of us on each side: the Right Rev.
Bishop of Swansea and Brecon, who never attended, the Very Rev.
Alan Richardson, who was very helpful, the Rev. Professor G. R.
Dunstan, who was the Anglican theological expert, and Mrs Kay
Baxter, who represented the women's angle on the question in the
Anglican Church.

We were, in addition to myself, the Rev. Geoffrey Litherland,
then Warden of the Deaconess Order, Dr Maldwyn Edwards,
Chairman of our work in Wales, Sister Margaret Siebold, Senior
Deaconess, and Miss Muriel Stennett, who represented the
women at work overseas.

The Commission met three times in open session informing
each other on what had been resolved and talked of in our
Churches. We also attempted some forecast of the possible
course of events in coming years within the two Churches and
made suggestions about the proceedings during Stage One of
the unification of the Churches, should either Church decide to
ordain women in the future unilaterally. A drafting committee
also met on two occasions.

In the upshot, the decisions come to can be summarised in the
concluding sentences of the report. 'In view of the uncertainty of
the Church of England on the issue of the ordination of women
we must therefore sound a note of warning and point out that the
task of those negotiating Stage Two (of the Union Scheme) would
include a new factor if there were different practices. We trust that
these could be resolved.' The best that could be said was that the
matter had been openly discussed on a bilateral basis. The Report

came to the 1968 Conference.

The second task remitted to me was to take the chair in
a Committee on the re-alignment of the Departments of the
Methodist Church. I was selected for this task after I had decided
to leave the Connexional level in our Church and return to the
task of individual church life at Eastbourne.

We had a very strong committee which included a
personnel manager of ICI and other experts in re-organisation,
both Ministerial and lay. It was a tremendous task involving
examinations of each Department and gathering impressions
far and wide as to their efficiency, such as a call on Lord Rank
who had backed the Home Mission Department so well and
so generously. When we met him he characteristically, handed
our draft scheme to an assistant to scrutinise and confined his
personal enquiries entirely to what our scheme would do for
evangelisation.

There were at the time thirteen Departments in our Church
and alongside of them a number of Connexional Committee not
attached to the Departments but existing separately. I drafted a
work scheme for the working party by reversing the two words
in our remit from Conference, by studying the function of
each department before studying structure. We went to each
Department and saw it ourselves, we talked with all the General
Secretaries of Departments and had each one create a scheme
of its work. We saw Chairmen of Districts and took opinions
far and wide. We became a mutually reliant team as we worked.
It must have been in part this mutuality which raised in my
mind at home one night the possibilities of advising Conference
to set up a Presidential Council. It could carry on the will of
Conference in the days between Conferences as the President was
in theory supposed to do. Throughout my Presidential Year this
had worried me. So much the President was supposed to do in
seeing Conference's will obeyed seemed to by-pass the very busy
President because of his travel.

In the upshot we produced for the 1969 Conference a

Scheme in which the thirteen Departments became seven
Divisions and incorporated much of the Committee work which
had existed outside of the Departments. To this we added the
Presidential Council of all the Divisonal Heads and sundry
balancing representatives to oversee the planning and work of the
whole. This Conference accepted, although the debate on it went
on into the Conference of 1970. The Divisions we proposed were;
Ministries, Education and Youth, Social Responsibility, Home
Mission, Overseas, Finance and Property with the Presidential
Council as co-ordinator. The Connexional Life of Methodism
now works on this basis.

In 1968 I made up my mind that I had done enough service
in the 'corridors of power' in our Church and determined to
leave the Missionary Society and go back to the work at the
ground level in a Circuit. The *Methodist Recorder* had once
called me the 'Most unecclesiastical President' in the long story.
I had discovered that I really was what the Recorder had said.
Chicanery, despotism and other blemishes on the top executive
class bored me intensely. I was on 68 committees and yet not part
of their work. I lived in a circuit but was not of it.

At that time Mr Eric Pigott of the *Methodist Recorder* was
a Circuit Steward in the Eastbourne Circuit and when we
lunched together one day, as was our duty, he asked me if I would
come, on leaving the Mission House, to become that circuit's
superintendent, stationed at the Eastbourne Central Church.
It was a providential thought. I talked this over with Gladys
and it suited her well. In the end I said I would consent to this
proposal going to the Stationing Committee for approval. It was
a breakthrough in the Mission House; previously any retiring
secretaries there had gone into superannuation and become
Honorary Secretaries living in the London Circle. I broke a
tradition, kept my name off any Overseas committees and have
never been back in the House since.

Peak 9 - FROM BEACHY HEAD

'Engage the enemy more closely'

Beginning the fortieth year of my ministry we journeyed down to Eastbourne, exchanging the tight communal situation of Kensal Rise for the sunshine and coastal climate of Eastbourne. The Manse we entered reminded us of our Portsmouth Manse for which we had exchanged London. Its large garden front and back gave Gladys, who loved gardens, all sorts of hopes. Margaret and her husband were just a few miles away at Crawley, life looked full of hope.

I had not been long in the circuit before I was out in the faithful Anglia and up on to the Downs. On the way up to Beachy Head there is a wonderful view of Eastbourne lying below with the sea lapping it.

The sea there is ever empty of shipping and stretches away across to our old enemy, France, uncluttered. On that first trip to the Downs my mind must have been irritated by this emptiness for it peopled the bay with the shipping one sees at Portsmouth, the Royal Navy in its strength.

The picture changed and there I imagined the ships of our enemies in great strength and Nelson's little ships scattered among them. They had lobbed their cannon shot into the enemy for hours and made nothing of it. Then Nelson's signal fluttered from his flagship. Not the now famous signal but another, it read, 'Engage the enemy more closely'.

The victory was to come not from the remote high command but from press-ganged matelots engaged in bloody battle, shiploads of them in close battle in the shrouds and at the rails.

As the downland vision of the sea faded I knew it for one

more God-given insight into what now lay before me. I had been
on the 'bridge' of things but now it was to be 'the shrouds and
rail' of a situation which bristled with the difficulties of personal
encounter with that town down there and its outlying villages.
Nine points of contact in the chapels of the Circuit, with people,
soul to soul.

That is precisely what it turned out to be. There are nine
churches of ours in the Eastbourne Circuit and it has three
ministers. The senior minister — the Superintendent — had
in my day the charge of the Central Church with its four
hundred or so members and its summer time pulpit where up
to a thousand worshippers gather on a Sunday morning and the
regular local members rally round the evening service. He is the
Superintendent of the rest and leader to the other ministers.
Four of the churches are within Eastbourne itself and are sited
according to very rigid changes in character of Eastbourne's
population.

Outside the town pride of place must go to Hailsham, a
budding town. There follow the villages down to such a tiny cause
as Blacknest, which then was strangely enough the pastorate of
the Central minister. There was one place, which in China we
would have called a Prayer Station, at Rushlake Green which
has now come to the Circuit Plan. Under the old system each
of these had its Trustee and other local committees which the
Superintendent had to attend, and they all claimed attention
from him in the course of his Sunday ministry. One of the town
churches had a big building scheme on during our time — St
Stephen's, a new area church.

At Central I was able, at last, to preach series of consecutive
sermons ranging right across the Christian system of theology
to my own delight and I hope theirs. I found my place in the
Eastbourne Christian Council. I found my place in welcoming
visitors to our Holiday Home at the Links, from which the total
household would come and occupy a block of seats on a Sunday
morning in the gallery at Central.

I married our own young folk and others, I baptised babies which I saw growing up later in our Sunday Schools. I laid to rest the bodies of old and tired people who had been part of our worship as they passed on from their retirement to the glories of the worship beyond. There was the three hundred strong Avenue House Old Folk's Club to see to. A joint venture, this, with the Eastbourne Social Service Civic Authority. What parties we had — every Friday seemed to be one.

I was in and out of homes and boarding houses regularly. Sometimes it would be the homes of people who had retired to grow beautiful gardens but were now past gardening. Sometimes it was the homes of those who had given up large gardens to live in town flats. Sometimes it was the homes of people who had been in Eastbourne all their lives. Rich homes, poor homes, happy homes and miserable. One roomed old folk's hide-outs took their place alongside the others. Now and again the Police would call me to a little one-room home of some old lady who had died all alone. They would ask me to go through her personal papers because they knew that she came to Central Church and I stood in for distant relatives or no relatives at all. I often gave God thanks for the psychological training I had experienced as a student and had completed at the Tavistock Clinic when I came home from Camp.

What problems lay behind the smiling face of sunny Eastbourne; it was rather like my surprise when I was taken from looking after hungry 'other ranks' in Italy and made to look after officers in Stalag Luft 3. Affluence only made problems more difficult to solve, or called out those which penury cannot provide.

What is to be done when you find yourself in a fine home but the love has gone out of the couple who live in it. The woman's children have gone and the man has no 'business' to go to every day? They sit there estranged but not consenting to say so, nagging each other into a welcome grave. 'I give them five years of gardening bungalow life and three of flat dwelling, then their property is on the market as they die', one House Agent said to me. 'We do all right, I don't know about them.'

Can anything be done with a glorious spinster who lives alone with her dog and has no other stimulus in her life when she has sucked dry all the other activities open to her? She has passed the 50th year of her days and now twenty at least years lie before her unfilled. She has served happily in London offices through her working life and has enough laid by to see her through as far as essentials are concerned but she has a spiritual malnutrition problem.

I passed from these problems of ageing people to the problems of young couples born and bred in Eastbourne who lived in tiny little houses with their children round their feet all the time and incapable of getting any new and more spacious housing in this tourist-supported town with its influx of pensioners sweeping into the place with capital enough to corner all the accommodation. Go away then, you tell them. There is a mother or a widowed dad round the corner, or even in with them. How can they?

The thriving Sunday School and Young People's Fellowship gave access to many other parents and to the children themselves. It is a mistake to imagine that children have no problems, sometimes one is led to think their life is nothing but.

Throughout the life of the church at Central there was no lack of talented leadership. The incoming of new blood from Methodist churches all over Britain at the top of the age scales gave us a host of trained men and women eager to give service in their new abode. This was also true of the other churches in the circuit which also had their incomers. Just to hear Central Choir was demonstration enough.

The whole Circuit was a rare example of the untruth of the idea that accretions to church membership come from the adolescent group only. They come from that source, of course, but the crisis of young newly weds, the pressures of the arrival of the family, the problems of mid-term marriage and the shock of retirement all contribute people who find a new spiritual element in life.

During most of our time in the Circuit I had the assistance at Central of a Wesley Deaconess — Sister Irene — who took a great part in the work among young people in particular and was a most earnest visitor in homes. Some things like the Women's Fellowship meeting she left to Gladys, who joined in much of the work, but in the Wesley Guild and other organisations she was always present with a motherly presence.

In fact, it was her withdrawal from the work which made me think we should not stay too long in the circuit. Village pressures grew. Cross-in-Hand, for instance, away at the extreme end of the circuit went in for massive reconstruction and expansion and its affairs took much time. There were changes of ministers. Dr Boys who had wrapped up the affairs of his corner of the circuit for years was called away. The minister at Greenfield Road church, a centre of close family life, moved and one had to settle the new men in and all the time keep the great Central church going. In our personal life Gladys was much older than me and showed signs of weariness with the constant pressure of the work. I was past the year for retirement myself. What of her?

One day, having lunch together at Synod the minister at Seaford, James Cooper, told me that the Mid-Sussex Circuit was looking for a Supernumerary minister to live at Uckfield and look after Lewes, Uckfield and Buxted little churches. This opening decided me; I officially retired and took this post. It was with many a heartache that I left Eastbourne, it still lives in my life and I often meet members of it and I frequently preach in its pulpits. Though it has had two ministers in the interval since I left, I still regard its folk as my folk.

We moved, therefore, into the adjoining circuit to Eastbourne and entered the lovely manse at Uckfield with its outstanding garden. I officially retired from the active work of the Methodist Ministry but I became an Active Supernumerary. Such men are the humblest and least protected men in the ministry. In these

days the Connexion could not do without them. Were they to
resign their jobs, there would be an enormous gap in the stations
throughout the Connexion; but for Conference they officially
do not exist. Most of them do on a quarter's stipend the work of
a younger minister. Many have returned from service overseas
and come back to Britain in this guise. Men who have spent a
life in the Home work are much more cagey than to take the
posts. Where you find one you find a real son of John Wesley.
Yet, strangely enough, they are the only men in our ministry who
live on a Congregational basis in a Connexional church founded
by Wesley. Fortunately the people in the local churches love
them dearly as they contribute a lifetime of acquired knowledge
to the personal problems of the church members and a wide
understanding to the life of the community in which they live.

I plunged into the life of my little three churches and soon
found that their struggle to exist took up for me the same burden
as had blessed my days down through the years gone. In Lewes I
found at first I could hope for new things. Lewes is the County
Town of East Sussex with nine parishes in it of the Anglican
Church and other Churches too. We had a group of four middle-
years men in it and seemed set for a more significant Methodist
presence. The deplorable Act which changed Local Government
took all four away from us to other jobs up and down the country
and left a gallant group of women to operate the church.

Uckfield church is unfortunately sited in a corner of the town
and, though more lively than Lewes church, struggles to hold its
own. It has a Sunday School and younger leadership but it seeks
to maintain its life at about 30 members. Buxted was a small
village church until new folk came in and among other things
founded a Youth Club first and then a joint Sunday School with
the Anglicans of one particular parish and grew to real village
significance.

There is a strange compulsion in weakness and I laboured
in this tiny corner of the Circuit which contained the thriving
coastal strip round Seaford and the more vivid areas round

Haywards Heath and Burgess Hill — parts of the London
commuter belt — as though they were those fortunate regions. I
rediscovered the Chinese principle that circuits must follow the
line of 'Community Flow' to succeed or be artificial. There is no
community flow between Haywards Heath and the coastal strip,
let alone into the 'Styx of Sussex' as folk called my area. People
'over there' would say that they mean 'the Sticks of Sussex'. I insist
that the real meaning is 'Styx', the river of death. It represents their
distaste for entering it.

It was after we had been in the manse at Uckfield a year or
more that the blow fell. Gladys had for a week or two had some
muscular pain in an arm which did not improve. I drove her over
to our doctor's house; he was away but a locum was in attendance.
He saw her and prescribed a simple salicylic which on the way
home I stopped and procured at Boots in Uckfield.

She took this medicine but was rather more in pain than
before. In the evening I telephoned Dr Simpson, now returned.
By this time I had her in bed resting. Just before he came she
went into a savage attack of pain. He immediately called for an
ambulance which came and gave her oxygen treatment for a
heart attack. The doctor was excellent and talked to her about
her nursing career as he ministered to her. When the ambulance
crew had relieved her pain he ordered her into Cuckfield Hospital
which is 15 miles from Uckfield. As she was lifted into the
ambulance he said to me 'Those men have done you a good turn.
They've saved your wife's life.'

Thinking that she would be kept a while in the hospital
I followed the ambulance in my car. She was in the casualty
department when I reached the hospital. One of the ambulance
men directed me to it. I got there but never saw her alive again.
One of the doctors attending her came out to me and said 'I'm
terribly sorry but your wife couldn't make it'.

I went in to see her. Her head lay to one side. Her face had
a look I had never seen before. It had a strange resignation as
though to say, 'I did my best to stay. I couldn't; the battle is fought

and I lost.' I was completely shocked, kissed her and left carrying
that sight with me. Her long years were over, her battles fought.
She had died alone without any farewell. As she had lived through
a thousand things, so she died: her sister 200 miles away, her
daughter who was only 15 miles away in ignorance, her partner so
near yet so far. She who had comforted so many, young and old,
went out as she had lived, alone in her own strength.

As I tidied up her affairs letters poured in. There were well
over a hundred of them and each had its story of some lovely
thing which had been done in a life. China colleagues, army wives
and army men, people in the circuits in which she had worked,
each recorded some deed largely unknown before.

The folk of Uckfield and the other two little churches were
wonderful. The Eastbourne people were also totally co-operative
and I arranged the funeral service at the Central Church there
at which there was a great congregation both at the church and
in the Eastbourne Crematorium. She was obviously loved by so
many at this our last active charge. I had the ashes brought to the
manse and after a few days to make arrangements, I set out for the
tiny village of Slingsby in Yorkshire and laid them in her father's
grave in the little churchyard there. 'Home is the sailor home from
sea and the huntsman home from the hill.' She had loved that
place and it had mader her.

Life for me began again then, the life of oneness after all the
years of twoness in the manse where companionship is needed
more than in the ordinary home. My daughter and her husband
did all they could from Crawley. Friends crowded round, but I
lived inside of my own life. There were still my churches.

One day I was looking back through the letters Gladys had
written to me during our forced separation of the War and was
astonished to see there something I had completely forgotten. In
the body of a long letter written from Ben Rhydding's evacuated
Hunmanby Hall School she commented on the lone life of Dr
Lofthouse who had written to her and went on, 'The thing I
would always want you to do, dear, if I were not there but had

gone on before, would be to find someone who would be kind. I haven't patience with the women who worry about their husbands marrying again. It is the best thing they can do.' This was simply one paragraph in a long and newsy letter. It came right out of the context of living.

There was only one person in my life to whom these conditions could apply. She was Miss Margret Forrest who had been my colleague and friend in the Mission House for nine or ten years and had herself worked there for fifteen. Like others on the staff there we knew each other at many levels as much as at the business level. I had visited her home, she had been to the Eastbourne manse, I had been in the home of her parents. Our friendship could have terminated when I left the Mission House and she had gone off to follow her desire by training to prepare young women for business life. She was by this time a student at Garnett College for adult teacher training at Roehampton.

Sussex born she was nevertheless a child of the north country from which her people had come and in which her relatives lived. She had been abroad with her parents to Australia where her father found his own skills were better catered for back in England and brought the family back.

Keen members of our Church, the whole family had been brought up in our traditions and she found work in the Church familiar ground. Being of adult years and no young girl, she found my own age to be no trouble to her and our friendship ripened and developed over a considerable time.

She gained the Teacher's Diploma of London in the Garnett College, the Diploma of Qualified Private Secretaries of the London Chamber of Commerce and then went out to her first teaching appointment at the Watford College of Further Education. The new profession, backed by the long working years in business life, soon proved her to be an excellent person for the young teenage and older girls and women.

We married in 1973 at Kentish Town Methodist Church, to which she had given long years of service, though there were more

fashionable churches nearer her home. It was a great occasion
attended by all kinds of friends and relatives from both our
families, her friends giving the reception in the church hall. We
had a honeymoon up in Northumberland based on Otterburn
and then came back to the manse at Uckfield. The churches
took her to their hearts immediately, especially the younger end
of Uckfield. Margaret, her husband and family very soon made
friends. The friendship between Margaret and Margret (Meg)
had ripened into something that will last the years. One had
the feeling that Margaret has found the sister she has never had.
Margret, on the other hand, has found two fine boys as 'step
grandchildren' who are a joy to her and she to them.

When at last I came to the end of five years in Uckfield we
pooled our resources by Margret's selling of her flat in London
and my savings and moved to a little house in a nearby village.

Meanwhile she had removed to Lewes Technical College and
I had channelled all my missionary and executive experience into
part-time lecturing with the Workers' Educational Association
on international affairs. These classes are a great joy to me, the
presentation and the meetings are most interesting and, to me, are
part of the non-circuit ministry of a minister.

This, with preaching in the two circuits round me and beyond
and the part-time chaplaincy of Laughton Lodge Hospital for
the mentally retarded, has kept me fully occupied. The Uckfield
years were similar to other years in other English circuits with the
added problem of coping with little churches, which the spirit of
our age had weakened to very near the moment of dissolution.
There is a special urgency about keeping intact the very basic
witness of little struggling churches in our day. When twenty
persons out of a village of 300 go to worship it is not a signal for
withdrawal but for wider, deeper, worship among the twenty.
They are the root from which tomorrow's development will
grow. There are heroes of the depressed years as there are of the

are advances. To keep swimming in the troughs between waves
is sometimes a more heroic effort than cresting the waves. Many
little churches today are doing precisely what the lone monasteries
did long ago in hostile Europe. Our service is to God, our worship
centred on His tremendous venture out over the whole world. In
village after village the neglected parish church or wayside Bethel
is the unique vertical structure in the area. All else is horizontal
and knows not that the tiny place links heaven and earth.

It is secluded in such villages that my Mountain Journey
comes to its end. We have only left it once and that was to catch
a breath of the tumultuous life of growing peoples out in Asia.
We went through Bangkok, the home of the Asian Christian
Conference, Singapore, that mass of racial unit, Hong Kong on
the lap of my beloved China, and down to Australia where so
many Western problems are tormenting a new people.

But here we are back in this ancient Sussex village and in its
placid life. Margret's work in Lewes Technical College injects
into our life the problems of young women and their men. The
village school injects the problems of children and their parents.
The WEA classes give us a place in the life of adult people in a
changing world, and both the parish church and the surrounding
twenty Methodist Chapels in two contiguous circuits give us
opportunities to serve. We are not stranded.

It is difficult to look back with an ageing body at the long trail
of the Chinese roads of the '30s; not quite so difficult to see again
the days of five years of war and three of prisondom. The years of
power in the Connexion seem farthest away than the others. That
is all gone; to interfere now would be madness. The pastoral years
in the circuits never quite go away; people from them pop up in
the mail or call perpetually.

I can honestly say that I put whatever I was at any particular
time whole-heartedly into the task at hand in the name of God.
I am glad that He made it a mountain road, that the turns and

twists of that road taxed me at the time and still do. My life has covered more than seventy years of a most tumultuous century. It had to be a stormy road. I began just two centuries after John Wesley saw the light. As best I could I have carried his light forward into our century. I am still glad that the motto of my old Handsworth College hangs above my head as I write saying, 'Quo monstrat dominus' — 'Whither the Lord points'.

The Gift of a Review

I hope that you have enjoyed seeing the world through the eyes of someone who has helped to shape it. Now you've finished this book, the best thing you can do to help others is to add a review on Amazon, sharing your thoughts and what you enjoyed the most.

Thank you so much for your gift of a review.

Tim Ridgway.

Visit Today

www.DouglasWeddellThompson.com

We have set up a website related to this book, and to other things related to the life of Douglas Weddell Thompson. On this website you will find things such as:

- Downloadable hi-res photos
- Links to recordings of Douglas' time made just after the Second World War
- A wall of "thoughts" to which you can add your thoughts, memories or ideas
- Links to further books and information about Douglas Weddell Thompson

Make sure you spend time on the website listening to the stories which Douglas told. You'll be further inspired!

Printed in Great Britain
by Amazon.co.uk, Ltd.,
Marston Gate.

4190356R00175